THE
CRUCIFIXION

Book 1

TimeLine:
1 CE – 1300 CE

David Birnbaum

Harvard Yard
PRESS®

$ 40.00 / set

THE CRUCIFIXION

David Birnbaum's *The Crucifixion* is a uniquely distinctive work on the extraordinary historical odyssey of the Jews during a pivotal slice of history.

This work focuses on the 1300 year time frame bracketing the emergence of Christianity in the First Century, followed by the Christianizing of the Roman Empire post-Constantine, and finally, by the ending of the Crusades c. 1300 CE.

Via the mode of an integrated TimeLine, the author focuses on the crushing historical forces at-play. The Jewish nation which entered this period, is unrecognizable from the Jewish nation which emerged....

* * *

Harvard Yard
PRESS®

Boston ⋆ New York

www.Harvard1000.com

(master site)

---

www.Philosophy1000.com

www.History1000.com

www.Spinoffs1000.com

www.YouTubeX1000.com

www.AmazonX1000.com

About the Author

Private scholar David Birnbaum is known in academic circles primarily as the author of the *Summa Metaphysica* series: an overarching metaphysics. He is a graduate of Yeshiva Dov Revel, Yeshiva University High School, CCNY and Harvard.

God and Evil (1988), the first book in the landmark **Summa Metaphysica** series, has been assigned as a Required Text at universities around the world, and was a Book of the Month feature selection of the Jewish Book Club. The work has gone through Five Printings and eighteen thousand copies to date. The author is known as a leading conceptual theorist.

The two-volume *Summa Metaphysica* series was crafted over a twenty-six year span, 1982–1988 and then 2001–2008. It was the prime focus of a major international academic conference at Bard College (Annandale-on-Hudson, NY), April 2012. [see www.Bard1000.com].

Jews, Church & Civilization - Birnbaum's seven-volume integrated Jewish TimeLine work – was crafted in the 2002–2012 period.

David Birnbaum's works have been used as course texts at Brandeis, Hebrew University, Yeshiva University, Hebrew Union College, Tel Aviv University, Emory, JTS, Bar Ilan, and Union Theological Seminary, among others. His works have been reviewed by dozens of leading academic journals worldwide.

A long time ago, he taught "The Science of Strategy" at the New School in NY.

He lives and works in Manhattan.

***

Library of Congress Cataloging–in–Publication Data

First Printing 2010

Birnbaum, David.

The Crucifixion Book 1 / David Birnbaum

ISBN 978–0–9843619–0–8

1. History.   2. Holocaust.   3. Canon Gospels.   4. Judaism.
5. anti–Semitism.   6. Jewish History.   I. Title

Harvard Yard
PRESS®
Boston * New York

Danny Levine, Managing Director

HarvardYardPress@gmail.com

an imprint of J Levine / MILLENNIUM

(Harvard Yard Press operates independently of Harvard University)

To contact author's representative:

fax: (212) 398–9438

DBprivate@aol.com

A CHRONICLE

Books by David Birnbaum

History–related

The Crucifixion
I and II

Jews, Church & Civilization
I, II, III, IV, V, VI and VII

Metaphysics–related

***

Summa Metaphysica series

God and Evil (1988)

God and Good (2005)

**spin–offs from
Summa Metaphysica:**

God's 120 Guardian Angels

The Lost Manual

Cosmic Womb of Potential

*

**"companion works" to
Summa Metaphysica
[artistic/graphic representations]**

Q4P I + II

Cosmic Womb of Potential I + II

Cosmic Tool Kit I + II

Cosmic Code I + II

THE CHURCH & THE JEWS SERIES BY DAVID BIRNBAUM

"David Birnbaum's latest book, *The Crucifixion: The Church & the Jews 1 CE – 1300 CE*, provides an amazing wealth of historical information on the struggles of the Jewish people in relation to Christianity during its first thirteen centuries of existence. Dedicated to the "Righteous Gentiles" who risked their lives to save Jews from Nazi persecution, the book nonetheless raises up to Christians a devastating portrait of their ongoing prejudice, hatred, and persecution. The timelines are exhaustive and the photos and maps illustrative. The book leaves the reader stunned into reflection...."

– Judith M. Kubicki
   Professor, Department of Theology, Fordham University
   President, North American Academy of Liturgy
   Former Academic Dean, Christ the King Seminary, NYS

"He (Fidel Castro) began this discussion by describing his own, first encounters with anti-Semitism, as a small boy.

'I remember when I was a boy – a long time ago – when I was five or six years old and I lived in the countryside,' he said, 'and I remember Good Friday.'

What was the atmosphere a child breathed?

'Be quiet, God is dead.' God died every year between Thursday and Saturday of Holy Week,
and it made a profound impression on everyone.

What happened?

They would say, 'The Jews killed God.'

They blamed the Jews for killing God!

Do you realize this?'"

– Fidel Castro

Writer Jeffrey Goldberg article
for *The Atlantic Monthly*
September 2010 issue
recounting his interview of
Former Cuban President, Fidel Castro

kol ha–olam ku–lo
gesher tzar m'od,
gesher tzar m'od

v'ha–i–kar, ha–ikar
lo l'fa–ched,
lo l'fa–ched klal

v'ha–ikar, ha–ikar,
lo l'fa–ched klal

*

All the world
is like a narrow, frail footbridge

But the important thing,
the really important thing…

is not to be afraid…
not to be afraid…at all…

*

– modern day Jewish folk song

"We should always be disposed to believe

that that which appears white

is really black,

if the hierarchy of the Church so decides."

— *Saint Ignatius of Loyola*
c. 1523 CE

Paper cannot wrap up a fire

– ancient Chinese proverb

Dedicated

to the

Righteous Gentiles*

* Valorous European and Asian non–Jews who, during the Holocaust, risked
their lives to save Jews from Nazi persecution. The known names and memories
are individually recognized at an official state tribute at Yad Vashem Holocaust
Memorial on the outskirts of Jerusalem, Israel. Individual tributes are located
along a memorial path of trees and gardens planted in their honor, commemorating
their extraordinary courage and compassion (www.YadVashem.org).

Overview of this Book

This work, *The Crucifixion*, is really *two–books–in–one* –

> **TimeLine:** 1 CE – 1300 CE
>   (but really informally 480 BCE – 1300 CE)

plus the crucial

> **First Century Focus:** 80+ inter–related Exhibits

The TimeLine
provides historical *context, overview, drama* and *texture*

The First Century Focus
then *gets to the guts* of the matter

Sincerely,

THE AUTHOR

a focused note to Catholic readers of this work

This work is measured, but direct.

It was quite carefully crafted over a multi-year period
to be as close as possible to 100% accurate.

One of the intents of the work is for the Catholic laity, in particular,
to more fully *come to grips* with the dimensions of the
(ongoing) impacting 'issues.'

*

As we are aware,
all our genetic coding is 99.9+ percent identical.

Ultimately, we all
sail the sea of life
on this planet
together.

*

Definition: Torah et al.

Definition: **Torah** *et al.*

The *Torah* refers to the Five Books of Moses (or Pentateuch).

The Torah is the first part of the 3–section TaNaKh (a.k.a. *Tanach*), the Jewish Canon (Holy Texts).

TaNaKh stands for –

Torah	The Law/Teachings
	a.k.a The Five Books of Moses
Neveim	Prophets
Ketuvim	Writings

The TaNaKh (a.k.a. Mikrah a.k.a. Miqra a.k.a The Masoretic Text) is composed of 24 books.
[Christianity accepts these same 24 books as divine (or divinely–inspired), but using the same texts, albeit more sub–divisions (e.g. Samuel I and Samuel II) arrives at a higher number than 24.]

The *Torah*, (when bound known as a *Chumash* or as *Chamisha Chumshei Torah*) in turn, incorporates:
Bereshit	(Genesis)
Shemot	(Exodus)
Vayikra	(Leviticus)
Bamidbar	(Numbers)
Devarim	(Deuteronomy)

The term "Hebrew Bible" is used by many to refer to the *Torah* alone (and that is how this work employs the term). However, the term "Hebrew Bible" is also used by many, including Christianity, to refer to the entire TaNaKh.

Christianity refers to* the TaNaKh, the Jewish Canon, the Hebrew Bible, as the "Old Testament."

Judaism collectively bristles at the term 'New Testament' juxtaposed against a so–called "Old Testament," as the juxtaposition and the term 'New Testament,' in particular –
implies an updated *divine* document,
implies that a contemporaneous witness is relating the vignettes related,
implies that a non–anonymous author stands behind the particular homily,
implies at least co–equal 'standing' to the *Torah*,
implies non–hyper–edited texts, and
implies *supersession* (i.e. that Christianity displaces Judaism).

To Judaism, there is only one Testament, and it is not "new."

However, the terms New Testament and Old Testament have been successfully implanted by the Church in global society.

---

* NOTE: The TaNaKh – the Hebrew Bible – ends with Chronicles II and the exhortation to rebuild the Temple. The so-called "Old Testament" – whose precise order was delineated by the Church Fathers – ends with Malachi, whose closing words are framed by Christianity as a prophetic foreshadowing of Jesus.

cont'd

Definition: *Torah* et al.

In Christianity, the term 'The Bible' sequentially incorporates two divisions:

> First Division: The Jewish Canon[a]

> Second Division: The Christian Canon

The core of the Jewish Canon is the Torah (the Five Books of Moses).

The core of the Christian Canon is the four Canon Gospels.

The Christian Canon is also known as the aforementioned New Testament a.k.a. Greek New Testament a.k.a. Greek Scriptures a.k.a. New Law.

The New Testament, while packaged back–to–back by the Church with the Old Testament, is simultaneously often (gravely) pejorative to both the letter and spirit of the TaNaKh (Jewish Canon), and to the Jews, the recipients and guardians of the *Torah* and of the TaNaKh, as a whole.

Thus the New Testament is consistently quite significantly derogatory to the Jews on three basic levels simultaneously:
  – to Jewish theology, tradition and law
  – to the Jewish nation as a whole, *collectively*
  – to the Jewish character *individually*

---

[a]see * on prior page

The first four works of the (27–work) New Testament are the Canon Gospels:
  "Matthew"
  "Mark"
  "Luke"
  "John"

The work fifth 'in standing' in Christendom's New Testament is "Acts" a.k.a Acts of the Apostles

*

The Christian "Passion Saga" – extrapolated from 'cherry–picked' *intense* vignettes from sundry Gospels (and then often intensely turbo–charged – and not necessarily benignly towards the Jews) – is *more often than not* highly toxic and incendiary towards the Jews, collectively and individually.

The Passion Saga was and is readily accessible to the Christian masses, and its message and imagery are readily comprehensible to even five–year–olds. For the 1300–year span covered by this book and beyond, the intense Passion Saga *de facto* becomes the Christian Bible's projection to the world. And it is a quite–highly toxic projection *vis à vis* the Jews.

Moreover, one should not assume that the humanistic posture in church towards the Jews of a random 2010 Presbyterian minister in Vermont, is emblematic of the posture towards the Jews of a random c. 500 CE Catholic cleric in Medieval France/Germany...

THE CRUCIFIXION

Book 1

TimeLine:
1 CE – 1300 CE

*

An Integrated

Jewish/Christian/Universal

focused timeline

*

You are in Book 1

Focus: The First Century

sub–Table of Contents
1 of 4

Focus: The First Century

sub–Table of Contents
2 of 4

Focus: The First Century

Focus: The First Century

sub–Table of Contents
4 of 4

c. 1250 BCE

the first two of the Ten Commandments:

I ²*אָנֹכִי֙ ה אֱלֹ-֔יךָ אֲשֶׁ֣ר הוֹצֵאתִ֗יךָ
מֵאֶ֥רֶץ מִצְרַ֖יִם מִבֵּ֣ית עֲבָדִ֑ים ³*לֹֽא-יִֽהְיֶ֥ה
לְךָ֛ אֱלֹהִ֥ים אֲחֵרִ֖ים עַל-פָּנָֽי:
II ⁴לֹֽא תַעֲשֶׂה-לְךָ֣ פֶ֣סֶל֙ וְכָל-תְּמוּנָ֡ה אֲשֶׁ֣ר
בַּשָּׁמַ֣יִם֙ מִמַּ֔עַל וַאֲשֶׁ֥ר בָּאָ֖רֶץ מִתָּ֑חַת
וַאֲשֶׁ֥ר בַּמַּ֖יִם מִתַּ֥חַת לָאָֽרֶץ: ⁵לֹא-
תִשְׁתַּחֲוֶ֥ה לָהֶ֖ם וְלֹ֣א תָעָבְדֵ֑ם כִּ֣י אָנֹכִ֞י
ה אֱלֹ-֔יךָ אֵ֖ל קַנָּ֑א ...

תורה שמות כ יתרו

I   ²I the LORD am your God who brought you
out of the land of Egypt, the house of bondage:
³You shall have no other gods besides Me.

II   ⁴You shall not make for yourself a sculptured
image, or any likeness of what is in the heavens
above, or on the earth below, or in the waters
under the earth. ⁵You shall not bow down to
them or serve them. For I the LORD your God
am an impassioned God,...—TORAH EXODUS 20: 2–5 YITRO

Lead–in to

"The Crucifixion"...

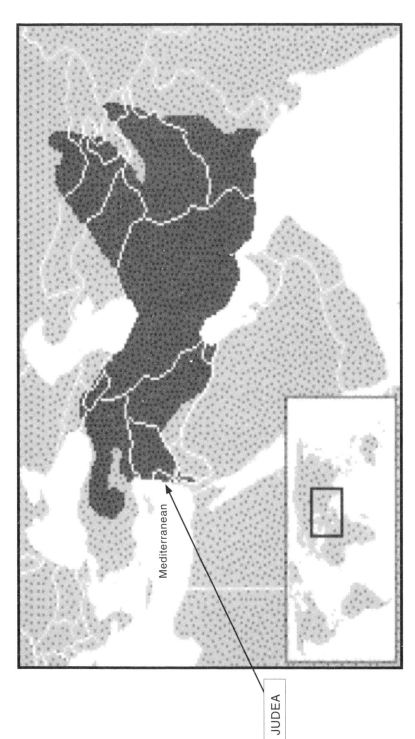

JUDEA

Mediterranean

Seleucid Empire
(shaded black)

source: www.wikipedia.org

Introduction

The introductory TimeLine [Lead-in #2] of this work,
"Crucifixion," commences 300 BCE, 23 years after the
death of Alexander the Great, and 31 years after pivotal
Battle of Gaugamela 331 BCE, which shifted the Near
East, the Levant and Judea, among other regions, from
Persian dominance to Greek control....

In turn, in 63 BCE, Roman general and master geopo-
litical player Pompey, politically maneuvering eastward,
absorbed what was left of the disintegrating Seleucid
Empire, into a Roman province – incorporating Judea...

By the year 1 CE, Judean King Herod's super–renovated
and gold–leafed extraordinary Temple II glistened on
its Jerusalem hilltop plateau, a Wonder of the Ancient
World, visible and awe–inspiring from the approaches
to Jerusalem.

Hillel (110 BCE – 10 CE) the renowned Jewish sage,
preached humanism and "love thy neighbor" as key Jewish
tenets; his philosophical standard bearers, the Pharisees,
would emerge as mainstream/normative Judaism.

The preeminent Roman rulers spanning the capture of Jerusalem by Pompey (63 BCE) and the three Jewish rebellions (through 135 CE) are listed along with some salient events relevant to our Integrated TimeLine during the period of latter days of First Roman Republic:

Early days Roman Empire Emperors

63 BCE
Cicero and Antonius are the two Roman Consuls
[Gen. Pompey readily captures Jerusalem 63 BCE after adroit alliance with one of the two contending Jewish forces in the internal Jewish civil war]

Various Roman 2–Consul leaderships
63 BCE–60 BCE

The First Triumvirate
60 BCE–53 BCE
Caesar/Crassus/Pompey

Pompey
52 BCE–49 BCE

Caesar
49 BCE–44 BCE
[Caesar crosses the Rubicon (river) 49 BCE]

Mark Antony / Octavian (Augustus) / Lepidus known as "The Second Triumvirate"
44 BCE–33 BCE
[Herod named tetrarch of Jerusalem 42 BCE]

Octavian (Augustus)
33 BCE–27 BCE
(but Octavian not ruling as emperor yet)

During subsequent period of Roman Empire:

continued (on next Left–side page)

Christianity would absorb some of Hillel's key humanistic motifs in the decades that followed his death.

The Jews, heirs to the heroic and glorious legacies of Moses, Mt. Sinai, David, Solomon and the Maccabees, stood at the very apex of Mediterranean civilization and society.

It was widely disseminated and/or suspected that something profound and cosmic had occurred *vis à vis* the Jews at Sinai. The Jews—and only the Jews—had this distinct claim on *destiny*.

In the year 1 CE, the ~7 million Jews represented approximately 2.8% of the world's population of approximately 250 million.

The Roman Empire was eventually to fall under the control of the Catholic Church by the mid–300s CE. It had been *de facto* Church policy since c. 68 CE to demonize and de–humanize the Jews. Now, with control of the *organs of state* of the Roman Empire, the Catholic Church would disseminate these themes with a vengeance. The Jews became total pariahs throughout the empire.

Between the years 68 CE and 1300 CE, the Catholic Church persuaded the world that "the Jew" was a cross between an evil *sub–human* and a conspiratorial *diabolical* entity.

Latter days Roman Republic Rulers

\# And the Roman emperors:

\# Octavian (Augustus a.k.a. Caesar Augustus
a.k.a. Augustus Caesar)
27 BCE to 14 CE
[Herod dies 4 BCE; Jesus born c. 5 BCE]

\# Tiberius
14 CE to 37 CE
[Jesus crucified by Pontius Pilate 33 CE]

\# Caligula
37 CE to 41 CE

\# Claudius
41 CE to 54 CE
["Letter to Alexandrians" (i.e. Alexandrian Jews)]

\# Nero
54 CE to 68 CE
[1st Jewish Revolt c. 67 CE;
General Vespasian dispatched to Judea]

\# ["Year of the Four Emperors":
Galba; Otho; Vitelius…Vespasian 68 CE]

\# Vespasian
69 CE to 79 CE
[son Titus ends Jewish Revolt I in 70–73 CE]

\# Titus
79 CE to 81 CE
[Arch of Titus; Vesuvius erupts 79 CE;
Fire of Rome 80 CE;
multi–year notable public romance with (Jewish 'royal') Berenice]

\# Domitian
81 CE to 96 CE

\# Nerva
96 CE to 98 CE

\# Trajan
98 CE to 117 CE
[2nd Jewish Revolt (Kitos) 115 CE–117 CE]

\# Hadrian
117 CE to 138 CE
[3rd Jewish Revolt (*Bar Kochba*) 132 CE–136 CE]

source: www.scaruffi.com/politics/romans.html

A random Roman Empire Jew would be born into this nightmare, and die 40–50 years later within its toxic envelopment, if he survived at all: isolated, denigrated, powerless – a shadow of the Jews in the non–Christian empires preceding the birth of Christianity.

By the year 1300 CE, the end of the last Crusade, the number of Jews had radically decreased. The historical estimates of the remaining Jews at that point (1300 CE) ranges from 1.4–3.0 million. So, at a maximum, assuming the figure was 3 million Jews, by the year 1300 CE, the Jews represented .0068 (approximately 7/10 of 1 percent) of the world's total population of 440 million.

Thus, calculating the decimation of the Jews very conservatively, the ratio of Jews in the world decreased from six million equaling .02181 (approximately 2.2 percent in year 0) of the world population, to three million equaling .0068 (approximately 7/10 of 1 percent in year 1300 CE) of the world's population over the 1300 year span.

Europe and the Mediterranean area
– at the time of the Crusades

JUDEA

Meaning, by the end of the Crusades, the Jews represented at a maximum less than 1/3 of their former *ratio* of the world's population prior to the advent of the Catholic Church. In absolute numbers, over the 1300 year span, the Jewish population, at a minimum halved, while global civilization grew by about 60 percent.

The statistics, of course, do not *tell the story*, by any means; they merely frame–out the skeletal parameters – of a grand multi–century saga of betrayal and infamy.

And of survival – physical and spiritual….

***

Note: The Black Death only made an appearance in 1348, after the time frame of this work, and outside the parameters of the above statistics.

end of Introduction

***

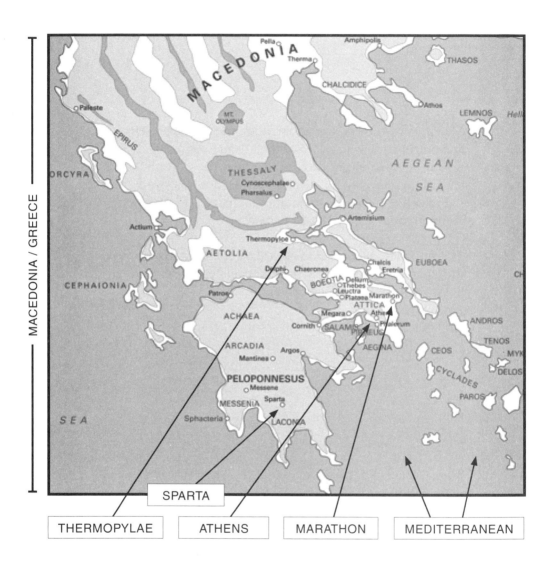

Ancient Greece (Macedonia)

Lead–in #1
480 BCE – 301 BCE

**pivoting around the
"The Spartan 300"**

"The 300" is the historic shorthand applied to the legendary Spartan (Greek) core defensive force commanded by King Leonidas I at the iconic Battle of Thermopylae (Greece) in August/September 480 BCE.

"The 300" were pitted against the Persian Empire's elite 10,000 "Persian Immortals," themselves a sub–component of the forward–force of 200,000+ soldiers of Xerxes I, Emperor of Persia. The total Persian expeditionary force mustered by Darius I numbered between 250,000 (the current consensus) and 2 million+ (historian Herodotus).

The massive Xerxes I invasion itself was a delayed response to the Athenian/Greek victory over the Persians at Marathon (Greece) ten years earlier (c. 490 BCE). The earlier Persian invasion had been orchestrated by Darius I (reign: 522 BCE – 486 BCE), the late father of Xerxes I.

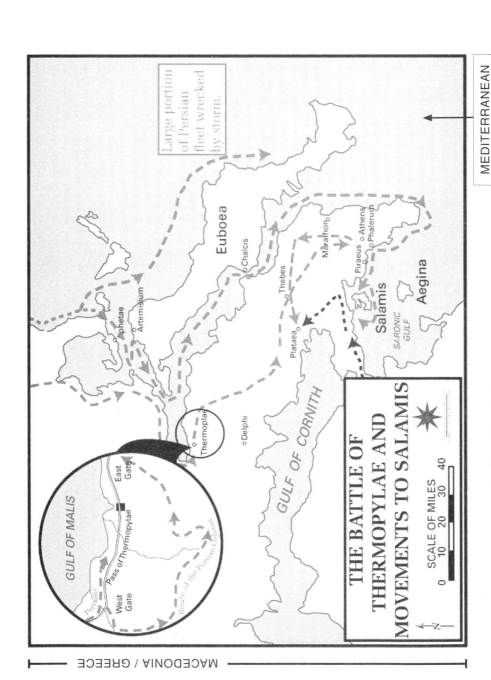

MACEDONIA / GREECE

MEDITERRANEAN

Large portion
of Persian
fleet wrecked
by storm.

Euboea

Chalcis

Thebes

Delphi

Plataea

Marathon

Athens
Piraeus Phalerum

Salamis

Aegina

SARONIC
GULF

Aphetae

Artemisium

Thermoplae

GULF OF CORNITH

GULF OF MALIS

West
Gate

East
Gate

Pass of Thermopylae

Route of the Persian Column

Pygelus

THE BATTLE OF
THERMOPYLAE AND
MOVEMENTS TO SALAMIS

SCALE OF MILES

0   10   20   30   40

N

source: The Department of History, United States Military Academy

The legend of "the 300" revolves around the *'last stand'* of the Spartan Greeks under King Leonidas. Understanding that defeat by the Persians was inevitable, Leonidas had sent the great bulk of the 7,000–strong Greek defensive force back home to safety, electing only to delay the Persian advance utilizing his elite "300" (plus 1,100 allied soldiers) in a suicidal martyr–gambit to block the crucial Thermopylae Pass, entryway to Greece.

According to lore, "the (valiant) 300" essentially *held their ground* in the narrow pass. The Persians, however, maneuvered around them through a back–road pass, revealed to Xerxes's troops by the traitorous Ephialtes. The Persians then attacked and slaughtered the "300" from two directions simultaneously.

The Persians won the battle of Thermopylae, but ultimately lost the war (Persian Invasion II). They also lost the next war (Persian Invasion III), approximately a year later.

***

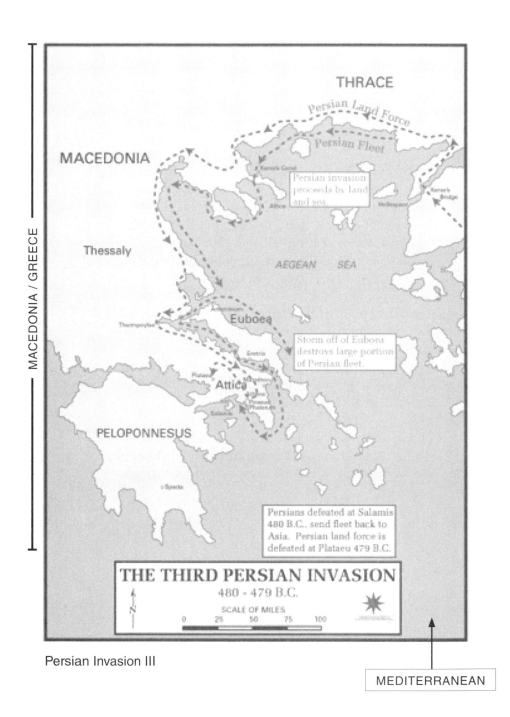

THRACE

MACEDONIA

Persian Land Force

Persian Fleet

Persian invasion proceeds by land and sea.

Thessaly

AEGEAN SEA

Thermopylae

Euboea

Storm off of Euboea destroys large portion of Persian fleet.

Eretria

Plataea

Attica

PELOPONNESUS

Salamis

Sparta

Persians defeated at Salamis 480 B.C. send fleet back to Asia. Persian land force is defeated at Plataeu 479 B.C.

THE THIRD PERSIAN INVASION
480 - 479 B.C.

N

SCALE OF MILES

0   25   50   75   100

Persian Invasion III

MEDITERRANEAN

MACEDONIA / GREECE

- *But where might the round and even "300"
  number have come from?*

The 300 warrior number may come straight from the
saga of (Israelite Judge–Warrior) Gideon (c. 1150 BCE),
whose super–elite 300–man Israelite strike force –
trumpets blaring, torches flaring, clay jars shattering –
psyched–out the Midianites, and put their much larger
army to rout.

So, 670 years before Leonidas fielded his "300" at Thermopylae in Greece, Israelite Commander Gideon fielded
his own "300" eastward in Canaan (Judea).

"When the 300 trumpets [of Gideon's troops] sounded,
the Lord caused the men throughout the [Midianite]
camp to turn on each other with their swords" (Judges/
Shoftim 7:17)

- *And, how does Xerxes relate to Jewish
  history, if at all?*

Xerxes I (reign: 485 BCE – 465 BCE) was most probably none other than Achashverosh (transliteration of
Ahasuerus). Both names – Xerxes and Ahasuerus – derive
directly from the Persian name *Khashayarsha*.

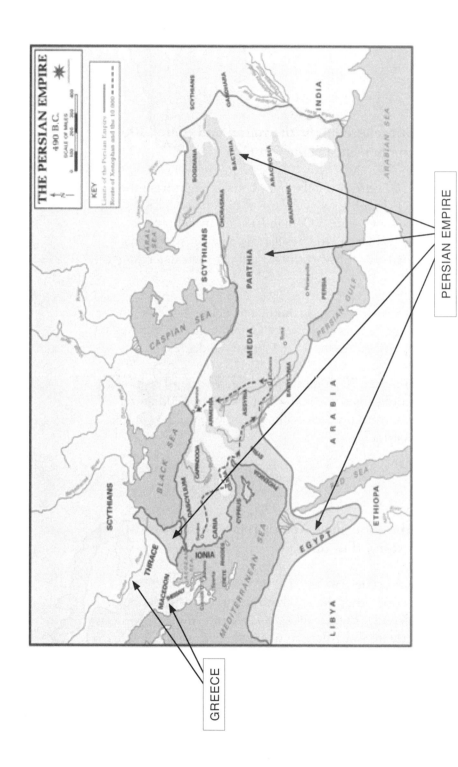

Greece/Macedon presents as almost 1/20 the size of the Persian Empire

source: http://ancienthistory.about.com

Achashverosh, was the Persian ruler who wed the legendary (Jewish Queen) Esther. She, in turn, saved the Jews, after some *fancy footwork* involving the king, from the evil Persian vizier Haman. The Jewish Holiday of Purim – celebrating the deliverance of the Jews from the evil Haman – is the result. [Purim is celebrated in March/April, always exactly four weeks before Passover.]

- ***What was the lineage of Xerxes?***

Xerxes I was the son of Darius the Great (reign 522–486 BCE), who had secured the throne of Cyrus the Great (reign 559–530 BCE) eight years after the death of Cyrus (530 BCE).

- ***And what is the context of Cyrus the Great here?***

Cyrus the Great (a.k.a Cyrus II) was the founder of the Achaemenid Persian Dynasty (559 BCE – 330 BCE), one of the world's great empires, not only in terms of land mass conquered, but in terms of contributions to civilization, as well. Among other contributions, the Persian Empire banned slavery in all its forms. As well, the *empire paradigm* followed by Cyrus (and later by Darius), assiduously respected the cultures and customs of the conquered peoples.

CYRUS THE GREAT
ILLUSTRATOR: ANGUS McBRIDE

Cyrus is introduced into Jewish history via the Book of Daniel. Trained in the Royal Court of Babylon, the young Jewish exile Daniel was called in by Belshazzar to decipher the *Writing on the Wall* (a.k.a. the Hand Writing on the Wall).

Prince Belshazzar was the son of Nabonidus (reign 556–540 BCE) destined to be the last king of Babylon. Nabonidus's predecessor Nebuchadnezzar (605–562 BCE), who died six years before Nabonidus assumed the throne – had destroyed (the Jewish) Temple I in Jerusalem – on the ninth Day of the lunar month of Av, 586 BCE.

Daniel 5:1–4 describes *Belshazzar's Feast,* wherein the Babylonian prince employed sacred vessels of the sacked Temple I of Jerusalem in a pagan feast. A disembodied hand then appeared writing on the wall. At loss to explain the cryptic meaning of the verses, Belshazzar summoned Daniel to interpret the writings, which Daniel did forthwith.

539 BCE: THE WRITING ON THE WALL
"THE FEAST OF BELSHAZZAR" (1635)
PAINTER: REMBRANDT

* "*Mene, Mene,*
Tekel,
Upharsin,"

* exact quote from Daniel

Addressing the Babylonian crown prince:

God has numbered the days of your kingdom
And brought them to an end;
You have been weighed on the scales – and found wanting;
Your kingdom is divided, and given to the Medes and
Persians

                           – Book of Daniel 5:26–28

Belshazzar is slain shortly thereafter. Advance troops of
Cyrus – emperor of the Medes & Persians – commence their
military assault on the capital city of Babylon. On October
29, 540 BCE, the Imperial High Command Cyrus the Great
himself entered the capital city of Babylon and detained
Belshazzar's father, Nabonidus, King of Babylon. The Babylonian Empire "was history." The Persians would swallow
the Babylonian Empire whole – 44 years after Babylonia's
Nebuchadnezzar has sacked the Holy Temple in Jerusalem.

Belshazzar

Dynasty XI of Babylon (Neo–Babylonian or Chaldean)

- Nabu–apla–usur (Nabopolassar) 626– 605 BCE

- Nabu–kudurri–usur (Nebuchadrezzar II (Nebuchadnezzar II) 605– 562 BCE

- Amel–Marduk 562– 560 BCE

- Nergal–šar–usur (Nergal–sharezer) 560– 556 BCE

- Labaši–Marduk 556 BCE

>>>
- Nabu–na'id (Nabonidus) 556– 539 BCE
  (and his son Belshazzar in tandem)

- Cambyses 538– 522 BCE

In 539 BCE, Babylon was captured by Cyrus the Great of Persia, and lost its independence. His son, Cambyses, was crowned one year later formally as King of Babylonia.

- *And how does Cyrus relate to Jewish history after his conquest of Babylon?*

Cyrus was indisputably the greatest ally and benefactor of the Jews in history – spanning the 3500 years of Jewish history.

Under Cyrus the Great of Persia, his *Edict of Restoration*, gave legal sanction to Jewish return to Jerusalem. In 538 BCE under the aegis of Cyrus's satrap, the legendary (Jewish) Zerubbabel (grandson of Judean King Jehoiachin) approximately 48 years after the Babylonian Exile (c. 586 BCE), approximately 42,000 Jews returned to Judea from Babylonia in this first wave of return.

Three years later, in 535 BCE, the rebuilding of the Temple (henceforth to be called Temple II) commenced under the aforementioned Persian Governor Zerubbabel. The rebuilding continued intermittently over the time span 535–515 BCE. The Jewish prophet Ezra, as well, oversaw the construction.

As noted above, Darius the Great (Darius I) had assumed the reigns of power of the Persian Empire in September 522 BCE, eight years after the death of Cyrus. Darius ratified the continued building of Temple II and was the emperor when Temple II was completed 516 BCE, and dedicated, 515 BCE.

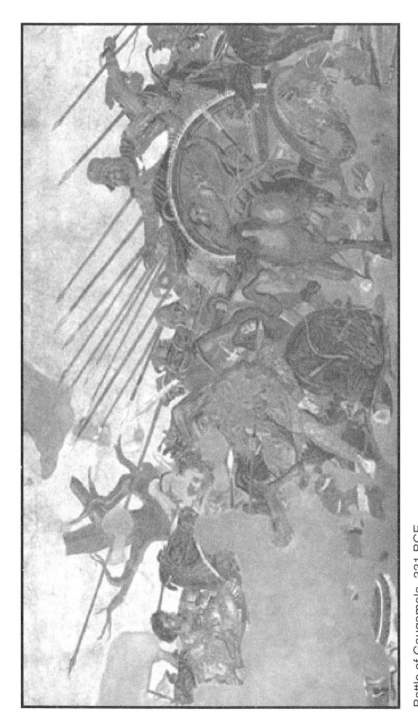

Battle of Gaugamela, 331 BCE

- *What was the denouement of the Achaemenid Dynasty?*

Down the road in Achaemenid Dynasty history, Darius III would fight 25–year–old Alexander the Great, who had marched eastward from Greece, at the Battle of Gaugamaela (Persia) in 331 BCE. The historic battle resulted in a massive victory for the Macedonians (Greeks) and the fall of the Achaemenid Persian Empire. The empire of Alexander the Great's empire would unfold eastward, victory after victory, upon the heels of the pivotal victory at Gaugamela.

When Alexander's empire, in turn, devolved upon his death in 323 BCE, one of the major successor states, the (Greco–Syrian–Near Eastern) Seleucid Empire (312–63 BCE) ended up with control of Judea, among other territories in its vast domain. Antiochus (reign: 175–164 BCE), a.k.a. Antiochus IV Epiphanes, nemesis of the Maccabees (revolt: 167–142 BCE), would come from this Seleucid line.

The ultimate triumph of the Jewish forces over the Seleucids, in 142 BCE, after 25 years of revolt, is commemorated by the Jewish holiday of Chanukah.

end of lead–in #1

480 BCE – 301 BCE

***

300 BCE: THE ABACUS

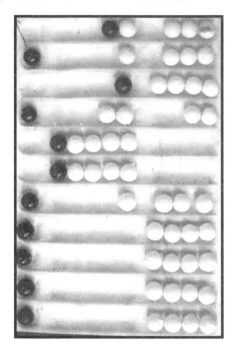

Older Abacus

Chinese Abacus

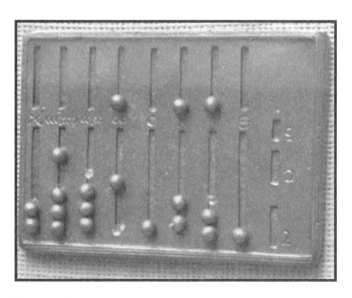

Roman Abacus

Lead–in #2
TimeLine
300 BCE – 1 BCE

300 BCE: EUCLID

Euclid, a Hellenist living in Alexandria, Egypt publishes *Elements*, a 13–volume treatise on geometry and the ancient Greek version of number theory.

Euclidean geometry employs, among other components:
- definitions
- postulates (axioms: highest level "laws");
- propositions (theorems derived from postulates);
- proofs of theorems.

Euclidean geometry is a self–contained construct of mathematical and formal logic of elegance and perfection.

Elements has been revised in over 1,000 editions, and is considered the most successful "textbook" ever written.

300 BCE: THE ABACUS

The Babylonians invent the earliest calculator, the abacus, in Mesopotamia.

287 BCE: ARCHIMEDES
"ARCHIMEDES THOUGHTFUL"
PAINTER: DOMENICO FETTI

289 BCE: TROPHY LIGHT HOUSE

Ptolemy II of Egypt builds the first–known large lighthouse on an island at the mouth of the Nile. The lighthouse is 400 feet high, and according to lore, could be seen from 40 miles away.

[Author – Equations regarding "horizon" would confirm the 40 mile possibility, but only if a fire–beacon lit the top of the lighthouse, to further project its visibility.]

287 BCE: ARCHIMEDES

Britannica –

"The most famous mathematician and inventor of ancient Greece. Archimedes is especially important for his discovery of the relation between the surface and volume of a sphere and its circumscribing cylinder. He is known for his formulation of a hydrostatic principle (known as Archimedes' principle) and a device for raising water, still used in developing countries, known as the Archimedes screw.

Far more details survive about the life of Archimedes than about any other ancient scientist, but they are largely anecdotal…

There are nine extant treatises by Archimedes in Greek: these include –

On Conoids and Spheroids deals with determining the volume.

On the Equilibrium of Planes (or *Centres of Gravity of Planes*; in two books) is mainly concerned with

287 BCE: ARCHIMEDES

Archimedes is said to have remarked about **the lever:** *"Give me a large enough lever*, and I will move the Earth."*

(an engraving from *Mechanics Magazine* published in London, 1824)

*and/or "a place to stand"

establishing the centers of gravity of various rectilinear plane figures *et al.*

The *Sand–Reckoner* is a small treatise that is a *jeu d'esprit* written for the layman—it is addressed to Gelon, son of Hieron—that nevertheless contains some profoundly original mathematics. Its object is to remedy the inadequacies of the Greek numerical notation system by showing how to express a huge number—the number of grains of sand that it would take to fill the whole of the universe.

Method Concerning Mechanical Theorems describes a process of discovery in mathematics. It is the sole surviving work from antiquity, and one of the few from any period, that deals with this topic. In it Archimedes recounts how he used a "mechanical" method to arrive at some of his key discoveries.

On Floating Bodies (in two books) survives only partly in Greek, the rest in Medieval Latin translation from the Greek. It is the first known work on hydrostatics, of which Archimedes is recognized as the founder.

Archimedes is known, from references of later authors, to have written a number of other works that have not survived. Of particular interest are treatises on catoptrics, in which he discussed, among other things, the phenomenon of refraction....

Archimedes' mathematical proofs and presentation exhibit great boldness and originality of thought on the one hand and extreme rigor on the other...

280 BCE: "PYRRHIC VICTORY"

King Pyrrhus

In antiquity, Archimedes was also known as an outstanding astronomer."

Encyclopaedia Britannica Online, http://www.britannica.com/EBchecked/ topic/32808/Archimedes (accessed July 1, 2009)

280 BCE: PYRRHIC VICTORY

The term "Pyrrhic victory" enters into the military lexicon courtesy of King Pyrrhus of Epirus [currently Greece + Albania], whose ultimately victorious army suffers awesome casualties in his victory over the Romans at Heracles (280 BCE) and Asculum (279 BCE) during what comes to be known as the Pyrrhic War.

After his casualty–heavy victories, King Pyrrhus is reported by Plutarch and Dionysius to have caustically noted, "One more such victory will utterly undo me."

Now, the obverse of a *Pyrrhic victory*, would be a **Pyrrhic loss** (with the term coined just now, here...*wink*). For example: In 2007 (Palestinian wing) Fatah was unceremoniously routed from Gaza by (Palestinian wing) Hamas; the denouement (at least to date) has been that Fatah, delinked from international–*problem–child* Hamas, has "advanced" on the world stage from its newly defined center–of–gravity on the more pivotal West Bank, while Hamas has "twisted and turned" back in forlorn (under–siege) Gaza.

273 BCE: ASHOKA OF INDIA

Ashoka the Great (304–232 BCE) ascends as emperor of the Mauryan Empire. He then conquers and unifies most of South Asia, along with parts of Afghanistan and Iran. After conquering the adjacent kingdom of

250 BCE: THE SEPTUAGINT (THE SEVENTY)

The Septuagint: A column of uncial text from 1 Esdras in the *Codex Vaticanus*, the basis of Sir Lancelot Charles Lee Brenton's Greek edition and English translation.

source: Plate XII. "The S.S. Teacher's Edition: The Holy Bible." New York: Henry Frowde, Publisher to the University of Oxford, 1896.

Kalinga in 265 BCE, Ashoka has regrets over his warlike tendencies, adopts Buddhism, and makes it the official religion of the Mauryan Empire.

In the 260s BCE, Ashoka grants increasing religious and social tolerance, as well as animal rights. He builds hospitals for the poor and for animals, and treats his subjects as equals regardless of class or creed. He promotes non–violence and republicanism. His historical zenith is probably the *Edicts of Ashoka*, which codify his historic reforms.

250 BCE: THE SEPTUAGINT (THE SEVENTY)

Greek King of Egypt, Ptolemy II Philadelphus, has 72 Jewish scholars translate the Five Books of Moses (as well as other books from the *Tanach*) into Greek.

Note: The title "The Septuagint" (a.k.a. "The LXX") comes from the Greek number 70 (rounded–off from 72).

One wonders…if they *rounded off* the precise number in their own title, whether they also *rounded off* the translations….

247 BCE: PARTHIA

Parthian kingdom, whose center of gravity is northeast Iran, founded in the Middle East and Near East during the Arsacid Dynasty.

Arch–enemy of the Roman Empire to the west, Parthia reaches its greatest extent around 150 BCE under Mithridates and lasts approximately 500 years. It was defeated in 224 CE by a vassal group, the Persians of the Sassanid Dynasty.

216 BCE: BATTLE OF CANNAE

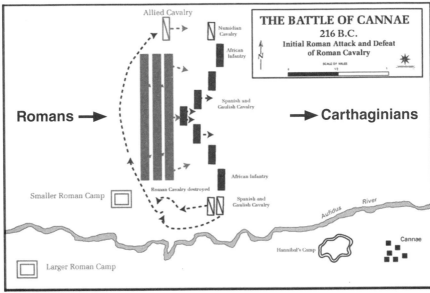

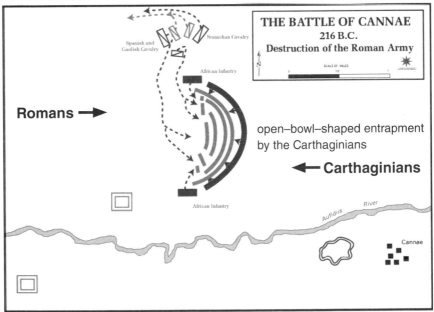

source: The Department of History, United States Military Academy

230 BCE: ARISTARCHUS

Greek mathematician and astronomer from Samos, an island off ancient Greece.

The first recorded person to place the sun, moon and planets in correct orientation with each other (known as heliocentric theory). Although the proposal of Aristarchus was rejected as wrong and impious, the world eventually caught up with his thinking – about 1800 years later – when Copernicus proposed the same theory c.1543 in the year leading–into his death. The *heliocentric theory* was finally "accepted" about 100 years subsequent to the death of Copernicus.

221 BCE: THE (FIRST) GREAT WALL OF CHINA

First Emperor Qin Shi, regarded by many as the founding father of China, builds a wall along 1,200 miles of China's northern border. The wall stands between 20 and 50 feet high and 18 and 30 feet wide. It has a roadway on top, along with many periodic stations and connecting towers.

The wall's more muscular successor, the 4,000–mile–long Great Wall, is built seventeen centuries later under the extraordinary Ming Dynasty.

216 BCE: BATTLE OF CANNAE

Carthaginian (centered in what is now Tunisia) General–in–Chief Hannibal crosses the Italian Alps (after marching through Iberia and Gaul) in the winter with 30,000–40,000 men, 6,000 horses and some surviving elephants. Although he is vastly outnumbered,

216 BCE: BATTLE OF CANNAE

HANNIBAL'S ROUTE OF INVASION
Third Century B.C.

SCALE OF MILES

0   1/4   1/2   3/4   1

N

Labels on map:

ATLANTIC O.

GAUL

SPAIN

Gades

Ebro R.

Cartagena

Saguntum

Massilia

Rhone R.

ALPS

Turin

Trebia R.

Ticinus River

Po R.

Rhone R.

Arminium

Arretium

Tiber R.

Rome

Capua

Cannae

Tarentum

ADRIATIC SEA

CORSICA

SARDINIA

MEDITERRANEAN   SEA

Messina

Sicily

Syracuse

Carthage

Zama

NUMIDIA

AFRICA

Hannibal's route of invasion

source: The Department of History, United States Military Academy

Hannibal annihilates the Romans' 87,000–man army at Cannae in southeast Italy, outside of Rome.

The Battle of Cannae is considered by many military historians, along with the Battle of Gaugamela (331 BCE), to be one of the greatest tactical feats in military history.

Rather than line up his forces head–to–head against the massed Romans, Hannibal assembles them in a V formation, with the point of the V pointing straight at the Romans.

When the Romans advance, Hannibal feigns weakness, and then gradually "collapses" the front of the V, steadily encircling the Romans. Hannibal then signals a full–scale attack from all directions. A massacre of the Romans ensues.

The extraordinary ignominious count of 50,000+ Romans killed in one day is a uniquely dark historic figure in military annals.

Eighty Roman senators, who came anticipating basking in the glory of a dramatic victory over Hannibal, were either killed or captured at Cannae.

Military historians speculate that if Hannibal had pressed his advantage and marched on nearby Rome itself, he would have prevailed. The weight of the evidence is, indeed, on that side of the argument. However, Hannibal paused, and Rome would not be caught vulnerable again for a long time.

Several Italian city–states hitherto aligned with Rome,

210 BCE: XIAN

CHINA

did defect to the Carthaginian side, however. They would ultimately regret that decision.

210 BCE: XIAN

Emperor Qin Shi dies. Buried next to his mausoleum in the Shaanxi Province of China is the Xian necropolis (meaning "city of the dead"), life–size *terra cotta* replicas of Qin's army.

Xian vies with Egypt's pyramids as the preeminent (surviving) man–made "wonder of the Ancient World."

The 8,000 clay replicas—in formation and in battle dress with weaponry and chariots—are believed to have taken 700,000 workers and craftsmen 38 years to complete.

The figurines, with an average height of about 6' 2.5" are actually about 25 percent bigger than the actual size of the local humans at the time.

Each figure has a unique expression and facial details. The figures vary in height, uniform and hairstyle in accordance with rank.

The clay battalions were discovered in 1974 subsequent to some pottery–fragment discoveries by a local farmer.

190–120 BCE: HIPPARCHUS

Greece: One of the great astronomers of antiquity. He was involved in the development of trigonometry and the astrolabe, the earliest known star chart. He was also a geographer and mathematician. Hipparchus spent the latter part of his life in Rhodes.

210 BCE: XIAN

Terra Cotta Army

175 BCE: ANTIOCHUS IV EPHIPANES

–ascends to the Seleucid throne. Original name: Mithridates.

Greek–Syrian Seleucid king Antiochus IV Epiphanes, successor to the Egyptian Ptolemies (who, in turn, are successors to Alexander the Great).

His adversaries called him "The Mad One."

(b. 215 BCE; d. 164 BCE)

168 BCE: *"LINE IN THE SAND"* / ANTIOCHUS

The Seleucid army from the east had invaded Roman Protectorate Egypt.

The Roman ambassador (Gaius Popillus Laenas) in Egypt confronts Seleucid King Antiochus IV and demands that Antiochus commit to withdraw from Egypt. The ambassador draws a circle in the sand around Antiochus. The Roman ambassador demands that Antiochus—prior to crossing the circle *line in the sand*—commit to withdrawing all his forces from Egypt, implying that Antiochus's breach of the circle in the absence of a commitment to withdraw, would provoke war with Rome. Antiochus hesitates, but then capitulates and commits to withdraw from Egypt. The Roman ambassador shakes his hand and Antiochus exits the circle in the sand. Antiocus subsequently indeed withdraws his forces from Egypt.

169 BCE: ANTIOCHUS IV OVERSTEPS

Having been stymied in Egypt and compelled to withdraw, Antiochus turns his attention to Judea.

c. 167 BCE: THE MACCABEAN (HASMONEAN) REVOLT COMMENCES

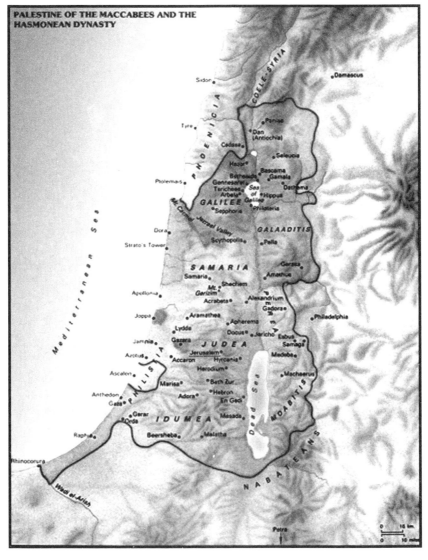

JUDEA

Antiochus asserts strict control over Judea, plunders Jerusalem and its Temple, suppresses Jewish religious cultural and religious observances, and imposes Hellenistic practices.

On December 25th 169 BCE he profanes the Temple. Among other acts, he orders a statue of Zeus erected inside, provoking the Maccabees (the Hasmoneans) into rebellion.

c. 167–162 BCE: THE MACCABEAN (HASMONEAN) REVOLT COMMENCES

The revolt is sparked and led by the Maccabean family of Jewish priest Matisyahu and his five sons: Jochanan, Simon, Ezra, Jonathan and Judah.

Matisyahu refuses to allow anyone to sacrifice to the Greek gods—and slays a Hellenistic Jew who attempts to do so.

The revolt is on.

> "Mi l'Adoshem, ai–lye"

> "He who is for God, follow me!"

> –Battle cry of Matisyahu the Maccabee

The Jews will follow him into battle, and will ultimately prevail, after two–and–a–half decades of battle.

167 BCE: MATISYAHU DIES

Son Judah succeeds him as preeminent leader of the revolutionary forces. While Matisyahu was more priest than commander, Judah is more commander than priest;

c. 167 BCE: THE MACCABEAN (HASMONEAN) REVOLT COMMENCES

"And he [the Maccabee brothers] crept under the elephant, and thrust him from beneath and slew it" (I Maccabees 6:48).

his actual taken name is "Judah the Hammer," i.e. Judah the Maccabee.

Judah the Maccabee, revolutionary commander, recaptures Jerusalem and rededicates the Temple on December 14, 164 BCE (25 *Kislev*).

The Jews are offered a compromise by the Greek–Syrians: religious freedom but under continued Greek rule. The Maccabees decline the offer. They have heard that line *before*.

The Maccabean insurgency will continue another 23 years in the endeavor to shake off Greek–Syrian rule totally, and to achieve political independence. One after the other, the sons of Matisyahu—the Maccabean commanders—are killed in battle. Judah is killed in 160 BCE, and his successor Jonathan is killed in 142 BCE. Another son is crushed by a charging Greek–Syrian military elephant in battle. Finally, in the same year, under the command of Judah's surviving brother Simon— priest, warrior and master statesman—the Greek–Syrians, now under Demetrius II, grant the Jews complete political independence (and religious freedom).

After 25 years of almost unrelenting battle against the regional successors of Alexander the Great, the Macabees have prevailed and secured total Jewish independence.

Under the command of Judah the Maccabee previously, the Jews had restored the Temple, complete with the miracle of the oil lamps. In commemoration of the miracle, Judah institutes the holiday Chanukah, when eight festive candles are lit for eight days each December (starting on the Hebrew calendar day *Kislev* 25).

142 BCE: ZUGOT PERIOD

from

Pirkei Avos

פרקי אבות

The Wisdom of the Fathers

AVOS I:12

HILLEL AND SHAMMAI RECEIVED THE TRADITION FROM THEM. HIL-LEL SAYS: BE OF THE DISCIPLES OF AARON, LOVING PEACE AND PUR-SUING PEACE, LOVING YOUR FEL-LOW MEN, AND DRAWING THEM NEAR TO THE TORAH.

הִלֵּל וְשַׁמַּאי קִבְּלוּ מֵהֶם. הִלֵּל אוֹמֵר הֱוֵי מִתַּלְמִידָיו שֶׁל אַהֲרֹן אוֹהֵב שָׁלוֹם וְרוֹדֵף שָׁלוֹם אוֹהֵב אֶת הַבְּרִיּוֹת וּמְקָרְבָן לַתּוֹרָה:

Dedicated priest, faithful son, triumphant battle commander, leader of Israel and liberator of Jerusalem, re–dedicator of the Temple, then killed in battle, Judah the Maccabee bequeaths an extraordinary legacy for the ages.

144 BCE: ROMAN AQUEDUCTS

The Romans develop hydraulic cement, which does not dissolve in water, allowing them to build major large aqueducts bringing fresh water to Rome. Eleven aqueducts, constructed over a period of 500 years, ultimately supplied the city of Rome itself.

142 BCE–40 CE: ZUGOT PERIOD

First rabbinical era; refers to the period when five successive pairs (*zugot*) of legal scholars ruled the *Beit Din HaGadol* (the Jewish supreme court).

The five pairs of *zugot* are:

- Jose ben Joezer + Jose ben Johanan
  (Maccabean period)

- Joshua ben Perachyah + Nittai of Arbela
  (John Hyrcanus period)

- Judah ben Tabai + Simeon ben Shetach
  (Salome Alexandra period)

- Sh'maya + Abtalion
  (Hyrcanus II period)

- Hillel + Shammai
  (Herod the Great period)

142 BCE: ZUGOT PERIOD

THE CRUCIFIXION

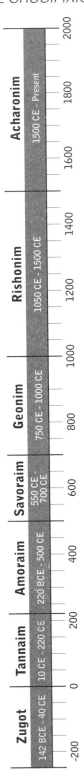

Zugot	142 BCE - 40 CE
Tannaim	10 CE - 220 CE
Amoraim	220 BCE - 500 CE
Savoraim	550 CE - 700 CE
Geonim	750 CE - 1000 CE
Rishonim	1050 CE - 1500 CE
Acharonim	1500 CE - Present

The (macro) rabbinical eras (with some significant overlap) are:

> Zugot – *just–described*
> Tannaim
> Amoraim
> Savoraim
> Geonim
> Rishonim
> Acharonim

135 BCE: HASMONEAN ASSASSINATION

Simon Maccabeus and his two sons are assassinated at the instigation of his son–in–law Ptolemy (the Judean, not the Roman general of the same name).

However, Simon Maccabeus's third son, John Hyrcanus, emerges from the maelstrom of the assassinations and assumes kingship. He incorporates an aggressive leadership style that includes the historically unusual forced conversion of the Idumeans (Edom) in the eastern regions of greater Israel, as well as a campaign against the Samarians (in middle–northern greater Israel) including the destruction of their temple on Mt. Gerizim.

130 BCE: PHARISEES

The Pharisee thrust in Judaism begins to emerge. Meaning, Judaism periodically developed tributaries. Sometimes these tributaries "dried up" and sometimes they flourished (and flourish to this day), The Pharisee thrust flourished, leaving the Sadducee camp to ultimately wither.

The Pharisees, with Hillel to be their iconic standard–bearer, were less authoritarian and more humanistic on

130 BCE: HASMONEAN LEGACY

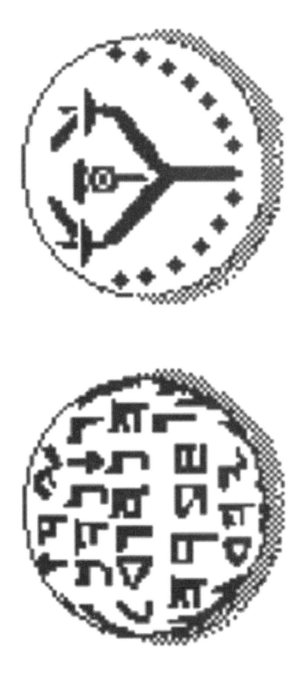

The coins of the Hasmoneans were filled on one side with text written in ancient Hebrew script, with the flip-side symbolizing their signature Menorah motif.

the ideological spectrum than the competing Sadducees.

The Pharisees were more into the "spirit of the law" than the technical dictates of the law. The so–called "Oral Law" – Rabbinic Law – Talmudic Law, is redacted (by Pharisee Judaism) from the so–called "Written Law" (of the Five Books of Moses). Of course, the "Oral Law" was ultimately written down—after it was debated—orally.

The Pharisees will eventually become essentially synonymous with Judaism post–Hillel, blossoming contemporaneously with the times of Jesus (who was himself a Pharisee).

Christian texts bizarrely invert the position of Jesus as *in opposition* to the mainstream and normative Jews, the Jewish–Pharisees. In reality, Jesus himself **was born and died a Pharisee.**

Furthermore, the Orthodox Jewish Pharisee Jesus followed precisely in the footsteps of—and precisely in the spirit of—the iconic humanistic Jewish–Pharisee sage Hillel (the Elder).

The sage Hillel (the Elder) preceded Jesus in the precise same locale—Greater Jerusalem—by precisely one generation.

Their respective humanistic ideologies are quite precisely *one and the same*. Verbatim.

The destruction of Temple II c. 70 CE, along with the destruction of the central Jewish authority and the subsequent ignominies unleashed by the Christianized Roman Empire post–Constantine, hundreds of years

130 BCE: HASMONEAN LEGACY

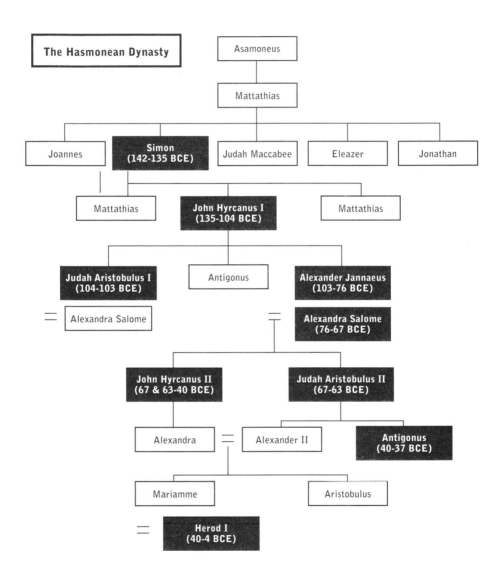

later, will give the development of the Talmud—
a Pharisee centerpiece—more centrality and importance.

130 BCE: HASMONEAN LEGACY

The legacy of Judah the Maccabee—"Judas Macabeeus"—
of extraordinary and victorious resistance and
redemption—is so powerful that 250 years later the
Romans will attempt to hunt down and slaughter all of
his descendants in Judea in order to preclude another
Maccabean leader from emerging to challenge them.
The later demonization by the Church of the name Judas
was possibly, as well, an attempt to undermine the Jewish
icon of the same name, aside from the Jews as a whole.

In 145 BCE, two decades after Judas Maccabeus defeats
Antiochus, his brother Simon Maccabeus sets up a
Maccabean Dynasty.

Thus a revolutionary and priestly family shifts gears
and asserts a royal claim to leadership, a claim far from
universally welcome by the Jews. A corruption–plagued
dynasty will then prevail for a hundred years before
becoming a client kingdom of Rome in 37 BCE, with the
installation of Rome–backed (technically non–Jewish)
Herod the Great as King of Israel.

The Hasmonean dynasty was the only independent
Jewish state in the four centuries after the destruction of
the kingdom of Judah by the Babylonians in 586 BCE,
and was essentially the last Jewish state prior to the
modern state of Israel (founded in 1948).

Vicious civil war between Hyrcanus II and Aristobulus II,
grandsons of Simon the Maccabee, presented political

130 BCE: HASMONEAN LEGACY

PAINTER: WOJCIECH STATTLER

The Romans dictating to the Jews (pre–rebellion), with the image of Mattisyahu approaching in the background.

and military vulnerability, which was then exploited by Roman general Pompey, who then adroitly and firmly secured control of Judea.

Later, when Pompey and Caesar die (48 BCE and 44 BCE, respectively), leading to yet another civil war in Rome, there is a brief Hasmonean resurgence backed by the Parthians, only to be crushed by Roman emperors Mark Antony and Octavian. By c. 6 CE, Rome will assert full control over Judea.

76 BCE: HER EXCELLENCY SHLOM–TZION

Commencement of the reign of *Shlom–Tzion* (Salome Alexandra), the only Jewish queen ever over Judea.

During her nine–year reign, Salome's son Hyrcanus II is named her successor and installed as High Priest. However, power apparently resided in the hands of his Machiavellian adviser, Antipater the Idumaean.

In sync with the Pharisees (Shimon ben Shetach, the head of the Pharisees, is said to have been Salome's brother) Salome reorganizes the Sanhedrin according to their (Pharisee/Sanhedrin) wishes.

This effectively re–morphs the Sanhedrin from a quasi *House of Lords* (of the aristocracy) which it had evolved into, back into a "supreme court" for the adjudication of religious matters, which was its very original mandate.

Salome was the last ruler to die as the head of a fully independent Jewish state in Israel until the formation of the modern state of Israel (2015 years later), in 1948.

68-63 BCE: ONE SPAN OF THE GREAT SANHEDRIN

source: www.campsci.com

73 BCE: SPARTACUS!

Former gladiator Spartacus leads a slave revolt back in Rome and initially defeats many Roman military forays at him.

Roman legions are brought home from abroad to deal with the insurgency.

After Spartacus is defeated and his army surrenders, all the insurgents are executed (crucified), with the 6,000 corpse–laden crucifixes lined–up along the Appian Way.

The Romans justify the execution of the surrendered army with the (spurious) assertion that "since the slaves had violated their employment contracts, they were liable for the death penalty."

67 BCE: HYRCANUS II MARCHES

Hyrcanus II reigns as king of northern Judea from 67 to 63 BCE.

Allied with Aretas, King of the Nabataeans, he marches on Jerusalem—the stronghold of his adversary Aristobulus. Both Hyrcanus II and Aristobulus were from wings of the Maccabeean dynasty.

During the siege of Jerusalem, the forces of Hyrcanus II commit two interrelated acts that incense the majority of the Jews and brand him forever:

1) The besieged forces in Jerusalem (under Aristobulus) had need of pascal lambs for the Passover rites, and negotiated the purchase of one* from the besieging forces—apparently for the huge sum of 1,000 drachmas. However, instead of

63 BCE: ROMAN GENERAL POMPEY...

Flight of Pompey from Pharsalia. [showing General Pompey in the Battle of Pharsalus (48 BCE): Caesar v. Pompey during "Caesar's Civil War," fifteen years after Pompey entered Judea]

source: www.heritage–history.com

sending a pascal lamb, the besieging Hyrcanus II forces malevolently and insultingly send a pig.

2) The pious ONI (Honi Hameagel), along for the march with the forces of Hyrcanus II, refuses to support Hyrcanus II after the pig incident and is consequently stoned to death by Hyrcanus II's forces.

The two actions in concert give Hyrcanus II a niche in infamy in Jewish lore. The internecine fighting also has other consequences—in that it gave the Roman General Ptolemy the opening he needed to soon *de facto* seize control of the country.

* Many rabbinic commentators say: **one/day** for each day of Passover, even though the parties were warring against each other. Some commentators go still further and say **one/day** was tendered ongoing to maintain the Temple rites.

68–63 BCE: ONE SPAN OF THE GREAT SANHEDRIN

Preeminent successor to the Great Assembly, noted above. An assembly of the 71 greatest Jewish judges and scholars of the time. Various Sanhedrins will appear periodically over a several hundred year span.

The august legislative–judicial–Halakhic body was one of the most esteemed institutions in Judaism's entire 3,000–year history.

According to both Roman and Jewish sources, the Sanhedrin ceased prosecuting capital cases after Rome asserted control over Jerusalem/Judea c. 6 CE.

When Rome co–opted the Sanhedrin c. 6 CE, by imposing the High Priest (which Rome selected) as head

57 BCE – 935 CE: SHILA (a.k.a. SILLA) DYNASTY

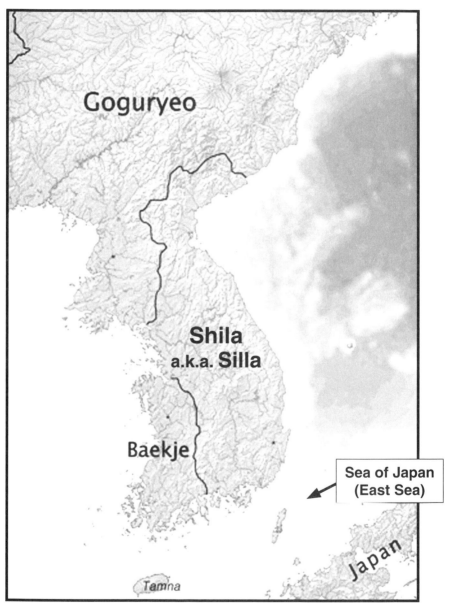

Shila (a.k.a. Silla) at its height in 576 CE.

of the Sanhedrin in lieu of the *nassi* (president), the prerogative of the Sanhedrin is effectively neutralized.

The co–opted and neutered Sanhedrin–shell of that era indeed later dissolves completely in 68 CE in the wake of the Roman military counter–onslaught, as the Jewish community in Judea implodes under Roman assault, destruction, and subsequent exile in the decade following–upon 68 CE.

63 BCE: ROMAN GENERAL POMPEY…

Roman general Pompey maneuvers for conquest of Judea.

He enters Judea with his forces and, allied for the moment with Hyrcanus II (of the Maccabeean dynasty), captures Jerusalem from Aristobulus (also of the Maccabeean Dynasty).

The internecine Jewish fighting between Hyrcanus II and Aristobulus had given General Pompey the opening to capture Jerusalem with minimal cost. The fighting was an offshoot of total Hasmonean squandering of the political capital bequeathed to them by Matisyahu and his son, Judah the Maccabee.

General Pompey first appoints (the weak) Hyrcanus II as a puppet–government symbol via the high priesthood, and dispatches Aristobulus, nemesis of Hyrcanus II and pretender to the Jewish throne, back to Rome in chains.

Meanwhile, the puppet Hyrcanus II not only has Pompey on his case, but the old intriguer Antipater. Twenty–three years later, in 40 BCE, Emperor Mark Antony will strip Hyrcanus II of all titles, and then bestow the kingship on Herod.

63 BCE: ROMAN RULERS: POMPEY >

Roman Rulers

Early days Roman Empire Emperors

> 63 BCE
> Cicero and Antonius are the two Roman Consuls
> [Gen. Pompey readily captures Jerusalem 63 BCE after
> adroit alliance with one of the two contending Jewish
> forces in the internal Jewish civil war]

> Various Roman 2–Consul leaderships
> 63 BCE–60 BCE

> The First Triumvirate
> 60 BCE–53 BCE
> Caesar/Crassus/Pompey

> Pompey
> 52 BCE–49 BCE

> Caesar
> 49 BCE–44 BCE
> [Caesar crosses the Rubicon (river) 49 BCE]

> Mark Antony / Octavian (Augustus) / Lepidus
> known as "The Second Triumvirate"
> 44 BCE–33 BCE
> [Herod named tetrarch of Jerusalem 42 BCE]

> Octavian (Augustus)
> 33 BCE–27 BCE
> (but Octavian not ruling as emperor yet)

> During subsequent period of Roman Empire:

continued (on next page)

63 BCE: ROMAN RULERS: POMPEY >

Latter days Roman Republic Rulers

And the Roman emperors:

> Octavian (Augustus a.k.a. Caesar Augustus
  a.k.a. Augustus Caesar)
  27 BCE to 14 CE
  [Herod dies 4 BCE; Jesus born c. 5 BCE]

> Tiberius
  14 CE to 37 CE
  [Jesus crucified by Pontius Pilate 33 CE]

> Caligula
  37 CE to 41 CE

> Claudius
  41 CE to 54 CE
  ["Letter to Alexandrians" (i.e. Alexandrian Jews)]

> Nero
  54 CE to 68 CE
  [1st Jewish Revolt c. 67 CE;
  General Vespasian dispatched to Judea]

> ["Year of the Four Emperors":
  Galba; Otho; Vitelius…Vespasian 68 CE]

> Vespasian
  69 CE to 79 CE
  [son Titus ends Jewish Revolt I in 70–73 CE]

> Titus
  79 CE to 81 CE
  [Arch of Titus; Vesuvius erupts 79 CE;
  Fire of Rome 80 CE;
  multi–year notable public romance with (Jewish 'royal') Berenice]

> Domitian
  81 CE to 96 CE

> Nerva
  96 CE to 98 CE

> Trajan
  98 CE to 117 CE
  [2nd Jewish Revolt (Kitos) 115 CE–117 CE]

> Hadrian
  117 CE to 138 CE
  [3rd Jewish Revolt (*Bar Kochba*) 132 CE–136 CE]

continued (on next page)

63 BCE: ROMAN RULERS: POMPEY >

> Antoninus Pius
> 138–161 CE

> Lucius Aurelius Verus
> 161–169 CE

> Marcus Aurelius
> 161–180 CE

> Commodus
> 180–192 CE

> Pertinax
> 193 CE

> Didius Julian
> 193 CE

> Septimius Severus
> 193–211 CE

> Caracalla
> 211–217 CE

> Geta
> 209–211 CE

> Macrinus
> 217–218 CE

> Elagabalus
> 218–222 CE

> Alexander Severus
> 222–235 CE

> Maximin
> 235–238 CE

> Gordian I
> 238 CE

> Gordian II
> 238 CE

> Pupienus
> 238 CE

> Balbinus
> 238 CE

continued (on next page)

63 BCE: ROMAN RULERS: POMPEY >

> Gordian III
> 238–244 CE

> Philipp "Arabs"
> 244–249 CE

> Decius
> 249–251 CE

> Hostilian
> 251 CE

> Gallus
> 251–253 CE

> Aemilian
> 253 CE

> Valerian
> 253–259 CE

> Gallienus
> 259–268 CE

> Claudius II
> 268–270 CE

> Quintillus
> 270 CE

> Aurelian
> 270–275 CE

> Tacitus
> 275–276 CE

> Florian
> 276 CE

> Probus
> 276–82 CE

> Carus
> 282–283 CE

> Numerian
> 283–284 CE

> Carinus
> 283–285 CE

continued (on next page)

63 BCE: ROMAN RULERS: POMPEY >

> Diocletian
> 284–305 CE

> Maximian
> 286–305 CE

> Constantius I
> 305–306 CE

> Galerius
> 305–311 CE

> Severus
> 306–307 CE

> Maximian
> 306–308 CE

> Maxentius
> 306–312 CE

> Maximinus Daia
> 308–313 CE

> Licinius
> 311–324 CE

> Constantine I
> 311–337 CE

> Constantine II
> 337–340 CE

> Constantius II
> 337–361 CE

> Constans
> 337–350 CE

> Julian
> 361–363 CE

> Jovian
> 363–364 CE

> Valentinian I
> 364–375 CE

> (East) Valens
> 364–378 CE

continued (on next page)

63 BCE: ROMAN RULERS: POMPEY >

> (West) Gratian
> 375–383 CE

> (West) Valentinian II
> 375–392 CE

> (West) Theodosius
> 379–395 CE

> Maximus
> 383–388 CE

> Eugenius
> 392–394 CE

> (East) Arcadius
> 395–408 CE

> (West) Honorius
> 395–423 CE

> Constantius III
> 421 CE

> Johannes
> 423–425 CE

> (East) Theodosius II
> 408–450 CE

> (West) Valentinian III
> 425–455 CE

> (East) Marcian
> 450–457 CE

> (West) Petronius
> 455 CE

> (West) Avitus
> 455–456 CE

> (West) Majorian
> 457–461 CE

> (East) Leo I
> 457–474 CE

> (West) Severus
> 461–465 CE

continued (on next page)

63 BCE: ROMAN RULERS: POMPEY >

> (West) Anthemius
> 467–472 CE

> (West) Olybrius
> 472 CE

> (West) Glycerius
> 473 CE

> (West) Julius Nepos
> 473–475 CE

> (East) Leo II
> 473–474 CE

> (East) Zeno
> 474–491 CE

> (West) Romulus Augustulus
> 475–476 CE

> (East) Zeno
> 474–491 CE

> (East) Basiliscus
> 475–476 CE

> (East) Anastasius I
> 491–518 CE

> (East) Justin I
> 518–527 CE

> Justinian
> 527–565 CE

> Justin II
> 565–578 CE

> Tiberius II
> 578–582 CE

> Maurice
> 582–602 CE

> Phocas I
> 602–610 CE

> Heraclius I
> 610–641 CE

continued (on next page)

63 BCE: ROMAN RULERS: POMPEY >

> Constantine III
> 641 CE

> Heracleon
> 641 CE

> Constans II
> 641–668 CE

> Constantine IV
> 668–685 CE

> Justinian II
> 685–695 CE

> Leontius
> 695–698 CE

> Tiberius II
> 698–705 CE

> Justinian II
> 705–711 CE

> Philippicus
> 711–713 CE

> Anastasius II
> 713–715 CE

> Theodosius III
> 715–717 CE

> Leo III
> 717–741 CE

> Constantine V
> 741–775 CE

> Leo IV
> 775–780 CE

> Constantine VI
> 780–797 CE

> Irene
> 797–802 CE

> Nicephorus I
> 802–811 CE

continued (on next page)

63 BCE: ROMAN RULERS: POMPEY >

> Stauracius
  811 CE

> Michael I
  811–813 CE

> Leo V
  813–820 CE

> Michael II
  820–829 CE

> Theophilus I
  829–842 CE

> Michael III
  842–867 CE

> Basil I
  867–886 CE

> Leo VI
  886–912 CE

> Alexander II
  912–913 CE

> Constantine VII
  912–959 CE

> Romanus I
  920–944 CE

> Romanus II
  959–963 CE

> Nicephorus II
  963–969 CE

> John I
  969–976 CE

> Basil II
  976–1025 CE

> Constantine VIII
  1025–1028 CE

> Zoe
  1028–1050 CE

continued (on next page)

63 BCE: ROMAN RULERS: POMPEY >

> Romanus III
> 1028–1034 CE

> Michael IV
> 1034–1041 CE

> Michael V
> 1041–1042 CE

> Constantine IX
> 1042–1055 CE

> Theodora
> 1055–1056 CE

> Michael VI
> 1056–1057 CE

> Isaac I
> 1057–1059 CE

> Constantine X
> 1059–1067 CE

> Romanus IV
> 1068–1071 CE

> Michael VII
> 1071–1078 CE

> Nicephorus III
> 1078–1081 CE

> Alexius I
> 1081–1118 CE

> John II
> 1118–1143 CE

> Manuel I
> 1143–1180 CE

> Alexius II
> 1180–1183 CE

> Andronicus I
> 1183–1185 CE

> Isaac II
> 1185–1195 CE

continued (on next page)

63 BCE: ROMAN RULERS: POMPEY >

> Alexius III
> 1195–1203 CE

> Isaac II
> 1203–1204 CE

> Alexius IV
> 1203–1204 CE

> Alexius V
> 1204 CE

> (Latin) Baldwin I
> 1204–1205 CE

> (Latin) Henry
> 1205–1216 CE

> (Latin) Peter of Courtenay
> 1216–1217 CE

> (Latin) Yolande
> 1217–1219 CE

> (Latin) Robert of Courtenay
> 1219–1228 CE

> (Latin) Baldwin II
> 1228–1261 CE

> (Latin) John of Brienne
> 1231–1237 CE

> (Nicean) Theodore I
> 1204–1222 CE

> (Nicean) John III
> 1222–1254 CE

> (Nicean) Theodore II
> 1254–1258 CE

> (Nicean) John IV
> 1258–1261 CE

continued (on next page)

63 BCE: ROMAN RULERS: POMPEY >

> (Nicean) Michael VIII
> 1259–1261 CE

> Michael VIII
> 1261–1282 CE

> Andronicus II
> 1282–1328 CE

> Michael IX
> 1295–1320 CE

> Andronicus III
> 1328–1341 CE

> John V
> 1341–1347 CE

> John VI
> 1347–1354 CE

> John V
> 1355–1376 CE

> Andronicus IV
> 1376–1379 CE

> John V
> 1379–1391 CE

> John VII
> 1390 CE

> Manuel II
> 1391–1425 CE

> John VIII
> 1425–1448 CE

> Constantine XI
> 1448–1453 CE

44 BCE: JULIUS CAESAR
"DEATH OF JULIUS CAESAR"
PAINTER: VINCENZO CAMUCCINI

63 BCE: MACCABEEAN RULE CONTINUES

Maccabean (Hasmonean) rule continues, but under the protection and supervision of Rome.

57 BCE – 935 CE: SHILA (a.k.a. SILLA) DYNASTY

1000–year golden empire on the Korean peninsula stressing peace, spirituality, and learning, particularly during its 500–year zenith from the 400s CE to the 900s CE. [This one paragraph alone does no justice to this extraordinary dynasty – author]

49 BCE: CAESAR CROSSES THE RUBICON

Jan 10: Roman General Julius Caesar defies the Roman Senate and crosses the Rubicon River (in Northern Italy) enroute with his armies to Rome itself.

Caesar seizes power and reigns as "perpetual dictator" of Rome. This marks the transition from the 450–year–old "Roman Republic" to the commencement of the "Roman Empire."

But Caesar's reign is to be short–lived....

44 BCE: JULIUS CAESAR

The Emperor of Rome is assassinated on the "Ides of March" (March 15).

"Et tu Brute?" ("You as well, Brutus?") exclaims Caesar to Brutus in Shakespeare's play *Julius Caesar*. Brutus, once a friend of Caesar's, had joined the rebels who assassinate Caesar, hoping to restore the Republic.

40 BCE: ROME

Mark Antony, details of a marble bust;

Vatican Museum, Rome

[There is an antecedent biblical parallel to the famous line "*Et tu Brute*" in Samuel I (*Shmuel Aleph*), written 900 years earlier:

"*Ha–gam Sha–ul ba–N'veim?*" ["*Is (King) Saul as well with these false prophets?*"]]

The rebels against Caesar are known as the Liberatores ("liberators"). After the initial knife thrust by a senator named Casca is deflected by Caesar, approximately sixty senators participate in the stabbing of the Emperor.

Although the assassins hoped to restore the Republic, the denouement is another civil war, which leads eventually to the (almost) permanent establishment of the Roman Empire (military dictatorship). Caesar's adopted heir, Octavius (later to be called Augustus) becomes emperor.

Caesar is front–and–center on the stage of world history, with details of his life recorded by many historians, including Plutarch and Strabo.

Caesar authored the work *Commentaries* on his military campaigns.

Caesar was a political rival of the famous orator Cicero, and we know Caesar somewhat (filtered, of course) from Cicero's oratory.

40 BCE: ROME

Emperor Mark Antony appoints Herod as King of Judea, but Herod assumes control only in 37 BCE, after Rome prevails in war against the invading Parthians.

40 BCE: ROME
"ANTONY AND CLEOPATRA" (1883)
PAINTER: SIR LAWRENCE ALMA–TADEMA

Mark Antony executes the leader of the Parthians, Antigonos.

Herod rises from a wealthy and influential Idumaean family. (The Idumaeans were successors to the Edomites, descendants of Esau a.k.a. Esav) in eastern Judea/West Jordan.)

As noted above, when the Maccabeean (Hasmonean) John Hyrcanus (Hyrcanus I) conquered Idumaea in 130–140 BCE, he required all Idumaeans to obey Jewish law or leave. Most Idumaeans apparently converted to Jewish practices at that point, but not necessarily including (*halachically* required) circumcision by the males.

Therefore, while King Herod identified himself as Jewish and was considered as such by much of contemporary Jewish society, nonetheless according to Jewish law he technically was not Jewish. Jewish history prefers to refer to him simply as Herod the Great.

In 40 BCE the Roman senate "elects" Herod as king of the Jews. Herod is, for sure, a kindred spirit to the Roman senate: He is power–crazed and homicidal, willing to murder his own children to advance his personal glory and power.

Ironically, the Romans, 73 years later, will mock Jesus with the same appellation. "King of the Jews" reads the placard placed around the neck of Jesus, as Pilate and functionaries crucify him.

In any event, matters come full–circle, with an Idumaean–neo–Jew displacing a Hasmonean as king of the Jews and of Judea. Thus, in a bizarre twist of history, while the Edomites were sidelined by the patriarch Isaac way back in biblical times, an Edomite/Idumaean ends up as ruler of the Jews.

31 BCE: THE BATTLE OF ACTIUM
"THE BATTLE OF ACTIUM"
PAINTER: LORENZO A. CASTRO

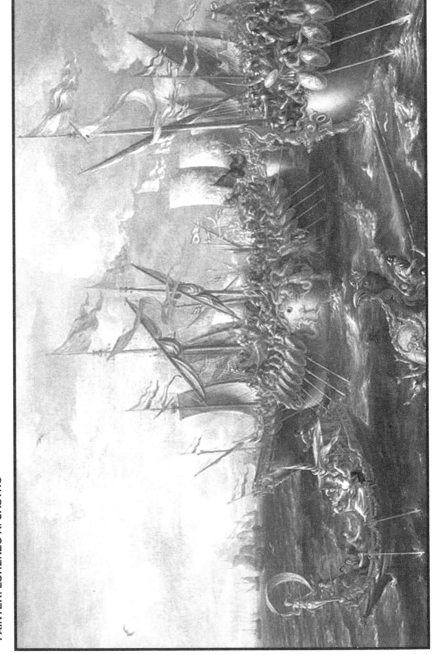

Note that, importantly, Herod was the second son of Antipater the Idumaean, the Machiavellian manipulator of Hyrcanus II until Antipater was poisoned in 43 BCE (possibly by Herod himself).

A tax collector is pinned with the poisoning of Antipater and executed by Herod, but historians are not so sure that Herod himself was not the culprit. One would be wise not to bet against Herod being the culprit here. It would later be manifest that one of the most dangerous positions to be in, was to be part of Herod the Great's nuclear family.

In any event, Antipater, who pulled the strings behind Hyrcanus II's rule, now exerts dominion from his grave over Judea via his son Herod.

Herod's brother–in–law and competitor, Aristobulus III, the high priest, will mysteriously drown at a party, as well. With Herod's father and brother both dead, Herod is free to concentrate on being Herod the Great.

31 BCE: BATTLE OF ACTIUM

Roman power–player Octavian defeats Mark Antony in a decisive naval encounter on the Ionian Sea, off the Roman colony of Actium in Greece.

The pivotal battle is considered to mark the completion of the transition from the Roman Republic to the Roman Empire (essentially a military dictatorship).

Octavian's fleet is commanded by the legendary commander Agrippa. Mark Anthony is supported financially by his lover, Cleopatra VII, Queen of Ptolemaic Egypt.

c. 22 BCE: HEROD THE BUILDER

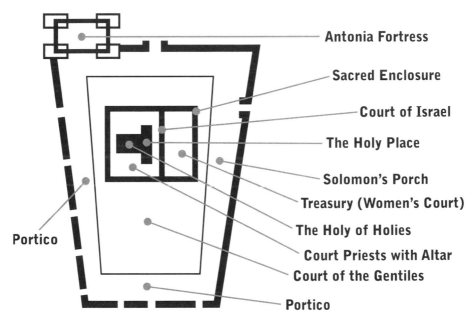

Antonia Fortress

Sacred Enclosure

Court of Israel

The Holy Place

Solomon's Porch

Treasury (Women's Court)

The Holy of Holies

Court Priests with Altar

Court of the Gentiles

Portico

Portico

The Temple Area

source: www.biblia.com

Octavian's victory enables him to further consolidate his power. He accepts the designations *princeps* ("first citizen") and "Augustus" (meaning "August One").

The rule of Augustus initiates a two–century era of relative peace known as the "Pax Romana," or "Roman Peace." But note that the first Roman war against the Jews takes place during this (presumably *relatively* peaceful Roman) era.

Sextilis, the eighth month of the Roman calendar, is renamed *August* in his honor.

29 BCE: HEROD THE SON–IN–LAW

Herod has his mother–in–law, Alexandra, executed.

28 BCE: HEROD THE BROTHER–IN–LAW

Herod executes his brother–in–law, Kostobar.

 c. 22 BCE: HEROD THE BUILDER

Herod commences major renovation and expansion of Temple II, rebuilt approximately 500 years earlier under the Persian satrap, the Jew Zerubavel.

The newly renovated complex is popularly called "Herod's Temple."

Herod's Temple complex will be somewhere between 5–15 times larger than Zerubavel's (approximately 500' x 165' complex).

With the entire Temple complex constructed on a perfectly horizontal carved–out plateau, and made of white stone, and with the central Temple itself

13 BCE: HEROD / THE OVER–ACHIEVER

Cacsarca Maritima, Mediterranean coast, Israel, 2008

Model of Herod's Temple, Israel Museum, 2008

source: www.bokertov.typepad.com

constructed exclusively of glistening white marble, Herod's Temple will be one of the Wonders of the World.

Counterpoised against Herod's glistening white Temple, where doves are sacrificed to God, 1,426 miles to the west is the symbol of Rome, the gladiator amphitheatre, where human prisoners were pitted against each other and wild animals, for daytime entertainment. The Roman state–sponsored gore and sadism in the public amphitheatre would only be trumped by the licentiousness in the Palace itself.

Before Herod can commence (the grandiose–planned) construction, the wary Jewish priesthood authority requires Herod to quarry at least all the foundation and central Temple stone.

They had good reason to be wary of Herod's planned construction: the largest foundation bricks were to weigh 628 tons. (We know the weight because these bricks still exist in place today).

Inasmuch as only *Kohanim* (the Jewish priest class) are permitted to enter the central zones of the Temple, 1,000 *Kohanim* were trained as masons and stone–cutters.

It is not clear how long the entire process took from start to finish; estimates range from three years to twenty–five years. But Herod was good at completing projects and an experienced mastermind. So, the central Temple was probably complete within two years, with the entire Temple Complex essentially complete within fourteen years (by 8 BCE).

> "He who has not seen the Temple of Herod,
> has never seen anything truly beautiful."
>
> – First Century BCE saying

12 BCE: EMPEROR AUGUSTUS INTERCEDES

Bust of Augustus (Octavian), wearing the Civic Crown.

Glyptothek, Munich.

Note: Temple functions (including *karbanot*, or animal sacrifices) apparently continued uninterrupted throughout construction (somehow).

20–35 BCE: THE FLEETING MINI–STATE

Two brothers Hanilai and Hasinai (Anilaeus and Asineaus) establish a short–lived "Jewish State" in the region of Nehardea (Persia/Babylon).

13 BCE: HEROD THE OVER–ACHIEVER

Herod completes Caesarea Maritima, the port city of Caesarea (Judea), in honor of his patron Caesar in Rome, with another temple, this one dedicated to the divine spirit of Augustus. Thus, Herod shows that he is an "equal opportunity temple builder": one for the Jews and one for the Romans.

12 BCE: EMPEROR AUGUSTUS INTERCEDES

Augustus stops Herod from putting both his sons (from his first marriage) on trial.

Herod executes them in 7 BCE anyway, as well as another son in 4 BCE.

And what of the Idumaeans (the Edomites)?

As if matters were not incredible enough, on the eve of the siege of Jerusalem by (Roman General) Titus around 69 CE, nearly 20,000 Idumaeans appeared before Jerusalem to fight on behalf of the (Jewish) Zealots.

The Idumaeans then subsequently apparently fade out of existence in the second century CE some time after

c. 10 BCE: HILLEL

PAINTER: ARTHUR SZYK

the multiple Jewish rebellions against Rome. Presumably, this fade–out of a loyal Jewish ally was not discouraged (if not actively aided and abetted) by Rome.

10 BCE: HEROD THE COMPLETER

Herod finishes adding an artificial harbor at Caesarea.

c. 10 BCE: HILLEL

Primacy of the Jewish sage Hillel (Hillel I), a.k.a. Hillel the Elder. Humanistic–focused Jewish sage and scholar, Hillel is one of the most important figures in Jewish history. Hillel is placed historically by chroniclers within at least three intersecting historical groupings of Jewish sages – the *Zugot*, the *Tannaim*, and the *Soferim*.

Cites "Love Thy Neighbor as Thyself" (Leviticus 19:18) as centerpiece dogma (as will Jesus in the generation right after him). Hillel is integral to the development of the Talmud and an intellectual/religious counter–point to Shammai.

"School of Hillel" (*Beit Hillel*) generally prevails in Talmudic debates.

Both Hillel and Shamai are sages in Jerusalem, their tenures and schools overlapping with the birth nearby of the to–be central icon of Christianity. Hillel's teachings, whose "time has come," are accepted and codified. Hillel: "That which is hateful to you, do not do to your fellow… That is the whole Torah: "all the rest is commentary."

8 BCE: HEROD THE TRULY GREAT

Work is completed on the final outer courtyards of

8 BCE: HEROD THE TRULY GREAT

source: www.notablebiographies.com

Herod's new Temple, a cutting–edge achievement.

c. 4 BCE: JESUS IS BORN

- Jewish population "worldwide": approximately 7 million (but heavily in the greater Mediterranean and Mesopotamian areas.

- Total world population: approximately 250 million

- So, the Jewish population as a percentage of total world population: approximately 2.8 percent. The vicissitudes of subsequent history will very significantly and steadily lower that percentage.

- Percentage of world's total Jewish population living in Herod's Judea: approximately 33 percent (2.31 million of the 7 million total "worldwide")

***

The most sophisticated societies at this point in time in the Americas, are apparently located along the Andes Mountains of Peru and in the central valley of Mexico.

The ancient city of Teotihuacán (Mexico) was built— probably by the Totonac people—in central Mexico starting 200 BCE. The largest pyramid of the city, the Pyramid of the Sun, was completed by 100 CE. The city reaches its zenith around 150–450 CE, when it is the center of a powerful culture, possibly radiating well over a thousand miles.

At its peak, the city housed 150,000–250,000 people, covered over 11.5 square miles, was laid–out in very broad avenues at right angles, and had a sophisticated underground water–conduit system. Most interestingly, the city had no fortifications or military structures.

3 BCE: HEROD THE GREAT DIES

The burial place of Herod the Great – The Herodium

source: www.bible–history.com

The city contained a special district for religious worship, with the above–noted Pyramid of the Sun— 214 feet, or 17 stories high—dominating the horizon.

The religious district centerpiece is a spectacular "Avenue (in honor) of the Dead," with an associated major plaza at its terminus, complete with architectural pond.

Note that the iconic Peruvian city of Machu Piccu ("the Lost City of the Incas"), with the nearby Cuzco administrative nexus, only comes into existence over a thousand years later, around 1450 CE.

3 BCE: HEROD THE GREAT DIES

3 BCE – 39 CE: HEROD ANTIPAS TETRARCH OF GALILEE

Whereas King Herod was relatively strong *vis à vis* Rome, his son Tetrarch Herod Antipas is weak—and successfully marginalized by Rome—and by the Roman procurator in Jerusalem. Herod Antipas's capital was in Tiberias, on the Sea of Galilee in north east Judea…

Matters will now move apace.

end of lead–in #2

TimeLine

300 BCE - 1 BCE

***

* *

Note: In early 2008 the total number of Jews in the world is approximately 14.8 million, representing nearly **1/5 of 1 percent** *of the world's population (of 6.7 billion)*

* *

The Crucifixion

TimeLine

1 CE – 1300 CE

0 CE: ONE HUNDRED YEARS INTO THE FLOURISHING *TANNNAIC* PERIOD

Books of Judaism

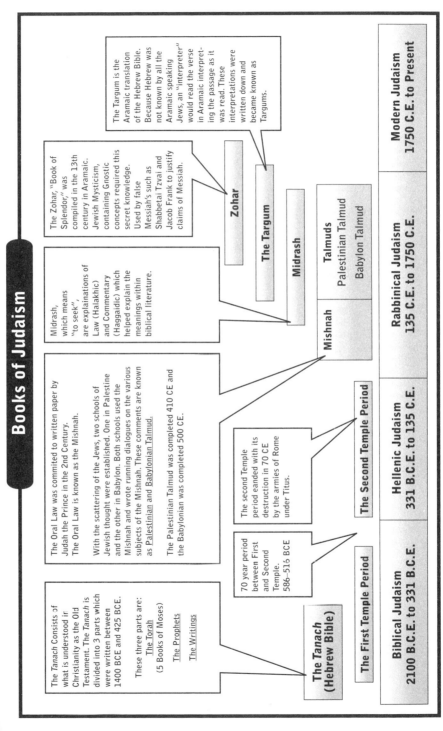

The *Tanach* Consists of what is understood ir Christianity as the Old Testament. The *Tanach* is divided into 3 parts which were written between 1400 BCE and 425 BCE.

These three parts are:
The Torah
(5 Books of Moses)
The Prophets
The Writings

The Oral Law was commited to written paper by Judah the Prince in the 2nd Century. The Oral Law is known as the Mishnah.

With the scattering of the Jews, two schools of Jewish thought were established. One in Palestine and the other in Babylon. Both schools used the Mishnah and wrote running dialogues on the various subjects of the Mishnah. These comments are known as Palestinian and Babylonian Talmud.

The Palestinian Talmud was completed 410 CE and the Babylonian was completed 500 CE.

Midrash, which means "to seek", are explainations of Law (Halakhic) and Commentary (Haggaidic) which helped explain the meanings within biblical literature.

The Zohar, "Book of Splendor," was compiled in the 13th century in Aramaic. Jewish Mysticism, containing Gnostic concepts required this secret knowledge. Used by false Messiah's such as Shabbetai Tzvai and Jacob Frank to justify claims of Messiah.

The Targum is the Aramaic translation of the Hebrew Bible. Because Hebrew was not known by all the Aramaic speaking Jews, an "interpreter" would read the verse in Aramaic interpreting the passage as it was read. These interpretations were written down and became known as Targums.

70 year period between First and Second Temple. 586–516 BCE

The second Temple period eanded with its destruction in 70 CE by the armies of Rome under Titus.

The Tanach (Hebrew Bible)

Mishnah

Talmuds
Palestinian Talmud
Babylon Talmud

Midrash

The Targum

Zohar

The First Temple Period	The Second Temple Period		
Biblical Judaism 2100 B.C.E. to 331 B.C.E.	Hellenic Judaism 331 B.C.E. to 135 C.E.	Rabbinical Judaism 135 C.E. to 1750 C.E.	Modern Judaism 1750 C.E. to Present

Common Era (CE) commences

Outline
Development of Christianity
the first 700 years:
a rough schematic

40-62 CE	Paul: **Embryonic Christianity**
62-100 CE	**The Greek Paulines:** Early Christianity
101-749 CE	**The Church Fathers**

1 CE: ONE HUNDRED YEARS INTO THE
FLOURISHING *TANNNAIC* PERIOD

– of the Talmud

The Tannaic period was of approximately 320 year
duration – from c. 100 BCE – 220 CE

(This is entirely a Pharisee continuum, as is, almost by
definition, the entire Talmud.)

Jewish law morphs via the Talmud from the written law*
of the Torah (the Old Testament) to the *redacted* law
of the Talmud, to be known as the "Oral Law" (even
though, as noted prior, the debates and conclusions are
ultimately written down in the Talmud itself).

The debates on the Oral Law, and the decisions of the
Tannaim (high level rabbinic scholars who are the actual
debaters in the Mishnah), are contained in the Mishnah.
[Also, supplemental to the Mishnah are the Baraita and
the Tosefta.] Perhaps, see quick–reference Wikipedia
online on keyword Talmud for easily–accessible
explanations of each: Baraita, Tosefta and, as well,
Aggadah].

The Talmud is hierarchical in its redaction. At the apex
is the *Torah*, the Five Books of Moses.

---

* According to rabbinic tradition, there was always some Oral Law
component to Jewish Law, even at Sinai; however, over time, the Oral
Law component became an ever-increasingly dominant component.

c. 1 CE: TRANSITION TO COMMON ERA

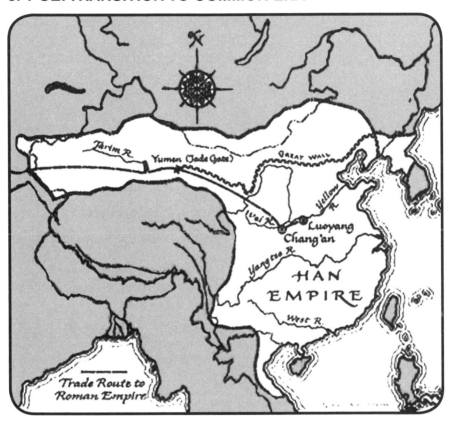

Map of China

from *A Traveler's Guide to Chinese History*, by Madge Huntington, © 1986 by Madge Huntington. Henry Holt and Company, Inc.

Next comes the Mishnah.

Basically, the Mishnah will interpret the Torah.

Then, the Gemara will interpret the Mishnah.

Mishnah (plus its supplements) + Gemara = the core of the Talmud = "the Shas"

Basically, the conclusions of the Gemara become *halacha*, or Jewish Law.

There are several important commentaries included in virtually all Talmuds. These commentaries would include, among others, Rashi and Tosefoth.

The major corpus of debate and discussion is the Gemara. The ratio of Mishnah to Gemara discussion is about 1:10.

[Note: the Baraita and Toefta are supplements to the Mishnah, and hierarchically come between the Mishnah and the Gemara.]

This is all somewhat difficult to understand, because in reality it is, indeed, complex.

As a historical note on the day–to–day reality, note that many of the Tannaim worked as craftsmen during business hours, as cobblers, charcoal burners, etc. In their parallel Jewish leadership world, they were teachers, rabbinics, judges, leaders of the people, and interlocutors with the Roman Empire.

6 CE: JUDEA OFFICIALLY BECOMES A ROMAN PROVINCE

The rise of the (Jewish) Zealots is a consequence.

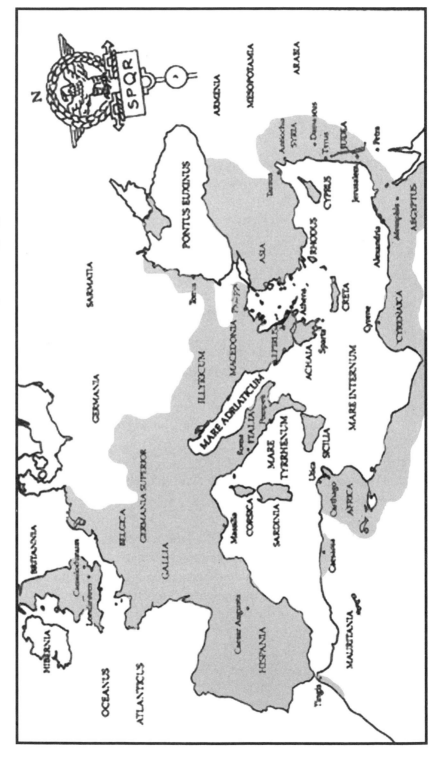

c. 1 CE: TRANSITION TO COMMON ERA: ROMAN EMPIRE (shaded grey)

Roman Empire from *The First Century: Emperors, God and Everyman* by William K. Klingaman. Copyright © 1990 by William K. Klingaman. Reprinted by permission of HarperCollins Publishers.

6 CE TENSION: Tensions will now rise as pagan Rome now takes over direct control of much of Judea, including Jerusalem, as well as the appointment of the High Priest. A tax revolt by the Jews is the first riposte. Judea will not see peace further that century.

As of this point, Rome, not the Jews, controls the Temple hierarchy. (Rome will appoint the historically notorious High Priest Caiaphas 21 years later in 27 CE.)

Jewish–Roman fighting will break out years later, in 66 CE. First, there will be a Roman police action as a consequence. This will ratchet–up into a full–scale Roman assault by 68 CE.

20 CE: JESUS OF NAZARETH PREACHES

Neo–Pharisee Jewish rabbi, teacher and healer, Jesus preaches mostly in the Galilee area of Israel until his crucifixion by Rome in 33 CE.

Since there is no contemporaneous or near contemporaneous more than fragmentary documentation of the life of Jesus, the various gospels, primarily those crafted in the c. 70–110 CE period, roughly 37–77 years after his death, project him onto the world stage.

Historically, the Jews are voluminous writers and obsessive record–keepers, but no (more than fragmentary) Jewish or other credible contemporaneous record (even within several decades of his execution in Rome) has ever surfaced documenting the life of Jesus. Compounding the problem, the Catholic Church had a *de facto* hammerlock for many centuries on any archival material potentially surfacing regarding his life, with a severe conflict of interest as the *de facto* archive controller. In any event, no contemporaneous documentation is known to us. Thus,

Timeline for the History of Jerusalem
(4500 BCE – 1967 CE)

4500–3200 BCE	**Chalcolithic Period**
3500 BCE	First Settlement
3200–2220 BCE	**Early Bronze Age**
2500 BCE	First Houses
2220–1550 BCE	**Middle Bronze Age**
1800 BCE	First City Wall
1550–1200 BCE	**Late Bronze Age**
1400 BCE	Mention of Jerusalem in cuneiform Amarna letters
1200–1000 BCE	**Iron Age I:** Jerusalem is a Canaanite (Jebusite) City
1000–539 BCE	**Iron Age II**
1000 BCE	King David conquers Jerusalem
960 BCE	King Solomon builds First Temple
721 BCE	Assyrians conquer Samaria. Refugees flee to Jerusalem. City expands onto western hill.
701 BCE	Assyrian ruler Sennacherib beseiges Jerusalem.
586 BCE	Babylonian destruction of Jerusalem.
539–322 BCE	**Persian Period**
539 BCE	Persian ruler Cyrus the Great conquers Babylonian Empire
516 BCE	Second Temple built
445–425 BCE	Nehemiah rebuilds walls. City confined to eastern hill
332 BCE	Alexander the Great conquers Judea
332–141 BCE	**Hellenistic Period:** Ptolemaic and Seleucid rule.
141–37 BCE	**Hasmonean Period**
141 BCE	Hasmonean Dynasty begins. Jerusalem again expands into the western hill
63 BCE	Roman General Pompey captures Jerusalem
37 BCE–70 CE	**Herodian Period**
37 BCE	Herod rebuilds Second Temple

cont'd

either documents never existed or they were lost or destroyed.

There is no reason to believe that Jesus was not, at least originally, one of several dynamic, humanistic, neo–messianic Jewish rabbinics/teachers of high–level consciousness in this spiritually hyper–intense era. Preaching to his Jewish flock, involved with healing and other spirituality, intersecting with John the Baptist, he was then crucified by Rome as a potential political threat.

Almost definitely of the Pharisee–Orthodox neo–Hillel–school, with a concomitant heavily humanistic thrust, Jesus had a religious–political following. The size of movement is unclear, but may have been small prior to crucifixion. With a religious–political following as a backdrop to his 'in your face' remonstrations in Jerusalem to the Romans and their lackeys in 33 CE, Jesus was perceived as over the Roman 'red–line' by the hyper–vigilant Roman military dictatorship of Pontius Pilate. It is not unlikely that Jesus was out of grace with the Roman–appointed, and hence co–opted, Sadducee High Priest Caiaphas, as well. There is no reason, however, to believe that the Sadducees conspired, let alone convened any assembly or court, to motivate Rome to execute him.

Note that sundry Temple and religious rabbinical authorities have been the subject of criticism and protest, often severe, by pluralistic Jewish religious groups for the past 3000 years. Indeed, at the time of Jesus, the (dominant, Temple–controlling Roman–co–opted) Sadducee priesthood of Judaism was under sustained and growing intellectual, political, and religious assault by the ascendant Pharisee wing of Judaism.

Timeline for the History of Jerusalem
(4500 BCE – 1967 CE)

>>>	30 CE	Jesus crucified by Rome
	70 CE	Romans destroy Jerusalem
	70–324 CE	**Roman Period**
	135 CE	Jerusalem rebuilt as Roman city
	324–638 CE	**Byzantine Period**
	335 CE	Church of the Holy Sepulchre built
	614 CE	Persians capture Jerusalem
	629 CE	Byzantine Christians recapture Jerusalem
	638–1099 CE	**First Muslim Period**
	638 CE	Caliph Omar enters Jerusalem
	661–750 CE	Umayyad Dynasty
	691 CE	Dome of the Rock built
	750–974 CE	Abassid Dynasty
	1099–1187 CE	**Crusader Period**
	1099 CE	Crusaders capture Jerusalem
	1187–1250 CE	**Ayyubid Period**
	1187 CE	Saladin captures Jerusalem
	1229–1244 CE	Crusaders briefly recapture Jerusalem twice
	1250–1516 CE	**Mamluk Period**
	1250 CE	Muslim caliph dismantles walls of Jerusalem. Population declines
	1516–1917 CE	**Ottoman Period**
	1517 CE	Ottomans capture Jerusalem
	1538–1541 CE	Suleiman the Magnificent rebuilds the walls of Jerusalem
	1917 CE–present	**Modern Period**
	1917	British capture Jerusalem
	1948	State of Israel established. Jerusalem divided
	1967	Israel captures Old City and reunifies Jerusalem

The then–challenging Pharisee wing has emerged as the overwhelming and exclusive corpus of Judaism subsequent to the destruction of the Temple in 70 CE.

The Sadducee priesthood power base imploded with the First Roman War, c. 68–71 CE.

While the Canon Gospels consistently posture Jesus in opposition to the Pharisees, and while the Canon Gospels then demonize the Pharisees (Judaism) across the board, this is a major divergence from the thrust of the actual historical record. The Temple leadership was Sadducee, not Pharisee as portrayed in the Canon Gospels. The primary challenge of Jesus was versus Rome, and symbolically versus the Sadducees in Jerusalem. He did not challenge the Pharisees. The center of gravity of the power–nexus of the Sadducees was in Jerusalem. As was that of Rome in Judea. Jesus himself was Pharisee or neo–Pharisee.

There were two *de facto* alignments, however subtle, and notwithstanding disagreements, however severe, intra–alignment:

The "In–crowd" power:
    the Romans
    the Sadducees (Jewish)

The "Out–crowd" theological–philosophical alignment:
    the Pharisees (ultimately normative Judaism)
    the (Jewish) Siccari (assassins)
    the Jewish Essenes (ascetics)
    the (Jewish) Zealots (armed rebels)

Trying to straddle both camps was Herod Antipater.

20 CE: JESUS OF NAZARETH: JUDEA

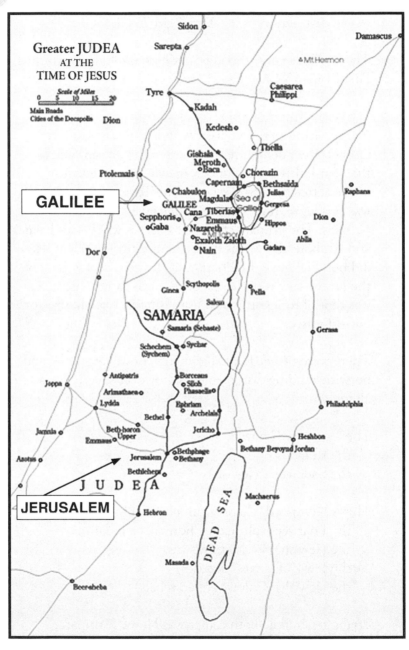

But, by and large Rome, which "had all the guns," *held all the cards*, of course.

Jesus was clearly aligned with the "Out–crowd" camp. The ("Out–crowd") Jews in due course launch full–scale rebellion against Rome, with, first insurgency in 66 CE, and then, by 68 CE, full–scale armed revolt against Rome, 33–35 years after the very same Roman leadership crucified Jesus. Thus, the (Pharisee–aligned) Jews are attacking the forces of the crucifier of Jesus. At this point, the allies of the gospel writers, political antagonists of the Jews, are well behind the lines. Back in the greater Turkey–area, the Gospel writers and associates commence composing and disseminating gospels.

While Jesus was thus Pharisee–aligned, the Gospels nevertheless cast Jesus as in opposition to the Pharisees (then, the insurgent Judaism, and today, normative Judaism).

Positioning Jesus as anti–Pharisee then breaches an opening for the gospels to paint normative Judaism in harsh brushstrokes. By flipping the very clear primary thrust of the historical role of the Pharisees *vis à vis* Jesus, the gospel writers are able to then position normative Judaism as adversarial to the teachings of Jesus. The historical truth, however, is that Jesus fought the (minority) Temple–controlling Sadducees, as did the Pharisees, a.k.a. the normative Jews.

Thus, the direct ancestors of the Twentieth Century Jewish teenager and Nazi–victim Ann Frank, were these very Pharisees—who were, as well, politically and theologically opposed to the Roman–Sadducee High

20 CE: JESUS OF NAZARETH PREACHES

Roman Empire taking over a farmer's land

source: www.latinrepublicans.org

Priest. Components of the Pharisee alignment took on Rome step–by–step.

Jesus was aligned in parallel with this insurgent Pharisee (mainstream Judaism) current in Judaism. Both Jesus and the Pharisees—normative Judaism today—launched insurgencies—whether political or armed—of one intensity or another, and in one form or another against both the Sadducee High Priest and the Romans. All Jews today are, indeed of the Pharisee / Hillel / populist / Oral Tradition / humanistic school of Judaism.

The Sadducee sect was a short–lived 200–year interlude from c. 150 BCE to 70 CE intersecting with the ministry of Jesus of Nazareth. The Sadducees aligned one wing of the priesthood with components of the Jewish social aristocracy, but never represented greater Jewish society at–large. The Sadducee power role steadily diminishes over the course of the First Century. The destruction of Temple II in 70 CE and the Roman onslaught/ persecution/expulsions finalized the implosion of the Sadducees.

The Talmud (embracing the Oral Tradition of Judaism) was crafted ongoing during this period by Pharisee Judaism, i.e. normative rabbinic Judaism. The Sadducees rejected the Oral Tradition.

The Sadducees rejected concepts of the *world–to–come*. Jesus embraced concepts of this genre. The Pharisees as a whole embraced the concept, among other divergences from the Sadducees.

However, the important "salvation" thrust in Christian theology regarding the world–to–come, is not an outgrowth of Pharisee theology.

Exculpate Rome

In 69–70 CE, with the Romans warring against the Jews, crushing the Jewish leadership and eliminating or enslaving the upper hierarchy of the Jews, the New Christian leadership may have wanted to align themselves a bit more with Rome and put more distance between themselves and the Jews, their spiritual front. Enter the gospel writers.

Re–coloring the Crucifixion saga of c. 36–37 years prior, may have been politically expedient, to put it mildly. It was, as well, an important survival maneuver vis à vis *on–the–rampage* Rome. Pontius Pilate, Roman Procurator, is thus repositioned by the Gospels as having been ambivalent about the Crucifixion of the iconic figure/deity of Christianity. Thus, even though Roman Procurator Pontius Pilate was de facto the *'one man band' prosecutor, judge, jury and executioner* of Jesus, the Gospels aggressively maneuver to tag their political nemesis, the Jews, with culpability.

Exculpate Rome. Blame the Jews. That theme would increasingly resound well across the empire. For the next millennium or two.

Pilate the Crucifier

Pontius Pilate was an *equal opportunity* crucifier, crucifying potential threats by the thousands. Ultimately, Pilate was crucifying so many Samaritans, that the Samaritan leadership vigorously protested to Rome. Pilate was subsequently stripped of his power and authority, and returned to Rome in disgrace to face charges.

Historian Josephus is dismissive of the Sadducees. Modern Orthodox Judaism probably considers them a short–lived, temporarily politically powerful, and overbearing (if not *reactionary*) group.

While evidence is not conclusive, the Essenes group of Dead Sea Scrolls fame was most likely a highly ascetic, purist, generally apocalyptic rabbinic breakaway (primarily) from the overbearing, possibly stifling, Sadducee priesthood group in Jerusalem.

Thus, the Jews are challenging the Sadducees on multiple fronts and in multiple formats –

- The Pharisees (current normative Judaism) challenged frontally theologically and philosophically, and ultimately prevailed.

- The ascetic Essenes challenged by self–imposed exile to the Qumran/Dead Sea area.

- The Jew Jesus challenged via a more highly–personalized, parochialistic approach. Jesus had common ground with normative Pharisee neo–Hillel Judaism, not with Sadducee, his antagonists, and the antagonists of what emerged as normative Judaism today.

- Meanwhile, the Jewish Zealots – *de facto* aligned and overlapping with Pharisee Judaism—are maneuvering to overthrow both Rome—and the "straddler" Sadducee High Priest, by violent means, ultimately by full–scale rebellion. To the (Jewish) Zealots, the Sadducee High Priest is a tool of the Roman Procurator and his Romans overlords. Both the High Priest and Rome are anathema. Two plagues joined–at–the–hip. But Rome held 99 percent of the levers

The Arrest of Jesus

From the Roman perspective, Jesus was doomed before Passover 33 CE commenced at sunset. Jesus was "over their 'red lines.'" For the Romans, Jesus of Nazareth represented their worst nightmare: an asserted miracle–worker, the leader of a Jewish messianic following – stirring up the throngs – from the very central court of the Temple – on the eve of Passover. Jesus was the very center–of–attention.

An adroit Roman plenipotentiary, Pilate's mandate was to maintain total control and order in Judea. And Pilate would most certainly fulfill his mandate.

Jesus, according to the Gospels (see also Gospel of John: 12:12–16) entered Jerusalem greeted by the people in a celebrated processional ("On the next day much people that were come to the feast, when they heard that Jesus was coming to Jerusalem took branches of palm trees, and went forth to met him, and cried, Hosanna: Blessed is the King of Israel that cometh in the name of the Lord"–John 12:12–13) on a symbolic white donkey, ("behold thy King cometh, sitting on an ass's colt" – John 12:15).

(The Pharisee Jew) Jesus was *throwing down the gauntlet* against the powers–that–be, whether the Sadducee High Priest or Pilate's Romans; the Priests may have run the *day–to–day* operations of the Temple, and the Priests may have been given some trappings of power, but the Romans held 99 percent of the reins–of–power.

Jesus was very clearly positioned by his words – and by those of his ardent followers – as a potential messianic savior. And his quasi–triumphant processional – through the legendary Golden Gate at the nexus of Judea – at this nexus–day of the year, the eve of Passover, accompanied by an entourage of disciples and followers, 'raised–the–stakes' even higher.

Jesus posed a maximal potential threat to Roman authority. There was no way the Romans could – or would – allow this potent threat to their power to gain further traction.

continued (on next Left-side page)

of power; the Sadducees, one percent at most. The impotent Sadducees were a fig–leaf for Roman rule over the Temple. The Zealots will ultimately lead the (recalcitrant) Jews into war with Rome. They want Judea rid of Rome, and its lackey.

In the post–Temple II era the Sadducees then disappear from history. Their Temple II–base is gone, and they are anathema to the populace, at–large.

The Essenes disappear from history as well, but come back with a vengeance through their scrolls* 2,000 years later.

The Zealots ultimately provoke Rome—into onslaught.

The Pharisees prevail over the Sadducees. The Pharisees were persecuted/decimated/exiled by the Romans and then, post–Constantine, persecuted and dehumanized by the ascendant Christian powers that be. The Pharisees are the Jews. They are the subject and focus of this entire timeline.

Jesus's original theology is apparently first morphed by Paul and then more radically morphed by the Greek Paulines. The emergent Greek Pauline sect, in turn, replete with a heavy influx of Mediterranean–area converts, morphs into what becomes normative Christianity.

In the four decades immediately commencing with the Roman assault on the Jews of 66–71 CE, the gospels emerge. The Jews are distracted at this point. The Jewish elite are being hunted and murdered by the Romans. At this point, the New Christian gospel–writers begin writing—about Jesus and the Pharisees (normative Judaism). It would appear that the historical record is

---

* reference encyclopedia entries: Dead Sea Scrolls; Lawrence Schiffman

The Arrest of Jesus
(continued)

Pontius Pilate, the Roman Empire's enforcer in Judea, most certainly knew quite, quite precisely where the messianic Jesus was, and most certainly Pilate didn't need any mysterious back–channel from one of Jesus' disciples to ascertain his whereabouts. On the contrary, the whole point of the Jesus processional into Jerusalem was to win the *hearts and minds* of those in Jerusalem, not to scurry *in the shadows*. By Gospel accounts, Jesus was, after all, *dead center* in the Temple Courtyard, preaching and debating – and, last but not least, creating significant uproar there, at "Ground Zero" of the nexus of Roman power, probably for up to three days running.

Note that the (walled) city of Jerusalem is not particularly large. It is approximately the same square–meter size as Manhattan's Central Park (which is 3 extra–long Manhattan 'avenue blocks' wide, by 51 street blocks long). And all entry and exit into the walled city of Jerusalem was quite easily monitored via its eight medium–sized stone gates (now there are 7). And while Central Park has trees and foliage, the city of Jerusalem does not, making anonymity even further difficult.

Jerusalem has and had many very low–lying structures. Foliage, no. Additionally aiding Roman monitoring of the Old City, ramparts (raised stone walkways running along the Old City's outer walls) – walkable then and now – surround the city, greatly facilitating observation and communication.

Jesus's trumpeted processional into the city leading–into the Passover holiday, as conveyed in the Gospels, had to be quite well–known within the walls of Jerusalem – to even the blind and deaf. His whereabouts, by definition, could not be "betrayed" *per se,* as it was Jesus and his disciples who had trumpeted his precise whereabouts to all to begin with.

Jesus was on 'center stage', basically telegraphing his dynamic presence and aura to the entire city and beyond..... This was very 'high drama' and very public drama under the very eyes of the Roman garrison headquartered at the edge of the same Temple colonnades.

Jesus is quite 'Front–and–Center.'

continued (on next Left-side page)

"textured" (i.e. distorted) in this 70 CE – 110 CE period by sundry gospel–tellers. While this is going on as a backdrop, Jesus is deified and the Jews are demonized in the Pauline Greek–aligned churches. The Virgin Mary starts to emerge as a central motif of the Christians. The Pharisee insurgent role in Judaism and Roman–controlled Judea is concomitantly turned inside out by the eventual gospel story tellers. The Pharisee role is inverted by the Canon Gospels as adversarial to Jesus, when, in reality, it is actually humanistically aligned with Jesus. All agree that the gospels were originally, as they are called, gospels, i.e. stories.

The *de facto* inversion of the historical alignments of Sadducee and Pharisee by the Canon Gospels opens the door for the gospels to demonize emergent normative Judaism. If emergent normative Judaism had been portrayed accurately as having been in basic humanistic alignment with Jesus, the gospel–demonization of those same Jews would have been awkward and unable to achieve traction.

That being said, with Christianity controlling the organs of the Roman Empire post–Constantine, and tailoring the history books of the Empire to suit their theological–historical–political objectives, and controlling the archives of 99.9 percent of the extant texts, and with the Jewish intellectual elite decimated, dispersed and under the heel of the Church, the actual reality of the life of Jesus will, respectfully, never be known to the world.

But the gospels not only invert the Pharisee and Sadducee roles, the voluminous gospels also neglect to mention five key points:

The Arrest of Jesus
(continued)

But then, magically, according to the Gospels, assorted iconic figures, the Sadducee High Priest and the disciple *Joudas*, are fingered – as having 'betrayed' the location of Jesus…

Meaning, as having allegedly 'betrayed' the locale of the 'Front–and–Center' Jesus, who had 12 disciples in–tow while causing an ongoing uproar in the face of the Roman garrison. Assorted diabolical 'betrayal and handover actions' are described.

But there is, of course, a fatal contradiction here…
Either one or the other:

Either, Jesus (with 12 disciples in–tow) caused a 3–day–uproar in the Temple Courtyard in front of the Roman garrison – and his whereabouts would be clearly widely known;

or –

If the whereabouts of Jesus and his 12 disciples were not widely known, he could not have possibly just previously have made a 3–day commotion under the very noses of the hyper–controlling Romans in the epicenter of Jerusalem.

Thus, respectfully, the basic foundation upon which this particular unrelenting (over–the–centuries) Jew–bashing plays out, is structurally unhinged. The 'foundation beams' of the entire 'betrayal' construct simply do not fit together.

* * *

1) The High Priest Caiaphas was Sadducee
   – and anathema to the Jews

2) A multi–faceted and almost wall–to–wall Jewish
   alignment was poised against Rome and
   (the Sadducee High Priest) Caiaphas

3) The Sadducees were soon to be relegated to the
   dustbin of history by the Jewish alignment

4) Caiaphas never had any independent power to
   begin with, and most importantly –

5) Jesus was in humanistic alignment with emergent
   mainstream normative Judaism (neo–Pharisee,
   neo–Hillel)

***

Now, if a dozen New Christian activists had sat around
a campfire on a hill overlooking the Bosporous waterway
in modern day Turkey in August of 70 CE, as their
political adversaries the Jews were being decimated by
the Romans in Judea, and if the 12 told the story of a
messianic Jesus, and elected to demonize their Jewish
political adversaries via gospel–vignettes, and then each
of the dozen dutifully missionizing activists went his own
way, retelling the tale in his own words and spin, the
result would not have been much different than the four
later–edited Canon Gospels we have today.

***

Note: Combining any religious authority with any
political power whatsoever is always a recipe for
trouble, across all civilizations and religions. The

20 CE: JESUS OF NAZARETH PREACHES

Roman soldiers collecting taxes

source: www.latinrepublicans.org

greater the power, the greater the abuses. The eventual near–absolute political power of the Roman Catholic church over the Roman Empire, would have intense consequences.

*

The current wisdom regarding the Essenes is that they were a Jewish group that flourished primarily in the 200 BCE – 100 CE era, roughly paralleling the tenure of the Sadducees in Jerusalem. Symbolically, and very generally speaking, the worldly Sadducees in the Jerusalem capitol were counterpoised against the ascetic Essenes in the Judea desert just outside of Jerusalem.

Many separate but related and interconnected groups of that period and of the Qumran/Dead Sea area intersected in their mystical and/or eschatological (world–to–come) and/or messianic and/or ascetic beliefs. Collectively, they are referred to as Essenes. Clearly there were divergences between them, as well as theological–philosophical morphings over the pivotal 300–year time span.

26 CE: PONTIUS PILATE BECOMES (ROMAN) GOVERNOR OF JUDEA

He will have near total power on a day–to–day basis. His tenure will last over a decade (c. 26–36 CE). In 33 CE Pilate will unilaterally sentence Jewish teacher and political challenger Jesus of Nazareth to death by crucifixion.

According to the contemporaneous Alexandrian Jewish philosopher/chronicler Philo (20 BCE – 50 CE), Pilate was "inflexible, he was stubborn, of cruel disposition, He executed troublemakers without a trial." Philo refers to

LARGEST ANCIENT EMPIRES

>>>

1. Achaemenid Persian Empire – 7.5 million km² or 2.9 million mi²
(under Darius the Great)

2. Han Empire – 6 million km² or 2.32 million mi²

3. Roman Empire – 5.7 million km² or 2.2 million mi² (under Emperor Trajan)

4. Macedonian Empire – 5.4 million km² or 2.08 million mi²
(under Alexander the Great)

5. Maurya Empire – 5 million km² or 1.93 million mi² (under Ashoka the Great)

6. Hunnic Empire – 4 million km² or 1.54 million mi² (under Attila the Hun in 441)

7. Seleucid Empire – 3.9 million km² or 1.51 million mi²

8. Gupta Empire – 3.5 million km² or 1.35 million mi² (under Chandragupta II in 400)

9. Sassanid Persian Empire – 3.5 million km² or 1.35 million mi²
(under Khosrau II in 626)

10. Parthian Empire – 2.84 million km² or 1.1 million mi²
(under Mithridates II 123–88 B.C.E)

11. Median Empire – 2.8 million km² or 1.08 million mi²

12. Neo–Assyrian Empire – 1.4 million km² or 540,543 mi²

13. Aksumite Empire – 1.25 million km² or 482,627 mi²

14. Egyptian Empire – 1 million km² or 386,102 mi²

15. Akkadian Empire – 650,000 km² or 250,966 mi²

16. Neo–Babylonian Empire – 500,000 km² or 193,051 mi²

Pilate's "venality, his violence, his thefts, assaults, abusive behavior, endless executions, endless savage ferocity."

–Philo, *On the Embassy of Gaius* Book XXXVIII 299–305

c. 26–29 CE: JOHN THE BAPTIST'S PREACHING AND BAPTIZING

29 CE: JOHN THE BAPTIST IMPRISONED

John the Baptist arrested by Herod Antipas (see Herodian Dynasty chart in appendix First Century).

John was imprisoned in the Herodian fortress of Machaerus, about 9 miles east of the Dead Sea (in modern–day Jordan).

At this time, there was one preeminent center of power: Rome, as personified by Pontius Pilate. There were two significantly subordinate, nominal centers of power in greater Judea given a modicum of deference by Rome: Herod Antipas to the northeast in secular matters, and the Sadducees at the Temple in Temple matters. Both Herod Antipas and the Sadducees High Priest were implanted in Judea by Rome, served at Rome's pleasure, and generally did nothing which might conceivably antagonize Rome.

There was another power center—the Jewish religious/ nationalist /Zealot–alignment—most certainly not given any standing by Rome. Quite the contrary; it was poised and coiled against Rome and the Sadducee High Priest.

John was beheaded by Herod Antipas in the early 30s CE (precise year unknown) as a threat to the local order.

The Alleged
c. 3:00–4:00 A.M. Sanhedrin Trial of Jesus

Modern scholarship dismisses the libel of a Sanhedrin Trial – as a *fabrication*. Any alleged Sanhedrin trial could only have taken place in "limbo time". Meaning, respectfully, it never happened. The 'construct' breaks down on multiple levels. There are multiple internal contradictions and mutually exclusive scenarios.

From a Jewish perspective it was *forbidden*. From a Roman perspective, a Sanhedrin Trial was *illegal*. Historically, it is *not plausible*. (The third and fourth Gospels, Luke and John, omit completely any alleged formal trial of Jesus by the Sanhedrin. Interesting, is that not, for such a potentially key event?)

The timing of an alleged Sanhedrin Trial does not jive; the sequences do not jive; the historical record does not jive; the Romans controlled all the levers of power. The Romans executed Jesus. But 'the crowd' will be manipulated by the resonance of the Gospels to call for Jewish blood. Aside from the impossible internal contradictions and discrepancies of the Gospels–construct regarding an asserted Sanhedrin Trial, one should note that no corroborative evidence has ever been produced in 20 centuries – that, indeed, any trial ever even took place.

As a 'backdrop' and for additional context, note –

- The Sanhedrin no longer held significant powers in 33 CE.

- The Sanhedrin did not meet at night, (and certainly not at 3 A.M. – 4 A.M. in the morning)

[The wives of the 70 year–old Sanhedrin judges might not have encouraged it.]

  [After a 4–hour multi–hour Seder in the 8 P.M – 12 P.M. zone, replete with four obligatory goblets of wine, the 60, 70, 80, 90 year–old Sanhedrin judges, may not have been in the mood to saunter for a 3 A.M. illegal tribunal.]

- The Sanhedrin never *sentenced* anyone to death over its entire multi–century span;

- The Sanhedrin did not meet on Jewish Holidays.

- The Sanhedrin no longer even *tried* 'capital cases' (death–penalty cases) (as noted explicitly in the Gospel of John, by the–way).

- The Sanhedrin did not hold surreptitious trials.

- The Sanhedrin required *bona fide* witnesses.

- The Sanhedrin required careful *due* process.

- The Sanhedrin met only in the Temple court; not in private dwellings.

- The Sanhedrin – 71 judges – could not possibly fit into a room in an Old City dwelling.

- The Sanhedrin did not hold 'snap trials' ever, nor would it be legally *(halachically)* allowed to.

continued (on next Left-side page)

33 CE: SHOWDOWN AT CAESAREA

Nonviolent/Passive Resistance #101

Pilate instructs his centurions to carry their official Roman ensigns (regimental battle standards bearing the Emperor's image) into Jerusalem under cover of darkness and deliver them to Antonia Fortress, contiguous to the Temple Complex.

The Jews are furious, as it smacks of paganism at the Temple complex.

Angry Jews from Jerusalem and the countryside assemble in Jerusalem and then march in protest 90+ miles to Pilate's seaside palace in Caesarea Maritima on the Mediterranean coast in protest.

Pilate refuses to budge. The regimental ensigns are to remain on the Temple Mount.

The protesters then bring the city center of Caesarea to a halt by staging a 5–day nonviolent sit–down strike – first opposite Pilate's palace.

Pilate still does not budge.

Then, after 5 full days, they assemble peacefully in the main public Square (*the agora*) to attempt to present a petition to Pilate.

Pilate refuses to accept the petition.

But, Pilate does mass columns of centurions, and threatens to "slice the Jews into pieces" if they do not return home immediately to Jerusalem.

The Alleged
c. 3:00–4:00 A.M. Sanhedrin Trial of Jesus
(continued)

- The Sanhedrin was led by its NASSI (president), not by the High Priest, as incorrectly asserted in the Gospel rendering.

- By definition, if a rump, run–away *entity* – large or small – was led by the High Priest, then whatever it was, if it ever existed at all, it was not the Sanhedrin.

- It would be illegal by Jewish Law to turn anyone over to Occupation Authorities.

- It would be *halachically* taboo to put any individual at–risk for crucifixion.

  (Notwithstanding John 19:6..."When the chief priests saw him, [at 5 A.M. in the morning????] they cried out, saying. Crucify him. Crucify him...)."

- If the Sanhedrin had ever sentenced anyone to death, it would have been precluded by its own internal regulations from carrying–out the execution on the same day as the sentencing; a separate session on a separate later day would have been required to formalize and proceed. Since there never was any Sanhedrin death sentence over the entire span of its history in any event, the issue is hypothetical and moot. However, it bears relevance to the fabrication in Christian lore.

Every individual Sanhedrin historically was under self–imposed restraint not to be labeled a *Bet Din Katlanit* – "a Killer Court." No Sanhedrin wanted to go anywhere near that appellation. Over multiple centuries, in different manifestations.

As noted in the text –

> "Any alleged capital trial by the Sanhedrin of Jesus is thus a convenient historical fabrication."
>
> – Lawrence Schiffman, Professor of Jewish History, NYU,
> "Double Injustice," (Journal of) Reform Judaism, April 2004

"The wholly suppositious trial of Jesus before the Sanhedrin is, points out Pierre van Passen in Why Jesus Died, pure fabrication, causing its utter rejection as unhistorical and untrue by a long and impressive line of savants [and scholars] from Reimarus and Strauss to Loisy, Guignebert and Eysinga."

– Betty McCollister, The Humanist, July–August 1993

* * *

The protesters do not budge.

Pilate orders his troops to draw their swords.

The Jews lie down, face up, their throats exposed.

Silence.

The Jewish protest leaders then announce to the Romans that all the protesters are fully prepared to die for their religious honor.

Pilate pauses.

–then backs down—and advises that the offending ensigns on the Temple Mount will, indeed, be removed from Jerusalem forthwith.

The 33 CE the Jewish protest leaders understood that, in principle, Rome wanted no bloodshed of non–threatening protesters, that Rome would tend to back down every time, as long as Roman honor was not challenged, no violence threatened or enacted, and no provocations offered.

In retrospect and hindsight, clearly this was the optimal route to "force Rome's hand," but the approach required thorough discipline and very carefully chosen encounters—with fully committed, disciplined and motivated protesters prepared to die.

So to recapitulate on the tactical chessboard:
If employed adroitly, moral authority + passive resistance + willingness to die + tight discipline, could trump Roman military might (peacefully).

33 CE: SHOWDOWN AT CAESAREA

PAINTER: MIHÁLY MUNKÁCSY

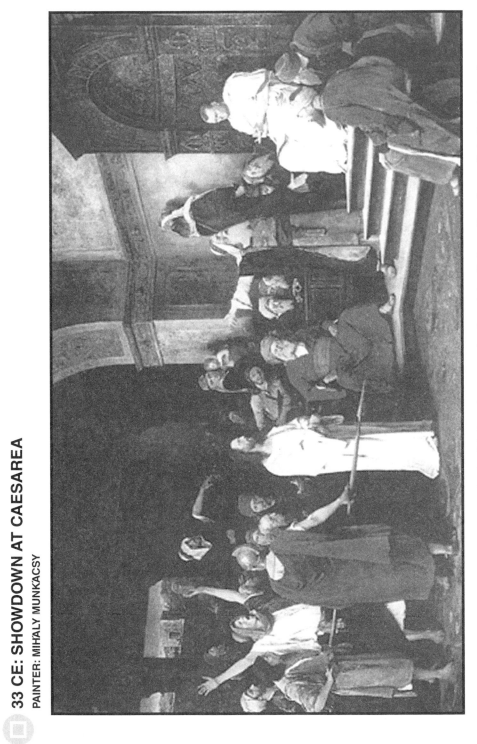

(Con–) artist attempting to co-opt iconic Jewish heroism saga by fraudulently inserting Jesus "into the picture."

Mohandas Gandhi and the legendary philosophy Satyagraha—resistance to tyranny through passive resistance civil disobedience—attributed to him in the mid–twentieth century had a clear predecessor 1,833 years earlier.

The astute First Century Jewish mastermind behind the "Caesarea Satyagraha," whoever he/she was, understood full well that the Romans wanted total local "control" but that if one yielded this to them, they would be vulnerable to disciplined, nonviolent moral protest.

What the Romans truly feared most of all, was an *out–of–control* nationwide conflagration. Rome did not want any local "matchstick" to light up any out of control "bonfire."

33 CE: JESUS CRUCIFIED

–by Roman procurator Pontius Pilate.

33 CE: THE BURIAL OF JESUS

Jesus, Mary, John and all the Twelve Disciples are Jewish, and, to the best of our knowledge, are buried well within the norms of Jewish tradition. Only starting primarily in the fourth century, post–Constantine, at which time much of First Century history is retouched by the dominating and domineering Catholic Church, are these key personages somehow morphed out of their very explicit and clear–cut Orthodox Jewish identities into more universal identities.

(continued on p. 167)

Map of normative Christian tradition re: Last Supper–related movements of Jesus, Old City of Jerusalem 33 CE

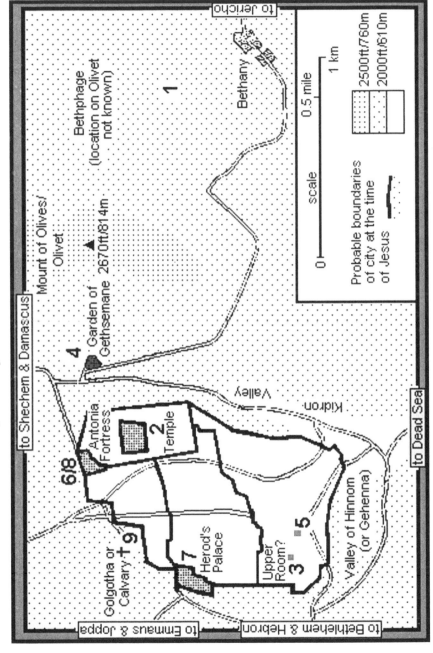

The Last c. 24 hours of Jesus

Points #2 > #8 delineate the movements of Jesus* – and the key episodic stops – during that 24 hour period – according to normative Catholic tradition.

The sub–journey of approximately 5–6 hour duration, which transpires between Point #4 > Point #5 > Point #6 > Point #7 > to Point #8, completely during the *Last Supper* night, which is asserted to include a full–scale trial, as well as the Pontius Pilate "Barabbas scene episode" (see exhibit First Century), had to occur *en toto* between close to midnight and daybreak. Meaning, all these *five iconic* events are asserted to have taken place in their entirety within a narrow middle–of–the–night approximately 6 hour time frame during the 'Last Supper' night.

The asserted "trial of Jesus" as well as the asserted "Barabbas scene episode" are wedged–into the key 'Last Supper' Night saga. These two asserted events, which might logically be conjectured to have lasted 4–6+ hours and 2–4+ hours each respectively, are both shoehorned in the approximately 6 hour time frame. Meaning, even at minimum time estimation, the two sagas alone would have essentially gobbled–up the entire approximately 6 hour time span, consequently leaving zero time for the other three sagas in the approximately 6 hour sequence. The historical veracity of either of these two iconic sagas – the 'trial' or the 'Barabbas' episode – occurring at all, is challenged aggressively by historians. As noted, these two "sagas" become the basis of 1900 years of anti–Semitism....prelude to the Nazi Holocaust.

* as per normative Catholic tradition

Note: Traversing and cross–cutting Old Jerusalem multiple times between 1 AM – 5 AM is no small feat in–and–of itself.

C. 36 CE: KINGDOM OF ADIABENE

"TOMB OF THE KINGS"

LITOGRAPHER: WILLIAM HENRY BARTLETT (NINETEENTH CENTURY)

Built outside the walls of Jerusalem by Queen Helena of Adiabene in the mid first century CE.

(continued from p. 163)

Only the apostle Judas Iscariot, singled–out to be demonized by the Church, is first demonized, and then markedly left with his full Jewish identity intact.

To be more specific, in fact the entire group – Jesus, his disciples and his family – were all Orthodox Jewish (Pharisees).

33 CE: MARY MAGDALENE

–The sole asserted witness to the asserted resurrection of Jesus.

Mary is Jewish, like the rest of the Disciples of Jesus, but the sole female.

She is later to be severely vilified and trashed by Pope Saint Gregory the Great—one of the four Latin Fathers of the Church—in the latter half of the 500s CE.

The vilification is basically terminated presumably once–and–for–all, by liturgical changes made in 1969 (1400 years after Gregory) in the Catholic liturgy.

This matter is important because Mary Magdalene is the sole witness to the assorted Resurrection of Jesus – to one of the two key pillar miracles of Catholicism, the other being the asserted Immaculate Conception. It is far from clear what would motivate Gregory to undermine "the witness."

c. 36 CE: KINGDOM OF ADIABENE

The conversion to Judaism of the kingdom of Adiabene (in the upper Tigris region, modern–day northern Iraq),

38 CE: BUCKING CALIGULA

PAINTER: EUSTACHE LE SUEUR

Caligula depositing the ashes of his mother and brother
in the tomb of his ancestors.

initiated by Queen Helena and her son Izates, marks the apogee of Jewish proselytizing in the Second Temple period both in the Parthian East and in the Greco–Roman world.

(Eli Barnavi, *A Historical Atlas of the Jewish People*. New York: Schocken Books, 1992)

38 CE: BUCKING CALIGULA

Five years after the Roman execution of Jesus in Jerusalem, Emperor Caligula in Rome declares himself a god and orders his statue to be set up at every temple and synagogue across the empire. Jewish riots subsequently break out in Alexandria, Egypt.

40 CE: ALEXANDRIA

Riots by the Jews again break out over the same (pagan Caligula) issue in Alexandria.

40 CE: PHILO

Hellenistic–Jewish philosopher Philo of Alexandria (a.k.a. Philo Judaeus) heads a delegation of Alexandrian Jews to Rome importuning Caligula regarding an anti–Semitic Alexandrian conflagration.

*

In Judaism, Philo is regarded more as a prominent historical hybrid (Jewish/Aristotelian) philosopher. The Alexandrian Philo himself may have liked being in that hybrid zone.

Philo is known for synthesizing Greek and Jewish thought.

40 CE: YAVNEH STIRS

Jews in Jamnia (Yavneh, Central Israel) destroy an altar

40 CE: PHILO

Philo of Alexandria

to Caligula (Emperor of Rome).

40 CE: CALIGULA PLAYS GOD

Angered by the destruction of the statue of himself in Jamnia, Caligula, back in Rome, *ups the ante* and orders that a statue of himself be erected in the Holy Temple of Jerusalem.

The Jews of Judea gear–up for revolt against Caligula and Rome. The Jews are *"locked and loaded."*

Fearing a conflagration, Roman governor of Syria (with dominion over Judea), Publius Petronius, slows down and delays the construction of the statue for nearly a year, *playing for time*.

Caligula is made aware of the delaying action, but is strangely *simpatico* to Publius's maneuver blocking his own (Caligula) request, inasmuch as while Caligula is somewhat mad, he is not suicidal. Quite the contrary. The salient point is that the Roman Governor is careful not to overplay his hand as regards Jewish religious honor. The local Roman rulers are attuned to the sensitivities of "Jewish honor," and, as a matter of policy, wish to avoid going over Jewish "red lines."

And the Jews of Judea in the first century have no shortage of red lines, of course. But the Romans, with dominion over the world's greatest empire, are sometimes wont to over–reach, sometimes with deliberate orders from Rome, sometimes through overly impetuous subordinates.

On some level, with the hubris of empire, and with their own hyper–aggressive Roman legions as a backdrop,

Execution #2

There is so much human blood spilled at Roman gladiatorial contests at the time of Jesus, that pleasantly aromatic "Stone Pine" trees are planted surrounding amphitheatres in foreign countries. Burning the pine cones will mask the smell of the blood. And, actually, the word "arena" itself actually means *sand*, a reference to the thick layer of sand necessary to soak up the running human and animal blood. The gladiatorial contests soaked the arenas with blood.

Thus, the dichotomy of the two emblematic structures

Jewish Temple v. Roman Amphitheatre

This is the symbolic backdrop.

sacrificing doves v. pitting humans against wild animals and each other

Two civilizations practically from different 'Ages of Man.'

Before the Jews shed Roman military blood at Beit Horon in 66 CE, the Roman Empire is wary of messing with the Jews. Not because it cannot crush them, but because it is wary of moving against this particular entity – as the Jews are unique: They have a claim on the 'spiritual high ground' – via their history, their books, their tradition – and via their symbolic Temple. As a religious–cultural–nation state, once warred–upon the Jews would be difficult to *bring to heel.*

Underneath the patina of fancy monuments and shiny battle shields, Rome was a debauched entity. Fairly consistently. Enslaving less–powerful sovereign entities; thoroughly morally corrupt at–the–top. *Survival of the fittest,* in its purest form.

The Israelite/Jews, on the other hand, *stuck to their knitting.* Worshipping their one god. Defending their historic turf. Iconoclastic and separate. One shiny marble temple included.

The powerful, but essentially debauched Roman Empire, had no particular taste to war on the Israelite/Jews: Tenacious; Proud; Heirs to Moses, David and Solomon. For, to truly destroy the Jews, one would need to destroy not only their (formidable) fighters – spiritual descendants of the Maccabees, and not only their symbolic (and extraordinary) Temple – a Wonder of the Ancient World – and not only their (legendary) books – asserted to be God–given, and not only their (formidable) intellectual–spiritual leadership; one would have to undermine or destroy not only their spirit, but also their reputation.

And that would be very, very difficult.

continued (on next Left-side page)

they are hard–wired to press to the max. The Jewish right–wing (or far right–wing), however, is not particularly interested in the nuances of the Roman macho psyche. With no referee to intervene, the two forces, one politico–military and one politico–spiritual, continuously grate against each other, intermittently skirmish, and are perhaps fated to eventually collide (not once, but three major times within a 70–year time-span, from 67 CE to 137 CE).

41 CE: CALIGULA ASSASSINATED

Caligula's assassination (unrelated to the Jews) in Rome ends that particular (putative *statue–in–the–Temple*) incendiary issue.

46–48 CE: THE FIRST MISSIONARY JOURNEY OF (St.) PAUL and (St.) BARNABAS

49–62 CE: (St.) PAUL MISSIONS TO THE GENTILES

St. Paul's Mission to the Gentiles: in Ephesus (53–56) (ancient Greece), and in Rome (60–62).

50 CE: NERO, 12, ADOPTED BY THE EMPEROR CLAUDIUS

c. 62 CE: COUNCIL OF JERUSALEM

a.k.a. The Apostolic Conference

The Council of Jerusalem (led by Paul) exempts Christians from the precepts of Jewish law.

Inasmuch as the Greek Paulines Christians radically undermine—and indeed, overthrow—the Orthodox

Execution #2
(continued)

That was the issue faced by both the Roman Empire and by the group religiously challenging the Jews – the Embryonic Christians. And when the Roman siege of the Old City of Jerusalem – housing this very Temple Complex – began in 68 CE, then, all of a sudden, as if on–cue, there was very significant and ongoing 'background static' undermining – with a vengeance – this very reputation. The slander–campaign against the Jewish reputation would be launched by assorted gospel writers (anonymously penned, but later attributed by the Church to specific historical Christians). The first gospel, "Mark" would be penned anonymously contemporaneous (c. 68 CE – early 70s CE) with the Roman siege and then destruction–of Jerusalem in 68–70 CE. All the four gospels chosen by one individual Irenaeus to be the Canon Gospels, in–concert – will *de facto* smear the Jewish reputation via several literary constructs.

Thus, while the Romans – via physical battering rams and crucifixes – physically assaulted and then destroyed the *cities* of the Jews, the Christians – via a fifty–year stream of literary smears – attack them from the rear, and relentlessly undermine their integrity and reputation.

Thus, a "second execution" takes place in the Canon Gospels: The "execution of the reputation of the Jews."

A viewing of the late 20th Century film – "The Passion of the Christ" – directed byAmerican Australian Mel Gibson – and derived quite directly from vignettes in assorted gospels – *will bring to the fore* how the stitching–together of various gospel–vignettes, cumulatively creates a highly toxic and diabolical Image of the Jew.

The previously well–earned 1500–year high–level–*reputation* of the Jews (up to the point of the Canon Gospels) is *de facto* "executed" via *literary–assassination* (counterfeit–sagas garbed in '*gospel truth*') in the four Canon Gospels. The former *bona fide* quite high–level Jewish *reputation* is then substituted–for by a counterfeit Gospel–construct: the Jew as a nefarious and diabolical entity.

Outgunned and outnumbered, exiled, and to some extent, enslaved, his institutions and leadership destroyed and dispersed, "the Jew" found himself in a sea of Romans and Christians and then Roman–Christians. And then found himself smeared relentlessly by the Catholic Church.

His reputation was doomed, as were, as a consequence, his fortunes – at least for c. 17–19 centuries – in the heart of Christian Europe. He was cast as a 'pariah.' He was painted as *evil*. And, after his 'reputation' was doomed, he and his descendants would be socially, legally and financially undermined. Shoehorned into the lowest stratum of society.

And then physically placed at–risk constantly. – *at risk* for his life – and for

continued (on next Left-side page)

Judaism of Jesus, and his successor James the Just, the true details and even the date of the Council of Jerusalem are shrouded in political positioning. The Church would like to date the Council of Jerusalem as early as possible (to 50 CE), and portray James as yielding somewhat on Jewish law as regards a class of converts.

This author believes that James the Just never yielded on *halachah*—Jewish law—and that the Council of Jerusalem may have taken place closer to (and perhaps after) his murder c. 62 CE. Indeed, in my opinion, it was probably James's stalwart defense of the Orthodox Judaism of his crucified brother, which resulted in his possibly politically–inspired lynch–murder.

60s CE: "Q"

A document, "Q" a.k.a. "the Logia" – hypothesized by some Christians to exist and to contain compiled writings concerning Jesus.

No document in part or in full is extant. Others believe that the hypothesis is but an attempt to date the roots of the Gospels closer to the time of Jesus. Additionally, a hypothesis is necessary to explain the too–close matching, often verbatim, of gospels "Matthew" and "Luke" (and "Mark") if they are indeed, the result of *witness to event* accounts. Meaning, experts explain, asserted *bona fide* credible independent accounts should be similar, but not verbatim—unless there is a source–document. But, no source–document has ever been produced.

This author believes there was, indeed, a very carefully calibrated source document, "Q" – a document which shaped the future contours of Christianity, but which

Execution #2
(continued)

the very lives of his children. And he and his children would indeed, ultimately be slaughtered, as a very, very direct consequence of all of the above.

The four Canon Gospels will perform this *de facto* 'trial and execution' four times–over. Since the Gospels are intended to be read sequentially, there is ample *resonance*. Even before layering–on Church sermons, plays, passion–sagas, dramatizations and related, all projecting the same inter–related toxic themes *vis à vis* the Jews. If one hypothetically, magically transported the four Gospels back–in–time to Abraham c. 1800 years prior, the progenitor of the Jews *himself* after reading the four Canon Gospels once–through, would himself probably become an anti–Semite. Let alone, a random seven–year–old Christian child being brought up in a random Christian home and church – exposed endlessly to this toxic stream – perhaps every Sunday and Christian Holidays, and perhaps often at bedtime via tale and saga.

As the Vatican cleric is quoted: c. "Give their minds to me when they are six – and they are mine forever."

As self–appointed *Judge, Jury and Executioner,* with eventual total control of the administrative and police organs of the Roman Empire, the Church will "shade the facts" and, indeed, "invent the facts." After *'railroading the conviction'* (not of Jesus, but of the Jews), *in–very–plain–sight* in the Gospels, the Church will *de facto* sentence (subsequent to Emperor Constantine's embrace of Christianity in the 300s) both the accused and its descendants – i.e. the Jews and their descendants – to centuries of ignominy and persecution.

Only the searing photographs – publicized in that late 1940s – almost 1900 years after the Gospel of Mark – of the emaciated and barely–alive Jewish prisoners, strewn across Nazi Death Camps – sometimes near pyres of emaciated Jewish corpses – with six million Jewish brethren murdered across the Nazi concentration–camp system as a backdrop – will make it "unfashionable" to be overtly anti–Semitic.

After the liberation from Egypt back in 1250 CE, the Jews bounced–back from slavery within a 59–100 year period; After the destruction of Temple I back in 586 BCE, the Jews bounced–back within a 50–100 year period; After the Nazi Holocaust the Jews bounced–back within a 50–100 year period.

But, after the destruction of Temple II in 70 CE, compounded by the literary gambit undermining of the Gospels and Passion Sagas, and the related ongoing relentless demonizations by the Catholic Church, the Jews would not bounce back for nineteen centuries.

It would be a brutal and solitary journey, unmatched by any people in the history of the planet.

* * *

included an embedded determination to foster deep–
rooted animus towards the Jews and laid the groundwork
for the demonizations to come. Meaning, a highly
politicized and manipulative document.

c. 60 CE: THE SICARII

–Extremist splinter–group of Jewish Zealots which
attempts to expel the Romans from Judea (c. 6–70 CE,
but primarily 50–70 CE).

The Sicarii concealed *sicae*—small daggers—under their
cloaks, hence the name of the group. At assemblies and
pilgrimages to Jerusalem, they assassinated their enemies,
enemy sympathizers and purported enemy sympathizers.
Apparently, they often "lamented" vociferously after the
killings to conceal and distract from their own role in
the killings. Sicarii means "dagger–men."

They are associated historically (along with the Zealots)
with the destruction of Jerusalem's food supply when the
city was under incipient Roman siege c. 66 CE—with
their (difficult to understand) "logic" being that their
actions would preclude negotiations with the Romans.
This action has not been viewed kindly by Jewish history.

One of their leaders, Eleazar ben Ya'ir, escaped the
Roman onslaught and fled with others to Masada, where
he became a preeminent leader in that resistance saga
and eventual mass–suicide.

62 CE: GESSIUS FLORUS

In Jerusalem, Roman procurator Gessius Florus steals
Temple taxes, further *bringing matters to a boil* and
strengthening the political position of the (Jewish)
Zealots, who continue to ratchet–up for rebellion.

The Money Changers

The (presumably Jewish) money changers near the Temple are demonized by the Church Fathers and in Church lore, Passion Sagas included. The vocation is given a contemptuous nefarious spin and taint.

Now, money changers – near the Temple – were employed –

(a) to change {repeat: change} (pagan) Roman coins
     to more 'politically–correct' (and *halachicly* correct) Judean coinage

(b) for the Passover Temple 'tax.'

(c) for the purchase of doves* *et al.* to sacrifice.

(d) to change sundry coinage from around the Mediterranean

(e) to change large Judean coinage for smaller Judaean coinage,
     appropriate to the purchase-price of the sacrificial animals.

Interestingly, the historian Ben-Sasson notes that between the years 28 and 32 CE in particular, [remember, the Jesus-saga is 33 CE] "the coins struck by Pilate bear **pagan symbols** in the form of cultic objects..."
All that coinage would be thoroughly taboo in the Temple proper.

The coinage had to be changed – by money changers. Known in contemporary times as "Currency Exchange," whether Deak Perera or American Express or Credit Suisse, *currency exchange* is in all key money center banks, any international airport worldwide, and often at major FIVE STAR hotels worldwide.

---

* NOTE: re: doves:
Korban 'OLAH,' the '*Olah*' sacrifice (the 'Burnt Offering') – the best known of the Temple II sacrifices – could be effected via cattle, sheep, goats or birds, depending on the offerer's means. The dove would be popular.

c. 62 CE: PAUL (beheaded)

Founder of Embryonic Christianity
–Executed by Rome – in Rome

c. 62 CE: JAMES THE JUST

–Murdered by parties unknown – in Jerusalem

c. 64 CE: PETER

–Crucified upside–down by Rome – in Rome

Early 66 CE: HELLENIST PROVOCATIONS

–of mainstream Jews in Galilee provoke a Jewish attack upon a small Roman garrison. It is hypothetically possible that Greek Paulines *had a hand in the provocations*.

This is the first shed blood. Roman blood.

It will prove a fateful turning point – both for the Jews at that time, and in the span of Jewish history. Shedding blood at any time is a very serious matter. Shedding the blood of the soldiers of the Roman Empire after Rome had given the Jews very considerable autonomy and (by Roman standards) prerogatives as regards the Temple State—was not, shall we say, optimal.

The Jews have just kicked "Superman" (i.e. the Roman Empire) in the shin. And "Superman" was not amused.

But, then again, neither was the Jewish politico–religious right–wing.

c. 64 CE: PETER
"CRUCIFIXION OF PETER IN ROME"
PAINTER: CARAVAGGIO

66 CE: FIRST JEWISH INSURGENT ACTIONS

–against the Roman Empire.

Caesarea, Upper Galilee, Judea.
(Nero has been Emperor of Rome since 54 CE).

> "Summer: Beginning of the Revolt. Resurgence of
> trouble in Caesarea; clashes with the procurator
> Florus in Jerusalem; Herod Agrippa II makes a public
> address in Jerusalem in a last attempt to prevent the
> insurrection; suppression by the Zealots of sacrifices
> in honor of the emperor; the Sicarii attacks Masada,
> killing the Roman garrison there. Moderate leaders
> ask for help from Agrippa and Florus, and 2000
> Roman horsemen arrive in the capital [Jerusalem] and
> occupy the Upper City; the rebels, holding the Lower
> City and the Temple Mount, besiege the Roman
> garrison. During the siege, the rebels kill [Sadducee]
> high priest Hanania and his brother Hezekiah. On the
> same day several Jews are killed in Caesarea leading to
> reprisals perpetrated by their brethren in other Greek
> cities. The Roman garrison in Jerusalem is destroyed."
> (A Histrorical Atlas of the Jewish People)

As noted, the price of internal civil war in Judea in
the century before Jesus between (Maccabean dynasty)
Hyrcanus II and (Maccabean dynasty) Aristobulus
was a mortal weakness, which General Pompey of
Rome exploited to gain control back in 63 BCE with
relatively minimal effort. The proud Judeans bristled at
the subsequent Roman rule, and the Zealots viewed the
Occupation through their own lens. The end–result of
the initial internecine Jewish fighting [in 63 BCE] was
ultimately to be an unmitigated national disaster on a
grand and historic catastrophic scale – commencing at
this point.

66 CE: FIRST JEWISH INSURGENT ACTIONS

> ***Jewish rebellions against Rome:***
>
> # First Major: 66 CE The Great Revolt;
>
> # Second Major: 115 CE–117 CE, the Kitos rebellion;
>
> # Third Major: 132–135 CE, the Bar Kokhba revolt
>   a.k.a. Bar Kosiba revolt
>
> # plus an additional (4th) significant revolt:
>   The "War against Gallus: 351–352 CE

Late 66 CE: BATTLE OF BET HORON PASS

Subsequent to the violence in the Galilee, Rome dispatches an expeditionary force, the Roman Twelfth Legion, as a *show of force* to quell the disturbances. A limited "police action." The Jewish nationalist–religious rebel forces, trying to throw off the yoke of Rome, elect to *up–the–ante* themselves…

The Roman Expeditionary force is ambushed by Jewish rebel forces at Bet Horon pass (the precise locale of an earlier Maccabean victory approximately 200 years prior) outside of Jerusalem. The Roman Twelfth Legion (Legio XII Fulminata) is routed—6,000 elite Roman legionnaires are killed in pitched battle with the Jewish Forces. To add to the Roman humiliation, the Twelfth Legion's battle standard (an eagle), has been lost (inviolably), to the Jewish insurgent forces.

The Jewish forces additionally seize dozens, if not hundreds, of artillery pieces and other armaments, to be used later in the defense of Jerusalem.

This triumph by the Zealot alliance will resound to the far reaches of the Roman Empire, but will prove one of the great "pyrrhic victories" (false/illusory victories) in the annals of humankind.

From the rebel perspective, the Jews had previously thrown off the yoke of the Syrian–Greek Empire 200 years prior, against all odds, and Rome has left the Jews no choice but to fight again for their freedom, dignity and honor.

An observer from the moon, surveying the vast power and tenacity of Imperial Rome, however, would say that the Jewish rebels were playing the ultimate doomed *long shot*.

The Roman god JANUS

All Jewish history, post–Gospels/Constantine/Augustine up through the Holocaust, will essentially be contending with *d e m o n i z a t i o n s* by the Gospels and related Church dramatizations. The Jews may not have paid much attention to the Gospels, and if they did, may not have taken these Gospel vignettes all that seriously, but the lower–stratum masses of Greater Europe had taken the Imagery quite seriously. Deadly seriously.

Like the mythological Roman god JANUS, the Catholic Church (of Europe in particular) would have two opposite faces:

LOVE THY BROTHER – as an exemplar – regarding Christians.

HATE THY BROTHER – as an exemplar – regarding the Jews.

THE FACE OF LOVE – to Christians.

THE FACE OF HATE – towards the Jews.

Theologically fully justified, by the Church, of course.

The ultimate betrayal – of Jesus's teachings – and of absolutely every-thing Jesus was all about, to begin with. Not to mention the targeting of Jesus's "mother nation." Not to mention, the ultimate hypocrisy.

* * *

But the same observer might have said the same when the Maccabees first took up arms against the Syrian–Greeks... or when Jewish leader Gideon, a thousand plus years earlier challenged Amalek... or when Prophetess Devorah challenged Canaan and prevailed... or when Moses challenged Pharaoh... and on and on with many *notches–in–the–gun–belt* of the Jewish nation.

Tenacious, tactically adept, highly motivated, with a legacy of victory, fighting on and for their homeland, and apparently perfectly willing to die for their freedom and honor, the Jewish rebel forces of Judea, empowered and emboldened by their belief in the God of Israel, would just as soon *bring their enemies down with them.*

With the Jews having played at the zenith of both the spiritual and temporal world on and off for 1,000 years, the Zealots of Judea were truly not interested in subjugation by pagan, idolatrous, licentious Rome. In isolation, the Bet Horon victory was glorious. But, in context, it brought the full wrath of a powerful, aggressive, wealthy, proud, marauding and, last but not least, slave–hungry empire down upon Judea. The rebels might be valiant and strong. But Rome was vastly stronger.

A tremor had gone throughout the far reaches of the Roman Empire. Having shown vulnerability, Rome would now need to send a counter–salvo back across the far reaches of the Empire.

Basically, an *immovable object* (Judean religious honor and freedom) had collided with the excesses of an *irresistible force* (Roman Empire dominion). But Rome knew a little about will and tenacity itself. And Rome maintained not only the will, but the resources and power–in–reserve, as well.

TRASHING the SYNAGOGUE

Judaism most certainly allows the *healing of the sick* on Shabbat, and most certainly *in the synagogue*. But the *Jews of the synagogue* in the Gospel of Mark (Mark 3:4) are castigated for their alleged "hardness of their hearts" (Mark 3:5) that they (the Jews, allegedly) might "accuse him (Jesus)" – and are then demonized for allegedly plotting to "destroy him" over Jesus's healing of a person in a synagogue – on the Sabbath.

"Destroy Jesus" over the healing on the Sabbath in a synagogue?

Why should the Jews destroy Jesus over the healing if the Jewish teacher Jesus was meticulously following Jewish Law?

Healing is a Divine imperative for the Jews – including on the Sabbath.

There is indeed a specific imperative *(halachah)* that *'Pikuach nefesh docheh shabbos'* – that one is definitely permitted, and indeed, absolutely mandated, to violate standard Sabbath prohibitions – in order that one might even have the possibility of saving a life...

And if the potential healing is in the synagogue itself, there is most certainly a clear imperative to effect the healing. Indeed the leader of the Synagogue is mandated to facilitate the rescue in whatever way possible. The absurd picture painted in Mark is a clear perversion of *halachic* reality. As is well–known to the central Church hierarchy both then – and now.

The gospel of Mark is in a cynical rush to show that Jewish law is insensitive. To undermine Judaism from yet another (false) angle. But to do so, Mark inverts Jewish law. Mark must turn it inside–out. Both *the letter and the spirit* of Jewish Law are inverted, to project his point.

* * *

For the rebels, at stake was greater autonomy and protected religious honor. For Rome, at stake was their control of a key geographic nexus–point, which completed, as well, their encirclement of the Mediterranean. But beyond the immediate geographic stakes, now at stake was the Roman *aura* of *invincibility* across the entire Empire.

Rome now poised to move in force against the Judean rebels.

Now, to protect their very thrones, Roman Emperors had become increasingly averse to major military campaigns, inasmuch as they would prove to be no–win situations for any emperor who engaged in one:

- If the campaign were stymied, the emperor would *lose face* and lose standing, and possibly lose power.

- If the campaign were successful, the victorious general, an *alpha male* to begin with, presumably now infused with surging popularity, could potentially march his victorious and pumped–up legions back right through Rome's gates, and potentially seize total power.

Only if an insurgency had threatened or humiliated the empire, would an emperor in the First Century unleash his Legions. And humiliation is precisely what the Judean insurgents had visited upon Rome.

Now, Rome had an appetite for slave labor, and an aversion to dependencies mowing–down its soldiers. Rebellions *here–and–there* provided "opportunity" as well. Therefore, for multiple reasons and considerations, some strategic, some tactical, some practical, Rome now had Judea *in its gun sights*.

66 CE: FIRST JEWISH INSURGENT ACTIONS

"ROMAN SIEGE AND DESTRUCTION OF JERUSALEM"

PAINTER: DAVID ROBERTS

Sculptured relief from the Arch of Titus, Rome.
Roman procession carrying the Holy Menorah into Exile to Rome.

Subsequently, over 20 percent of the entire Roman expeditionary army was mobilized for battle, and marched into Judea—one army from the north; one from the south—to crush the electrifying Jewish revolt.

As for Jerusalem itself, Jerusalem was an internationally recognized *trophy city*, and Rome, master of symbolism, was not oblivious to the magnitude of Jerusalem's global projection and importance.

67 CE: FIRST JEWISH–ROMAN WAR

Sometimes called The Great Revolt.

In 66 CE Roman Emperor Nero appoints General Vespasian to launch a Roman police action; however, by c. 67 CE the Roman "police action" has morphed post–Bet Horon into an all–out assault campaign by the Roman Empire.

Vespasian headquarters himself at Caesarea Maritima, on the Mediterranean coast, with 60,000 professional soldiers under his command.

68 CE: DESTRUCTION OF QUMRAN

(Site of the Dead Sea Scrolls, in the desert southeast of Jerusalem)

68 CE: ROME GAINS THE UPPER HAND IN JUDEA

By 68 CE, Jewish resistance in the north has been crushed by Vespasian, including the Jewish stronghold of Gamla in 67 CE. About a year after the death of Nero, in 69 CE, Vespasian heads back to Rome to take the title of Emperor (on the heels of The Year of the Four Emperors' internecine power struggle in Rome).

67 CE: FIRST JEWISH–ROMAN WAR
"DESTRUCTION OF THE SECOND TEMPLE"

Roman troops (on the right)

Vespasian delegates his son Titus to complete the Judean campaign, and to break the stalemate surrounding the siege of Jerusalem.

Total death estimates in Judea over the course of the nearly 4 year war hostilities range from 600,000–1,300,000 Jews.

Josephus states that during the siege of Jerusalem, 500 people were crucified each day in front of its walls. (The figure sounds high, although it is widely disseminated and Josephus enjoys high credibility to this day. Note that Josephus's account of Jerusalem is, in particular, somewhat compromised by his *calls for Jewish surrender* during the siege.)

The carnage was apparently gruesome:
"There was no room for crosses and no crosses for the bodies." –Dumont

By the end of the siege, hundreds, and possibly thousands, of crucified Jewish bodies encircled Jerusalem on the surrounding encircling Roman moat–road.

Note: This encircling moat–road was built at the same height as the walls of Jerusalem to isolate and starve Jerusalem.

The historian Josephus, a contentious Jewish personality, scholar, rebel commander (and neo–traitor), is the primary source of information for this period. It is hard to categorize Josephus, but it is clear that he adapts facts: His works are not always 100 percent consistent. His depiction of events, in particular, is suspect, as he was beholden to his Roman patrons, particularly Titus (who maintained him after his first career as a Jewish commander in the northern revolt). However, his overall credibility among scholars is relatively high, interestingly enough. Perhaps this is because he has no real competition as a chronicler

68 CE: DESTRUCTION OF QUMRAN

Dead Sea Scroll caves

of the Jews of this era. If Josephus is stripped of credibility, there is not all that much for a focused scholar of that period to do here. However, in my eyes Josephus does have true credibility in one specific circumstance: when his historiography is to the detriment of Rome.

69 CE: THE CANON GOSPELS

The embryonic Canon Gospels of Mark and Matthew appear first.

The exact dating remains amorphous.
The four Canon Gospels are written and appear over the 69 CE – 110 CE period, later to become canonized as "The New Testament."

"Mark"   (author unknown; the writing is not contemporaneous with the narrative; hundreds of years later ascribed by the Church to Mark the Evangelist)

"Matthew" (author unknown; the writing is not contemporaneous with the narrative; hundreds of years later ascribed by the Church to Matthew the Evangelist)

"Luke"   (author unknown; the writing is not contemporaneous with the narrative; hundreds of years later ascribed by the Church to Luke, the companion of Paul) [oldest surviving manuscript dates to approximately 200 CE]

"John"   (author unknown; the writing is not contemporaneous with the narrative; hundreds of years later ascribed by the Church to John) [This is "John the Evangelist," not the earlier iconic 'John the Baptist']

***

69 CE: THE CANON GOSPELS
in context of TimeLine

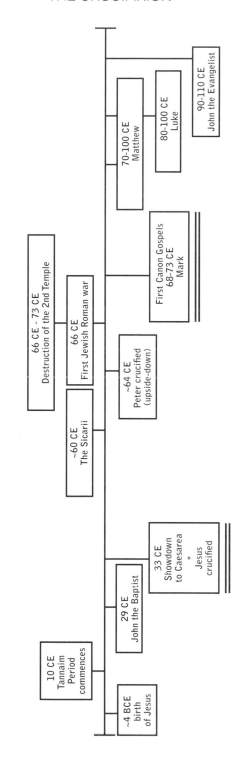

10 CE
Tannaim
Period
commences

~4 BCE
birth
of Jesus

29 CE
John the Baptist

33 CE
Showdown
to Caesarea
*
Jesus
crucified

~60 CE
The Sicarii

~64 CE
Peter crucified
(upside-down)

66 CE
First Jewish Roman war

66 CE - 73 CE
Destruction of the 2nd Temple

First Canon Gospels
68-73 CE
Mark

70-100 CE
Matthew

80-100 CE
Luke

90-110 CE
John the Evangelist

All four personages above are known as Evangelists. The precise identities of the four writers are not accepted outside of Church dogma. The Church basically assigned the identities.

All four Gospels were originally written in Greek, different that the language(s) that Jesus and his disciples used—which were Hebrew Aramaic.

The four Gospels were 4 out of 20–50+ gospels known to have existed.

The dates (noted above) which most of the world ascribes to the writings of the Gospels, diverge from the dates (approximately 10–20 years earlier) which the Church ascribes to them.

Conceptually, the closer the gospels were written to the actual key events of the early 30s CE, the more credibility they would have.

The Gospels were intended for a far different audience (primarily the neo–pagan populace) than the Jewish common people to whom Jesus had preached, and to whom the original Embryonic Christians proselytized in the earlier part of the First Century.

All four of the Gospels are almost definitely written in the greater Turkey–Syria.

The four Gospels are divergent on the key and crucial timing of the death of Jesus:

- One gospel places the death on *Erev Pesach,* the day leading–into Passover, Nissan 14. (Meaning, no Last Supper)

69 CE: THE CANON GOSPELS

re: "Matthew" labeling the Jews as 'hypocrites' (thrice)

"Woe unto you, scribes and Pharisees, hypocrites! For ye pay tithe of mint and anise and cummin, and have omitted the weightier *matters* of the law, judgment, mercy, and faith: these ought ye to have done, and not to leave the other undone." (Matthew 23:23)

"Therefore when thou doest *thine* alms, do not sound a trumpet before thee, as the hypocrites do in the synagogues and in the streets, that they may have glory of men. Verily I say unto you, They have their reward.

...And when thou prayest, thou shalt not be as the hypocrites are: for they love to pray standing in the synagogues and in the corners of the streets, that they may be seen of men. Verily I say unto you, They have their reward." (Matthew 6:2, 5)

(note: Jesus was a Pharisee)

re: some authenticity issues

The inter–relationships between the contents of the respective four Canon Gospels are often problematic: ***

1) The wording of some passages are too precisely similar between different gospels (between Mark, Luke and Matthew, in particular) if these passages were not simply copied from another gospel or inserted later simultaneously by an editor.

2) Some of the key vignettes in the four gospels are too contradictory or mutually exclusive (e.g. the timing of the Crucifixion in relation to the First Night of Passover).

source: (King James) version *The Holy Bible*. Philadelphia: National Publishing Company, pp. 996 and 1020.

[Some terminology explanations –
Jewish calendar days starts at nightfall.
Pesach means Passover.
Erev means the day leading into, so *Erev Pesach* means
    the day leading–into Pesach.
Nissan is a Hebrew month, a lunar month.
Nissan 14 is the day leading–into Passover.
Pesach (Passover) starts at sundown/sunset between
Nissan 14 and Nissan 15.]

• Two of the Gospels place the death of Jesus during
  the daytime after the Passover Seder, meaning on the
  first day of Passover, Nissan 15. (Thus, the normative
  Passion saga comports to these two.)

• The fourth Gospel places the death of Jesus after the
  first day Passover, meaning a day or two (or three) after
  Nissan 15.

The actual personages, Mark, Matthew, Luke and John
are all believed by mainstream academia to have died
well prior to the dates ascribed to the writing of their
respectively named gospels. This leaves the true authorship
of the Catholic Canon to *persons unknown*.

The Gospels as we know them today, were edited during
the period of Constantine 272–317 CE (+/–100 years).
The Church position would be that they were not edited.

The primary purpose of the Gospels, originally narrations
by Christian/Church advocates, was to expound the
glory of Jesus. This objective is axiomatic among secular
historians. Jesus is, as well, graphically portrayed/related as
the victim of treachery and betrayal. The specific treachery
and betrayal ascribed by these unknown gospel writers,

THE CRUCIFIXION

AN OVERVIEW OF 1700 YEARS OF JEWISH PERSECUTION

Anti–Judaism: Persecution of Followers of the Jewish Religion: (in Christian Europe)

Initial persecution of Jews was along religious lines. Persecution would [usually] cease if the person converted to Christianity.

- **306:** The church *Synod of Elvira* banned marriages, sexual intercourse and community contacts between Christians and Jews.
- **315:** Constantine published the *Edict of Milan*, which extended religious tolerance to Christians. Jews lost many rights with this edict. They were no longer permitted to live in Jerusalem, or to proselytize.
- **325:** The *Council of Nicea* decided to separate the celebration of Easter from the Jewish Passover. They stated: *"For it is unbecoming beyond measure that on this holiest of festivals we should follow the customs of the Jews. Henceforth let us have nothing in common with this odious people..."*
- **337:** Christian Emperor Constantius created a law, which made the marriage of a Jewish man to a Christian punishable by death.
- **339:** Converting to Judaism became a criminal offense.
- **367–376:** [St.] Hilary of Poitiers referred to Jews as a perverse people who God has cursed forever. [St.] Ephroem refers to synagogues as brothels.
- **379–395:** Emperor Theodosius the Great permitted the destruction of synagogues if it served a religious purpose. Christianity became the state religion of the Roman Empire at this time.
- **380:** The bishop of Milan was responsible for the burning of a synagogue; he referred to it as *"an act pleasing to God."*
- **415:** The Bishop of Alexandria, [St.] Cyril, expelled the Jews from that Egyptian city.
- **415:** St. Augustine wrote, *"The true image of the Hebrew is Judas Iscariot, who sells the Lord for silver. The Jew can never understand the Scriptures and forever will bear the guilt for the death of Jesus."*
- **418:** St. Jerome, who created the Vulgate translation of the Bible wrote of a synagogue: *"If you call it a brothel, a den of vice, the Devil's refuge, Satan's fortress, a place to deprave the soul, an abyss of every conceivable disaster or whatever you will, you are still saying less than it deserves."*
- **489–519:** Christian mobs destroyed the synagogues in Antioch, Daphne (near Antioch) and Ravenna.
- **528:** Emperor Justinian (527–564) passed the Justinian Code. It prohibited Jews from building synagogues, reading the Bible in Hebrew,

continued (on next Left-side page)

is, respectfully, historically untenable (see exhibit in appendix, the First Century).

Thus, given all of the above, the fact that some Gospels may intersect on a given anecdotal point, especially on a particular vignette – or a portion of a vignette – defamatory to the Jews, does not necessarily mean that the particular incident ever occurred as related. The incident, recounted or constructed decades after the actual point in time of the storied vignette, either added to the glory of Jesus, or detracted from the "standing" of the Jews. Even though the Jews were not proactively competing for the non–Jewish (neo–pagan) audience, Judaism as a Group/ Religion/Theology is consistently portrayed in toxic terms and imagery in the Gospels. Part of the Christian logic to the neo–pagan audience of the time would presumably be that—if the Jews are bad, and we (the Christians) are the breakaway, we must be *right*.

In any event, hypothetically, a band of a dozen politically– savvy Christian politico–religious advocates, perhaps integral to the embryonic core leadership, meeting together near Greater Jerusalem in 68 CE, observing the Jewish leadership being decimated by Vespasian, and the Jewish central authority imploding in–front–of–their eyes, grasps the "historic moment." With the Jewish elite immobilized and distracted, if not demolished totally, there is a historic vacuum. He whose saga resonates across the Judean terrain will *win the hearts* of the neo–pagan inhabitants of the Middle East and perhaps beyond. The outlines of the core saga–to–be–told are crystallized by this Christian vanguard. (The gospels are then crafted and written "back home" either by these same persons or by compatriots in the greater Turkey–Syria area.

The politico–religious *raconteurs/advocates* then each go

AN OVERVIEW OF 1700 YEARS OF JEWISH PERSECUTION
[continued]

assemble in public, celebrate Passover before Easter, and testify against Christians in court.

- **535:** The *"Synod of Claremont decreed that Jews could not hold public office or have authority over Christians."*

- **538:** The *3rd and 4th Councils of Orleans* prohibited Jews from appearing in public during the Easter season. Prohibited marriages between Christians and Jews. Prohibited Christians from converting to Judaism.

- **561:** The bishop of Uzes expelled Jews from his diocese in France.

- **612:** Jews were not allowed to own land, to be farmers or enter certain trades.

- **613:** Very serious persecution began in Spain. Jews were given the options of either leaving Spain or converting to Christianity. Jewish children over 6 years of age were taken from their parents and given a Christian education

- **694:** The 17th Church *Council of Toledo*, Spain defined Jews as the serfs of the prince. This was based, in part, on the beliefs by Chrysostom, Origen, Jerome, and other Church Fathers that God punished the Jews with perpetual slavery because of their responsibility for the execution of Jesus.

- **722:** Leo III outlawed Judaism. Jews were baptized against their will.

- **855:** Jews were exiled from Italy

- **1050:** The *Synod of Narbonne* prohibited Christians from living in the homes of Jews.

- **1078:** *"Pope Gregory VII decreed that Jews could not hold office or be superiors to Christians."*

- **1078:** The *Synod of Gerona* forced Jews to pay church taxes

- **1096:** The *First Crusade* was launched in this year. Although the prime goal of the crusades was to liberate Jerusalem from the Muslims, Jews were a second target. As the soldiers passed through Europe on the way to the Holy Land, large numbers of Jews were challenged: *"Christ–killers, embrace the Cross or die!"* 12,000 Jews in the Rhine Valley alone were killed in the first Crusade. This behavior continued for 8 additional crusades until the 9th in 1272.

- **1099:** The Crusaders forced all of the Jews of Jerusalem into a central synagogue and set it on fire. Those who tried to escape were forced back into the burning building.

- **1121:** Jews were exiled from Flanders (now part of present–day Belgium)

- **1130:** Some Jews in London allegedly killed a sick man. The Jewish people in the city were required to pay 1 million marks as compensation.

- **1146:** The Second Crusade began. A French Monk, Rudolf, called for the destruction of the Jews.

continued (on next Left-side page)

their own separate way, passing on their series of anecdotal vignettes either verbally or written, easily setting the stage for their own or "offspring Gospel manuscripts" appearing one to five decades later. Potentially to be heavily edited in turn by the Church central authority in the second to fifth centuries.

Adulatory to Jesus; consistently highly defamatory to the Jews. Christened into the newly Christianized Roman Empire in the fourth and fifth centuries, the Gospels will resonate across a continent *de facto* controlled lock–stock–and–palace by the Christian central authority, now with total control of the *organs of state* of Rome.

As noted, the four particular gospels were selected out of a greater pool of perhaps 20–50 gospels by the early Church Fathers (initially apparently by second Century Irenaeus in particular) to be the official Church canon (core theological text), hence the name The Canon Gospels.

The "Canon Gospels" were initially "canonized" by (later–to–be Saint) Irenaeus [of Lyons] c. 185 CE. This was later re–ratified (and possibly re–edited) by the Council of Rome 382 CE and by other synods to follow in the *triumphant over Rome* Christian fourth century.

As noted, the fourth century marked the *de facto* conversion of the Roman Empire to Christianity, with the full power of the Empire now behind Christianity. At this point the Jews are decimated, scattered and marginalized. However to the newly–aligned Roman–Christian hierarchy, the politically irrelevant Jews had one, and final, more crucial role to play: historical scapegoat *cum* evil polarity.

Eager to distance newly–Christianized Rome (now the Church's purview) from Rome's crucifixion of Christ

AN OVERVIEW OF 1700 YEARS OF JEWISH PERSECUTION
[continued]

- **1179:** Canon 24 of the *Third Lateran Council* stated: *"Jews should be slaves to Christians and at the same time treated kindly due of humanitarian considerations."* Canon 26 stated that, *"the testimony of Christians against Jews is to be preferred in all causes where they use their own witnesses against Christians."* (4)

- **1180:** The French King of France, Philip Augustus, arbitrarily seized all Jewish property and expelled the Jews from the country. There was no legal justification for this action. They were allowed to sell all movable possessions, but their land and houses were stolen by the king.

- **1189:** Jews were persecuted in England. The Crown claimed all Jewish possessions. Most of their houses were burned.

- **1205:** Pope Innocent III wrote to the archbishops of Sens and Paris that *"the Jews, by their own guilt, are consigned to perpetual servitude because they crucified the Lord... As slaves rejected by God, in whose death they wickedly conspire, they shall by the effect of this very action, recognize themselves as the slaves of those whom Christ's death set free..."*

- **1215:** The Fourth Lateran Council approved canon laws requiring that *"Jews and Muslims shall wear a special dress."* They also had to wear a badge in the form of a ring. This was to enable them to be easily distinguished from Christians. This practice later spread to other countries.

- **1227:** The *Synod of Narbonne* required Jews to wear an oval badge. This requirement was reinstalled during the 1930's by Hitler, who changed the oval badge to a Star of David.

- **1229:** The Spanish inquisition starts. Later, in 1252, Pope Innocent IV authorizes the use of torture by the Inquisitors.

- **1261:** Duke Henry III of Brabant, Belgium, stated in his will that *"Jews... must be expelled from Brabant and totally annihilated so that not a single one remains, except those who are willing to trade, like all other tradesmen, without money–lending and usury."*

- **1267:** The *Synod of Vienna* ordered Jews to wear horned hats. Thomas Aquinas said that Jews should live in perpetual servitude.

- **1290:** Jews are exiled from England. About 16,000 left the country.

- **1298:** Jews were persecuted in Austria, Bavaria and Franconia. 140 Jewish communities were destroyed; more than 100,000 Jews were killed over a 6 month period.

- **1306:** 100,000 Jews are exiled from France. They left with only the clothes on their backs, and food for only one day.

- **1320:** 40,000 French shepherds went to Palestine on the Shepherd Crusade. On the way, 140 Jewish communities were destroyed.

- **1321:** In Guienne, France, Jews were accused of having incited criminals to poison wells. 5,000 Jews were burned alive, at the stake.

continued (on next Left-side page)

approximately 300 years earlier, the Canon Gospels—
in the form incorporated by the Church at the same
time it gained supreme status in Constantine's Roman
Empire—will attempt to shift as much blame as possible,
and direct as much anger as possible—at the Jews. The
ramification is that a powerful and lethal dynamic is set
in motion, which would ultimately cause suffering and
death, to millions, through this very day…

The Jews of the First Century at the time of Jesus,
politically neutered by Rome, and under the military
heel of Rome, would be surprised to read in the Gospels
of the fourth century (were they to travel forward in time
to read them) that the Jews had any power at all in the
First Century. These Jews would also be quite surprised
to read that in the early morning hours after long late–
night Seders, 55 to 95–year–old Sanhedrin members
were apparently up at approximately 3 A.M., illegally
convening outside the Temple, illegally adjudicating
on the Passover Holiday and illegally getting anywhere
near the Halachic taboo against handing over a Jew to
occupying authorities. These Jews of the First Century
would be quite surprised to hear that in the early morning
Jewish mobs were gathering and howling. (When is the
last time one saw a Jewish mob, let alone at 5 A.M., let
alone on a Jewish Holiday, let alone howling?) And, all
this after four goblets of wine per Jew at the Seder? And
factoring in 3–5 hour (quasi endurance test) Seders for
each Jewish family going into the midnight hour of the
very night, just several hours prior?

This work is concerned with Jewish history. But the
toxic resonance of several asserted key vignettes,
defamatory to the Jews, scattered across the Canon
Gospels and later woven inextricably into the core
"Passion" saga (the centerpiece of Christian lore)

AN OVERVIEW OF 1700 YEARS OF JEWISH PERSECUTION
[continued]

- **1347+:** Ships from the Far East carried rats into Mediterranean ports. The rats carried the Black Death. At first, fleas spread the disease from the rats to humans. As the plague worsened, the germs spread from human to human. In five years, the death toll had reached 25 million. England took 2 centuries for its population levels to recover from the plague. People looked around for someone to blame. They noted that a smaller percentage of Jews than Christians caught the disease. This was undoubtedly due to the Jewish sanitary and dietary laws, which had been preserved from Old Testament times. Rumors circulated that Satan was protecting the Jews and that they were paying back the Devil by poisoning wells used by Christians. The solution was to torture, murder and burn the Jews. *"In Bavaria...12,000 Jews... perished; in the small town of Erfurt...3,000; Rue Brulée...2,000 Jews; near Tours, an immense trench was dug, filled with blazing wood and in a single day 160 Jews were burned."* In Strausberg 2,000 Jews were burned. In Maintz 6,000 were killed; in Worms 400..."

- **1354:** 12,000 Jews were executed in Toledo.

- **1374:** An epidemic of *possession* broke out in the lower Rhine region of what is now Germany. People were seen *"dancing, jumping and [engaging in] wild raving."* This was triggered by enthusiastic revels on St. John's Day – an Christianized version of an ancient Pagan seasonal day of celebration which was still observed by the populace. The epidemic spread throughout the Rhine and in much of the Netherlands and Germany. Crowds of 500 or more dancers would be overcome together. Exorcisms were tried, but failed. Pilgrimages to the shrine of St. Vitus were tried, but this only seemed to exacerbate the problem. Finally, the rumor spread that God was angry because Christians had been excessively tolerant towards the Jews. God had cursed Europe as He did Saul when he showed mercy towards God's enemies in the Old Testament. Jews *"were plundered, tortured and murdered by tens of thousands."* The epidemic finally burned itself out two centuries later, in the late 16th century.

- **1391:** Jewish persecutions begin in Seville and in 70 other Jewish communities throughout Spain.

- **1394:** Jews were exiled, for the second time, from France.

- **1431+:** The *Council of Basel "forbade Jews to go to universities, prohibited them from acting as agents in the conclusion of contracts between Christians, and required that they attend church sermons."*

- **1453:** The Franciscan monk, Capistrano, persuaded the King of Poland to terminate all Jewish civil rights.

- **1478:** Spanish Jews had been heavily persecuted from the 14th century. Many had converted to Christianity. The Spanish Inquisition was set up by the Church in order to detect insincere conversions. Laws were passed that prohibited the descendants of Jews or Muslims from attending univer–

continued (on next Left-side page)

will have a lethal effect on the Jews for over nineteen centuries.

The Canon Gospels become the basis for the Passion (saga), known also as "the Passion of the Christ." The Passion saga relates the (Church's version of) events of the days flanking the death of Jesus, with particular emphasis on the 24 hours flanking the Last Supper (*Seder*) on each side.

An individual "toxic to the Jews" vignette within the Passion saga may not always have appeared originally in more than one of the four Canon Gospels. But, may be incorporated, nevertheless, into the local Passion saga and often, significantly more intensely shaded and far more incendiary than in the original Canon Gospel itself.

Thus, the origins of the Gospels themselves are obscure, key internal contradictions exist within their texts, the historical veracity and precision of the stream of anti–Jewish vignettes in them is highly dubious, and it is universally accepted that the gospels were not written contemporaneous with events.

Finally, the Gospels themselves are not in accord internally on the crucial timing of very key events. Yet the Jews, politically powerless in the early Common Era centuries, and the historical ideological nemesis and whipping boy – straw man of the Church Fathers, will conveniently be caricatured and painted diabolically by later local Passion sagas, whose building blocks are extracted selectively from the four gospels, and then dramatically spun, *case by case*. With ominous consequences for the Jews and their descendants stretching–forth over the centuries.

AN OVERVIEW OF 1700 YEARS OF JEWISH PERSECUTION
[continued]

sity, joining religious orders, holding public office, or entering any of a long list of professions.

- **1492:** Jews were given the choice of being baptized as Christians or be banished from Spain. 300,000 left Spain penniless. Many migrated to Turkey, where they found tolerance among the Muslims. Others converted to Christianity but often continued to practice Judaism in secret.

- **1492 (Jan):** 100,000 Jews expelled and 3000 killed in Sicily (a Spanish province since 1411). 1400 years of Jewish history disappears almost overnight.

- **1497:** Jews were banished from Portugal. 20,000 left the country rather than be baptized as Christians.

- **1516:** The Governor of the Republic of Venice decided that Jews would be permitted to live only in one area of the city. It was located in the South Girolamo parish and was called the *"Ghetto Novo."* This was the first ghetto in Europe. Hitler made use of the concept in the 1930's.

- **1517:** The Venice Ghetto was established.

- **1523:** Martin Luther distributed his essay *"That Jesus Was Born a Jew."* He hoped that large numbers of Jews would convert to Christianity. They didn't, and he began to write and preach hatred against them. Luther has been condemned in recent years for being extremely anti–Semitic.

- **1540:** Jews were exiled from Naples.

- **1543:** Martin Luther, distressed by the reluctance of Jews to convert to Christianity wrote *"On the Jews and their lies, On Shem Hamphoras"* :

  "What then shall we Christians do with this damned, rejected race of Jews?

  - o *First, their synagogues or churches should be set on fire,*

  - o *Secondly, their homes should likewise be broken down and destroyed... They ought to be put under one roof or in a stable, like Gypsies.*

  - o *Thirdly, they should be deprived of their prayer books and Talmuds in which such idolatry, lies, cursing and blasphemy are taught.*

  - o *Fourthly, their rabbis must be forbidden under threat of death to teach any more...*

  - o *Fifthly, passport and traveling privileges should be absolutely forbidden to the Jews...*

  - o *Sixthly, they ought to be stopped from usury. All their cash and valuables of silver and gold ought to be taken from them and put aside for safe keeping...*

continued (on next Left-side page)

The Passion sagas are highly dramatic and *more often than not*, quite intense. In general, they position "the saintly" v. "the demonic" for their audiences. And the Jews will uniformly be conveniently cast in the "demonic role."

Generally, the only question is – *how demonic?* Impressionable Christian youth—over the centuries— introduced in childhood, by a combination of priest(s), parent(s), and teachers—to the "diabolical and demonic Jew" amalgam, will inevitably carry the toxic imagery embedded in their psyches for the duration of their journey through life.

The Jews are cast as radically more demonic in European medieval Passion sagas, than in 21st century American Passion sagas. Thus, contemporary American Christian audiences may not grasp the dimension of the vituperation employed. But the contentious 2003 American film *The Passion of the Christ* (Mel Gibson's handiwork), crafted under the rubric of *holy writ*, provides a partial insight as to how *hatred of the masses* towards the Jews can be promulgated and disseminated via dramatizations of the sufferings of Jesus and spinning of the background context.

While the Church will trumpet "Love thy Neighbor" as its asserted core doctrine, it will *by and large*—on an ongoing basis—lace the soil of Europe with "toxicity to the Jews." And any local demagogue will conveniently *harvest the hatred* along the timeline of the seventeen centuries following Constantine. Greater Europe will become an ongoing *killing field* for the Jews. Hatred will find a permanent and secure residence in Europe. But Jewish residence and life will be more tenuous, and somewhat "less secure."

Note the authoritative work *The Anguish of the Jews* by Edward H. Flannery* (Macmillan, NY, 1965).

AN OVERVIEW OF 1700 YEARS OF JEWISH PERSECUTION
[continued]

> o *Seventhly, let the young and strong Jews and Jewesses be given the flail, the axe, the hoe, the spade, the distaff, and spindle and let them earn their bread by the sweat of their noses as in enjoined upon Adam's children...*
>
> *To sum up, dear princes and nobles who have Jews in your domains, if this advice of mine does not suit you, then find a better one so that you and we may all be free of this insufferable devilish burden – the Jews."*

- **1550:** Jews were exiled from Genoa and Venice.
- **1555 (July 12):** A Roman Catholic Papal bull, *"Cum nimis absurdum,"* required Jews to wear badges, and live in ghettos. They were not allowed to own property outside the ghetto. Living conditions were dreadful: over 3,000 people were forced to live in about 8 acres of land. Women had to wear a yellow veil or scarf; men had to wear a piece of yellow cloth on their hat.
- **1582:** Jews were expelled from Holland

[note: There is a gap (here from 1582 > 1806) in the Robinson timeline – author]

Antisemitism: Persecution of Jews along Racial Lines:

Previous persecution was directed at believers in Judaism. Jews could escape oppression by converting to Christianity. Subsequent attacks against Jews were racially motivated; the Jewish people were viewed as a separate race.

- **1806:** A French Jesuit Priest, Abbe Barruel, had written a treatise blaming the Masonic Order for the French Revolution. He later issued a letter alleging that Jews, not the Masons were the guilty party. This triggered a belief in an international Jewish conspiracy in Germany, Poland and some other European countries later in the 19th century.
- **1846–1878:** Pope Pius IX restored all of the previous restrictions against the Jews within the Vatican state. All Jews under Papal control were confined to Rome's ghetto – the last one in Europe until the Nazi era. On 2000–SEP–3, Pope John Paul II beautified Pius IX; this is the last step before sainthood. He explained: *"Beatifying a son of the church does not celebrate particular historic choices that he has made, but rather points him out for imitation and for veneration for his virtue."*
- **1858:** Edgardo Mortara was kidnapped, at the age of six, from his Jewish family by Roman Catholic officials after they found out that a maid had secretly baptized him. He was not returned to his family but was raised a Catholic. He eventually became a priest.
- **1873:** The term *"anti–Semitism"* is first used in a pamphlet by Wilhelm Marr called *"Jewry's Victory over Teutonism."*
- **1881:** Alexander II of Russia was assassinated by radicals. The Jews were blamed. About 200 individual pogroms against the Jews followed.

continued (on next Left-side page)

* I first read Flannery's work when I was researching a term paper on anti–Semitism in high school c. 1966. *The Anguish of the Jews* © 1965 remains to this day one of the iconic, breakthrough works of all–time. Note for the record that Flannery sub–titles his work 'Twenty–three centuries of Anti–Semitism.' Thus, Flannery is trying to posture that anti–Semitism pre–dated Christianity. On this particular score, however, the sainted Catholic priest Edward H. Flannery, was trying to defend the indefensible. Isolated local flare–ups between culturally competing groups cherry–picked from the span of four tumultuous centuries pre–Christianity, simply do not qualify for the term 'anti–Semitism,' the virulent cancer that was to terrorize and cut down millions over the nineteen centuries to–date, subsequent to the Christian Fathers. [See also www.shofars.org/persecution/default.htm]

***

Preoccupied with defending their lives, freedom and religious honor from the assaulting legions of Rome in front of their city walls, the First Century Jewish intellectual elite was "somewhat distracted."

The first wave demonizations was being spun hundreds of miles to the northwest in greater Turkey–Syria emanating "coincidentally" just then from the *first wave* gospels. The gospel–spin would trash the legacy of an industrious and highly-educated spiritual–based group into a diabolical, blood–thirsty mob. But the Glory of Christ had to be expounded and promulgated.

Nineteen hundred years later, a random 7–year–old Jewish Polish girl, one of hundreds of thousands of Polish Jewish youngsters, as just one example of 1+ million Jewish children murdered by the Nazis, would face an average of 2–5 days of starvation–torture and

AN OVERVIEW OF 1700 YEARS OF JEWISH PERSECUTION
[continued]

("Pogrom" is a Russian word meaning *"devastation"* or *"riot."* In Russia, a pogrom was typically a mob riot against Jewish individuals, shops, homes or businesses. They were often supported and even organized by the government.) Thousands of Jews became homeless and impoverished. The few who were charged with offenses generally received very light sentences.

- **1893:** *"...anti–Semitic parties won sixteen seats in the German Reichstag."*
- **1894:** Captain Alfred Dreyfus, an officer on the French general staff, was convicted of treason. The evidence against him consisted of a piece of paper from his wastebasket with another person's handwriting, and papers forged by anti–Semitic officers. He received a life sentence on Devil's Island, off the coast of South America. The French government was aware that a Major Esterhazy was actually guilty. (The church, government and army united to suppress the truth. Writer Emile Zola and politician Jean Jaurès fought for justice and human rights. After 10 years, the French government fell and Drefus was declared totally innocent. The Dreyfus Affair was world–wide news for years. It motivated Journalist Theodor Herzl to write a book in 1896: *"The Jewish State: A Modern Solution to the Jewish Question."* The book led to the founding of the Zionist movement, which fought for a Jewish Home- land. A half–century later, the state of Israel was born.
- **1903:** At Easter, government agents organized an anti–Jewish pogrom in Kishinev, Moldova, Russia. The local newspaper published a series of inflammatory articles. A Christian child was discovered murdered and a young Christian woman at the Jewish Hospital committed suicide. Jews were blamed for the deaths. Violence ensured. The 5,000 soldiers in the town did nothing. When the smoke cleared, 49 Jews had been killed, 500 were injured; 700 homes looted and destroyed, 600 businesses and shops looted, 2000 families left homeless. Later, it was discovered that the child had been murdered by its relatives and the suicide was unrelated to the Jews.
- **1905:** The Okhrana, the Russian secret police in the reign of Czar Nicho- las II, converted an earlier anti–Semitic novel into a document called the *"Protocols of the Elders of Zion."* It was published privately in 1897. A Rus- sian Orthodox priest, Sergius Nilus, published them publicly in 1905. It is promoted as the record of *"secret rabbinical conferences whose aim was to subjugate and exterminate the Christians."* The Protocols were used by the Okhrana in a propaganda campaign that was associated with massa- cres of the Jews. These were the Czarist Pogroms of 1905.
- **1915:** 600,000 Jews were forcibly moved from the western borders of Rus- sia towards the interior. About 100,000 died of exposure or starvation.
- **1917:** *"In the civil war following the Bolshevik Revolution of 1917, the reactionary White Armies made extensive use of the Protocols to incite widespread slaughters of Jews."* 200,000 Jews were murdered in the Ukraine.

continued (on next Left-side page)

stench in a sealed Nazi cattle–car, in debasement and grime, watching her family *starve to death*, before probably being "gassed to death" with her mother, if she somehow survived the cattle–car torture–ordeal, upon arrival at a Death Camp—as a very, very direct consequence of the cumulative continued and ongoing demonizations by the Catholic Church pervasively over the seventeen to nineteen centuries to come.

The Church would like to portray itself as a victim of Nazism, as opposed to its *hatred for the Jews* progenitor.

But, *words tend to have wings.*

***

69 CE: *YAVNEH FOUNDED BY JOHANAN BEN ZAKKAI*

The great Yeshiva of Yavneh (Jamnia) – founded by Rav Johanan ben Zakkai, the leading Pharisee, with the acquiescence of General Vespasian, who was laying siege to Jerusalem.

Johanan ben Zakkai was a key *tanna* (sage of the Mishnah).

Britannica –

"Even before 70 CE, he acted as a leading representative of the Pharisees in debate with priestly and Sadducean authorities. (The Pharisees stressed rigorous observance of the Law, inclusion of the oral tradition as normative, and an interpretative adaptation of traditional precepts to new situations; the Sadducees, an elitist conservative group, accepted only the Written Law as authoritative and were more literalist and static in their interpretation.) Johanan's school was apparently famous, and one in search of learning would go to extremes, if need be, to be admitted there. Furthermore, Johanan was opposed to the

AN OVERVIEW OF 1700 YEARS OF JEWISH PERSECUTION
[continued]

- **1920:** The Protocols reach England and the United States. They are exposed as a forgery, but are widely circulated. Henry Ford sponsored a study of international activities of Jews. This led to a series of anti–Semitic articles in the Dearborn Independent, which were published in a book, *"The International Jew."*

- **1920:** The defeat of Germany in World War I and the continuing economic difficulties were blamed in that country on the *"Jewish influence."*

- **1920's, 1930's:** Hitler wrote in *Mein Kampf: "Today I believe that I am acting in accordance with the will of the Almighty Creator: by defending myself against the Jew, I am fighting for the work of the Lord."* The Protocols are used by the Nazis to whip up public hatred of the Jews in the 1930's. Widespread pogroms occur in Greece, Hungary, Mexico, Poland, Rumania, and the USSR. Radio programs by many conservative American clergy, both Roman Catholic and Protestant, frequently attacked Jews. Reverend Fr. Charles E Coughlin was one of the best known. *"In the 1930's, radio audiences heard him rail against the threat of Jews to America's economy and defend Hitler's treatment of Jews as justified in the fight against communism."* Other conservative Christian leaders, such as Frank Norris and John Straton supported the Jews.

  Discrimination against Jews in North America was widespread. Many universities set limits on the maximum number of Jewish students that they would accept. Harvard accepted all students on the basis of merit until after World War I when the percentage of Jewish students approached 15 percent. At that time they installed an informal quota system. In 1941, Princeton had fewer than 2 percent Jews in their student body. Jews were routinely barred from country clubs, prestigious neighborhoods, etc.

- **1933:** Hitler took power in Germany. Jews *"were barred from civil service, legal professions and universities, were not allowed to teach in schools and could not be editors of newspapers."* (3) Two years later, Jews were no longer considered citizens.

- **1934:** Various laws were enacted in Germany to force Jews out of schools and professions.

- **1935:** The Nazis passed the *Nuremberg Laws* restricting citizenship to those of *"German or related blood."* Jews became stateless.

- **1936:** Cardinal Hloud of Poland urged Catholics to boycott Jewish businesses.

- **1938:** On NOV–9, the Nazi government in Germany sent storm troopers, the SS and the Hitler Youth on a pogrom that killed 91 Jews, injured hundreds, burned 177 synagogues and looted 7,500 Jewish stores. Broken glass could be seen everywhere; the glass gave this event its name of Kristallnacht, the Night of Broken Glass.

continued (on next Left-side page)

policy of those who were determined on war with Rome at all costs. By quitting beleaguered Jerusalem according to most accounts in 70 CE (though it is possible that he left as early as 68 CE) and being brought to the Roman camp, he somehow succeeded in getting permission to set up an academy in Jamnia (Jabneh), near the Judaean coast, and there he was joined by a number of his favorite disciples. Two of them, Eliezer ben Hyrcanus and Joshua ben Hananiah, who are credited with having smuggled their master out of Jerusalem in a coffin, were to become, by the end of the century and the beginning of the following one, the leading teachers of their generation and had a profound influence on the greatest scholars of the next generation.

By establishing in Jamnia a major academy and authoritative rabbinic body, Johanan fixed the conditions for continuing Judaism's basic traditions after the destruction of the Temple; and that, by his lively sense of the need for reinterpreting inherited concepts in new circumstances, he laid the foundations on which Talmudic and rabbinic Judaism built their structure.

Of all the Palestinian Jewish sages of the first century A.D. [CE], none apparently proved so fundamentally influential in his own time and for subsequent generations of scholars and spiritual leaders as Johanan ben Zakkai. In the history of Talmudic literature and thought, Johanan is rightly seen as continuing the Hillelite tradition, although this should not be interpreted to mean that he inherited only Hillel's teachings."

Encyclopaedia Britannica Online, http://www.britannica.com/EBchecked/topic/304443/Johanan–ben–Zakkai (accessed July 1, 2009)

***

Yavneh, a west–central Judean town, 7 km (4.35 miles)

AN OVERVIEW OF 1700 YEARS OF JEWISH PERSECUTION
[continued]

- **1938:** Hitler brought back century–old church law, ordering all Jews to wear a yellow Star of David as identification. A few hundred thousand Jews are allowed to leave Germany after they give all of their assets to the government.

- **1939:** The Holocaust, the systematic extermination of Jews in Germany begins. The process only ended in 1945 with the conclusion of World War II. Approximately 6 million Jews (1.5 million of them children), 400 thousand Roma (Gypsies) and others were slaughtered. Some were killed by death squads; others were slowly killed in trucks with carbon monoxide; others were gassed in large groups in Auschwitz, Dacau, Sobibor, Treblinka and other extermination camps. Officially, the holocaust was described by the Nazis as subjecting Jews *"to special treatment"* or *as a "solution of the Jewish question."* Gold taken from the teeth of the victims was recycled; hair was used in the manufacture of mattresses. In the Buchenwald extermination camp, lampshades were made out of human skin; however, this appears to be an isolated incident. A rumor spread that Jewish corpses were routinely converted into soap. However, the story appears to be false.

- **1940:** The Vichy government of France collaborated with Nazi Germany by freezing about 80,000 Jewish bank accounts. During the next four years, they deported about 76,000 Jews to Nazi death camps; only about 2,500 survived. It was only in 1995 that a French president, Jacques Chirac, *"was able to admit that the state bore a heavy share of responsibility in the mass round–ups and deportations of Jews, as well as in the property and asset seizures that were carried out with the active help of the Vichy regime."*

- **1941:** The *Holocaust Museum* in Washington DC estimates that 13,000 Jews died on 1941–JUN–19 during a pogrom in Bucharest, Romania. It was ordered by the pro–Nazi Romanian regime of Marshal Ion Antonescu. The current government has admitted that this atrocity happened, but most Romanians continue to deny that the Jews were killed on orders from their government.

- **1942:** From JUL–28 to 31, almost 18,000 inhabitants of the Minsk ghetto in what is now Belarus were exterminated. This was in addition to 5,000 to 15,000 who had been massacred in earlier pogroms in that city. This was just one of many such pogroms during World War II.

- **1946:** Even though World War II ended the year before, anti–Semitic pogroms continued, particularly in Poland.

east of the Mediterranean, remained the center of Jewish rabbinical authority, centered in the Yeshiva of Yavneh [Yavneh Academy], for 62 years, until the Bar Kochba Revolt (c. 132 CE), when the city of Usha in western Galilee superseded it, evolving as the 130s CE center of rabbinic Judaism.

69 CE: YEAR OF THE FOUR EMPERORS (in Rome)

–ends with the election of Vespasian who inaugurates the Flavian dynasty. During the same year, there are internal Jewish conflicts in Jerusalem; the Zealots terrorize the population; Jerusalem's moderates are purged.

70 CE: DESTRUCTION OF TEMPLE II

Simeon Bar Giora becomes military commander of the Jewish rebels in Jerusalem; the final conquest of Jerusalem by Titus' troops transpires; the Roman troops sack the town and burn down the Temple; Vaspasian replaces the auxiliary troops with a permanent garrison (the "Tenth Legion") and transforms Judea into a province administered by a governor of praetorian rank.

70 CE: ACHER

Elisha ben Abuyah, a.k.a. Acher, a storied rabbinic, appears in a cryptic but legendary *bereita* (hi–level Talmudic segment).

   "Four entered the vineyard"
       "*arba nichnasu l'pardes*"
     Ben Azzai, Ben Zoma, **Acher** (Elisha be Abuyah) and Akiva
   Ben Azzai *looked and died*
   Ben Zoma *looked and went mad*

70 CE: YAVNEH FOUNDED BY JOHANAN BEN ZAKKAI

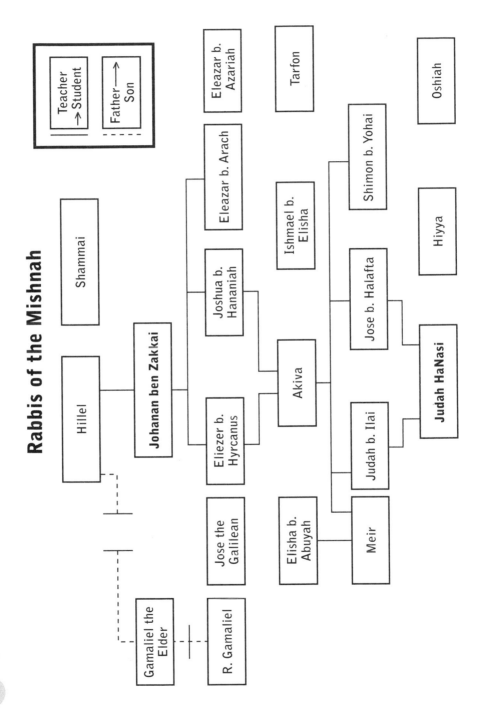

Rabbis of the Mishnah

Teacher → Student

Father → Son

Shammai

Hillel

Johanan ben Zakkai

Eleazar b. Arach

Joshua b. Hananiah

Eliezer b. Hyrcanus

Eleazar b. Azariah

Tarfon

Ishmael b. Elisha

Akiva

Jose the Galilean

Elisha b. Abuyah

Shimon b. Yohai

Jose b. Halafta

Judah b. Ilai

Meir

Oshiah

Hiyya

Judah HaNasi

Gamaliel the Elder

R. Gamaliel

Acher *destroyed the plants*
Akiva *entered in peace and departed in peace*

There are many interpretations. One of the preeminent interpretations runs as follows:

Four high level rabbinics engaged in the philosophical challenge of *"theodicy"*
i.e. if there is a God who is all–powerful and all–merciful, why is there gross evil?

Ben Azzai looked and died
Ben Zoma looked and went mad
Acher then rejected classic religion
Akiva entered in peace, and departed in peace

73 CE: MASADA!

Masada Fortress, Negev Desert (west of the Dead Sea) subsequent to the destruction of Temple II in nearby Jerusalem during Jewish–Roman War I (which peaked about 2 years prior).

"Last Stand of the Jews" and eventually, mass–suicide of the 960 Jewish "Zealot" rebels against Rome's 20,000–man Tenth Legion.

Masada, under the leadership of Eleazar ben Ya'ir, held out for three years…

Masada, a former Herodian retreat/refuge, is/was located in the Judean desert south of Jerusalem, just west of the Dead Sea. The Zealots used Masada as a base to raid and harass the nearby Roman troops. The Roman governor of Judea, Lucius Flavius Silva marched against Masada

70 CE: *ACHER*
OLD CITY of JERUSALEM WALL
incorporating TOWER of DAVID

Oil on canvas by Rhoda Birnbaum

with Roman Legion X (Tenth Legion) Fretensis, and laid siege to the fortress.

After the besieging Romans failed in repeated attempts to breach the defense, they elected to construct an earthen ramp, using thousands of tons of stones and earth. At the point that the Romans had 99 percent completed their massive siege ramp, and were poised for their final assault the next day, the "1,000" Jewish rebels of Masada made a decision to commit mass–suicide that night rather than fall into the Roman hands the following day.

Heads of families slew their families. Then, the men drew lots as to who would slay the others.

Two thousand years down the road, troops of the Israeli Armored Corps and the Givati Brigade and other IDF (Israeli Defense Forces) troops would take their oath of duty at high noon atop the sun baked plateau of Masada, overlooking the Judean desert far below.

> *"Masada shay–nit lo ti–pol"* . . .
>
> *
>
> "Masada shall not fall again"

 77 CE: TACITUS

Tacitus enters political life in Rome at age 22.

But his historical works *to come* will be his legacy.

Tacitus's Germania (98 CE), "Histories" (105 CE), and "Annals" (117 CE) are his most prominent works.

73 CE: MASADA!

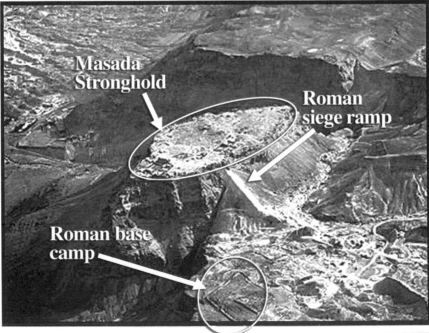

Masada
Stronghold

Roman
siege ramp

Roman base
camp

source: www.truthnet.org

A well–studied – and key – excerpt from Annals by Tacitus on the death of Jesus –

"Christus [Christ] from whom the name is derived…was executed at the hands of the procurator Pontius Pilate in the reign of Tiberius."

"…at the hands of Pontius Pilate." Period. Very explicit.

Like the Arabic accounts, and, indeed, like the Arabic accounts of Josephus, there is no mention at all of any participation or collaboration of any Jews whatsoever, or by the (Roman–appointed) Jewish High Priest or of any trial or institutional action by the Sanhedrin.

79–81 CE: ROMAN EMPEROR TITUS

Reign of Titus, Vespasian's son.

81–96 CE: ROMAN EMPEROR DOMITIAN

Reign of Domitian who persecutes Jews and those who converted to Judaism. "The tax on the Jews was exacted with particular rigor; it was also imposed on the proselytes who lived in the fashion of the Jews without declaring themselves Jewish and on those who, concealing their origin, tried to avoid the tributes imposed on this nation. "I remember seeing, when I was hardly an adolescent, a procurator examining a ninety–year–old man to see if he were circumcised" (Suetonius, *Life of Twelve Caesars*, "Domitian," VIII, 12).

96–98 CE: ROMAN EMPEROR NERVA

Benign reign of Emperor Nerva. A coin, minted after he abolished the extortionist procedure of taxing the Jews,

(continue four pages hence)

77 CE: TACITUS

Cornelius Tacitus

PLATE XIV

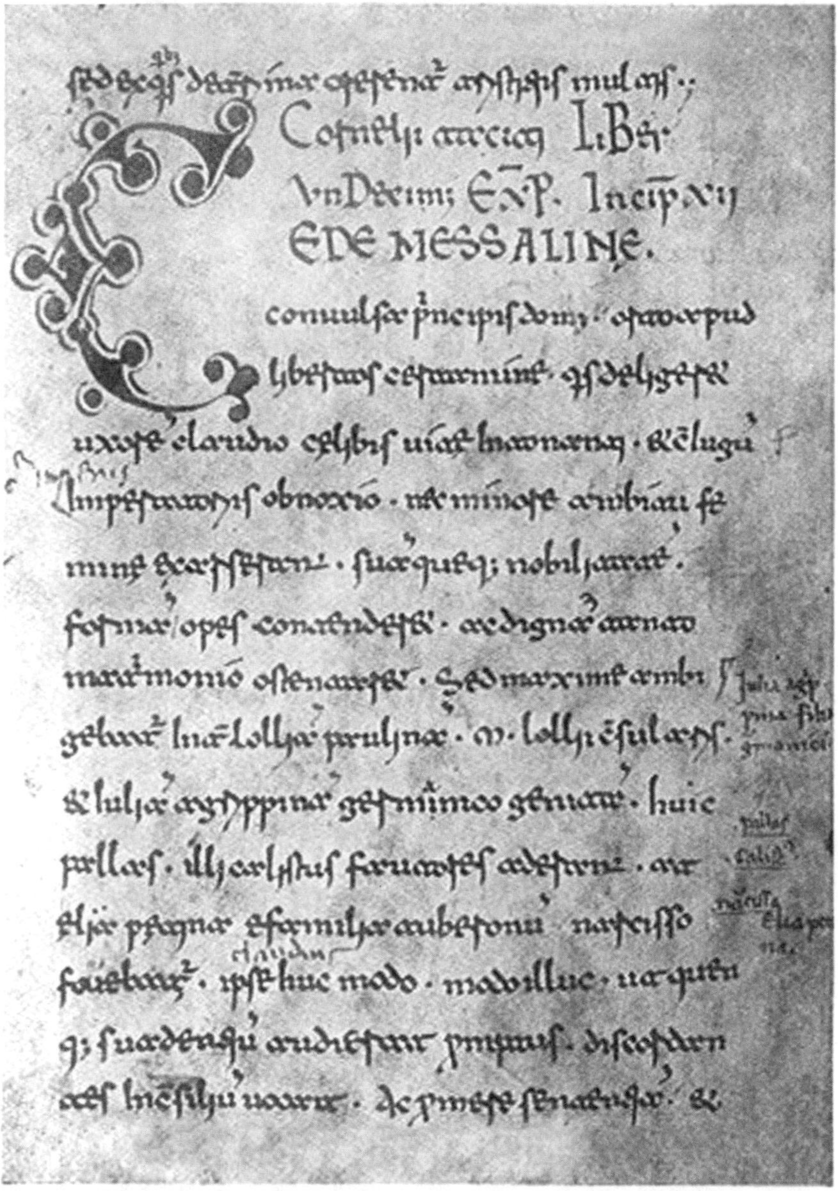

Sample manuscript of Tacitus

source: www.tertullian.org

100 CE: SHUOWEN JIEZI (DICTIONARY) COMPILED

The cover of a modern reprint of a Northern Song–Dynasty Edition of *Shuowen Jiezi*

(continued from p. 221)

bears the inscription: *Fisci iudaici calumnia sublata* ("to efface the shame of the Jewish tax").

98–117 CE: REIGN OF ROMAN EMPEROR TRAJAN

100 CE: SHUOWEN JIEZI (DICTIONARY) COMPILED

China: by Han scholar Xu Shen

Supersedes the more basic first known Chinese dictionary, the *Erya* (200s BCE) [author unknown].

The Shuowen Jiezi is a sophisticated early second century Chinese dictionary (from the Han Dynasty). It is ultimately presented to Emperor An (of Han) by Xu Chong, the son of Xu Shen, two decades later, in 121 CE.

Timing is apparently *everything*.

c. 100 CE: RABBI AKIVA TRAVELS TO NEHARDEA

Rabbi Akiva travels to Nehardea (Babylonia) to announce the Hebrew leap year. This is the first time that the sources mention a noted Jewish sage from Palestine active in the Babylonian Diaspora.

100 CE: LEGITIMACY

The early Church Fathers, as any new religious movement, would need to secure and protect their legitimacy as a religion. "Borrowing" key iconography from Judaism, they would need to fully secure their legitimacy *vis à vis* Judaism in particular. As the legitimacy of Judaism, direct heirs of Sinai, is somewhat difficult to undermine, and as the Church Fathers did

Saints & Angels
v.
Demons & Devils

Having been less than successful recruiting from the Jewish populace, the Early Christians will pivot to draw their recruits heavily and
overwhelmingly from the neo–Pagan and neo–Gnostic denizens of the
extended Roman Empire. The Byzantine Empire will come later.

While the concept and power of –
Saints & Angels
vs.
Demons & Devils
thoroughly "*gets past*" the Jews,
who have all been hard–wired monotheistically
over the 1500+ years since Abraham,
the duality–themes note above will hit deeply embedded psychic buttons
among the neo–Pagans and neo–Gnostics and their descendants.

Following this line–of–thinking,
the Early Christian leadership
will, indeed, *step–by–callous–step*
"set up" the Jews, their political and theological nemesis,
to play the role of "*Demons & Devils*".

The Church will 'succeed' in this score, probably beyond its dreams.

The Church will then juxtapose its litany of Saints & Angels
counter–posed against the "*demonic*" & "*diabolical*" Jews.
In the Gospels, Christianity is painted icon–by–icon in the brushstrokes
of "the heavenly and celestial." And, of course, as "victim" – of the diabolical and evil (Jews). Even though the Jews are a miniscule minority.

cont'd

not want to undermine 'Sinai' and/or the (Jewish) Bible, *per se*, the Church would employ a different tack.

The gambit that the Christians would take would be to steadily but surely undermine the character–reputation of the Jews. The Jews may have been distracted by the Roman invasion and expulsion from focusing much on the Christians. But the Christians were certainly focusing and polemicizing about the Jews. *Step by step* over the decades, and then over the centuries, this *character assassination* would proceed: first obliquely, then directly, and then directly and venomously.

The *stage is first set* in the gospels themselves. The Christian Fathers in the first several Common Era centuries then ratchet–up the intensity. Once hatred is sown, it tends to have a *life of its own*, or in the case of the Jews, probably more accurate to say – *a death warrant all its own.*

As the power of the Church increased by a quantum jump—with the *de facto* conversion of Constantine in the 300s CE—the Church did not back off from the concerted denigrations; but, rather, increased the intensity of the defamations and de–humanizations. Not only would the Jews be off–balance, and not in a position to politically or intellectually challenge the legitimacy of the Church, the Jews would be lucky to be left breathing.

*

Historically, Roman soldiers arranged the crucifixion of Jesus *start to finish* by this brutal Roman execution mode.

There were no tribunals before the execution. No tribunals were needed, any which way, as Pontius Pilate had absolute power over these 'local matters.'

Saints & Angels
v.
Demons & Devils

(continued)

Christian theology, dogma, and light culture will methodically aggressively paint the Jew – the torch–bearer of the Ten Commandments – as
the total antithesis of everything and anything positive and redemptive.

The duality of the themes will resonate powerfully in medieval times
among the masses of Europe.

Sixteen centuries after Constantine, and acutely alert and sensitive to
Pagan motifs, the neo–Pagan Nazi movement in the mid-twentieth
century, will *"play out"* this string.

The Nazis, just as the Catholic Church which had paved–the–way before
them, will first demonize and dehumanize the Jews. Once demonized,
the Jews will be 'fair game' for persecution and or slaughter.

While the Catholic Church had counter–posed Saints vs. the Jews,
the Nazis will juxtapose the fantasized *"Superman Aryan"* *vs. the Jews.*

Same wine, different flasks. Parallel diabolical manipulation of the
masses. diabolical manipulation of the masses.

While the Catholic Inquisition will burn suspected Jews at–the–stake,
the Nazis will burn the Jews *in the crematorium.*

In both events, the smoke of the bodies of Jewish children and their
parents will ascend heavenward....

* * *

The Jews under Rome were powerless to affect the outcome *either which way.*

The Romans feared sedition. The Romans executed many protagonists who threatened upheaval or worse. The Romans were messiah–averse. The Romans crucified lesser threats than Jesus.

Any hypothetical (Jewish) co–operation or collusion, even tangential, with Rome on this sordid matter would have been not only against Jewish law, but also contrary to the Jewish *modus operandi* spanning many centuries. Jesus may have been a threat to Rome, but Jesus does not appear in one single Jewish rabbinic text contemporaneous with that period.

So, how did the Jews become labeled by the Church as "Christ killers"?

With Rome ascendant, and the Church Fathers eager to recruit the inhabitants of the Roman Empire, increasingly the historical record is re–spun by the ascendant Church to diminish the role of Roman Procurator Pontius Pilate, and to increase, somehow, the alleged participation and capability of the Jews.

It would seem to be a challenging task to turn WHITE into BLACK, but that is the basic scenario.

101 CE: JOSEPHUS DIES

Jewish–born, Roman–captured, historian Josephus Flavius dies in Rome (at age 64), (where his patrons maintained him), ending a quite unique tenure on this planet, controversial to this day.

101 CE: JOSEPHUS DIES

The romanticized woodcut engraving of Flavius Josephus appearing in William Whiston's translation of his works.

[b. 37 CE (4 years after the crucifixion of Jesus); d. 101 CE]

110 CE: ONKELOS

Authors *Targum Onkelos* (on the Torah)

–Aramaic exposition of the *pshat* (basic meaning) of the Five Books of Moses.

Onkelos (35–120 CE), a nephew of Titus, is one of Judaism's most illustrious converts, having entered his works into the core of the *Masorah* (the Jewish core chain of theological tradition, "Written Law" and "Oral Law").

115 –117 CE: OVERVIEW: "KITOS" JEWISH REVOLTS

a.k.a. Jewish Revolt II

Major revolts by Diaspora Jews in Cyrene (Cyrenaica), Egyptus (Egypt minus the Sinai Peninsula), Cyprus, and Mesopotamia.

The rebellions were ultimately crushed by the Roman legionary forces, chiefly by the Roman general Lustus Quietus, whose name ultimately gives the far–flung conflict its name, as "Kitos" is a later corruption of the name.

c. 115 CE: FOCUS: **START** OF "KITOS" JEWISH REVOLTS

Beginning of the Jewish revolt in Cyrenaica (the eastern coastal region of modern–day Libya). According to Greek sources (Eusebius and Dio Cassius), the Jews of Cyrene, led by their "king" Lukuas, enter Egypt. The Egyptian Greeks, finding refuge in Alexandria, retaliate by massacring the

Interlinear text of Hebrew Numbers 6.3–10 with Aramaic Targum Onkelos from the British Library.

source: Plate IX. *The S.S.Teacher's Edition: The Holy Bible.* New York: Henry Frowde, Publisher to the University of Oxford, 1896.

110 CE: ONKELOS

Midrash, Genesis Rabbah 70:5

"[For the Lord your God] befriends the ger, providing him with food and clothing" (Deuteronomy 10:18), the ger Onkelos asked Rabbi Eliezer:

"Is that the reward for the ger, food and clothing?" "Is then that a small thing in your eyes?" replied Rabbi Eliezer. "When our ancestors asked for bread and clothing, they would make a vow (Genesis 28:20). Meanwhile G–d comes and offers it to the ger on a platter!" Then Onkelos visited Rabbi Joshua, who began to comfort him with words:" "Bread' refers to the Torah, as it says, 'Come, eat of my bread' (Proverbs 9:5), while 'clothing' means the [scholar's] cloak. When a man is privileged to [study the] Torah, he is privileged to perform God's precepts. Moreover, they [the proselytes] merry their daughters into the priesthood, so that their descendants may offer burnt offerings on the altar."

Jews in that city. Lukuas' Jewish rebels overrun the country until a Roman army defeats them. The Jewish community in Alexandria is then almost annihilated.

The local troubles extend onto the island of Cyprus where a Jewish revolt, led by a certain Artemion, kills thousands. When the revolt is crushed, Jews are Jews are officially forbidden to set foot on the island ever again....

116–117 CE: AIDING THE PARTHIANS

Babylonian Jews take an active part in the Parthian resistance against the invasion of (Roman Emperor) Trajan's troops.

116–117 CE: CONTINUATION: "KITOS" REVOLT / JEWISH REVOLT IN MESOPOTAMIA

Revolt in Mesopotamia: Trajan (reign: 98–117 CE) orders his general Lusius Quietus to expel or exterminate all Jews in the region; Quietus kills tens of thousands, a deed which earns him the rank of praetor, then of consul, and the position of governor of Judea which becomes a consular province in 117. A second legion, probably the *Secunda Trajana*, is positioned in the northern part of the country. Upon the death of Trajan; the new emperor Hadrian (reign 117–138 CE) evacuates the lands in the East conquered by his predecessor, dismisses Lusius Quietus, and severely punishes the Greeks who had persecuted the Jews in Alexandria.

120–129 CE: HADRIAN RECONSTRUCTS

Reconstruction of towns in the East raises false hopes that the new emperor (Hadrian) intends to rebuild Jerusalem.

120–129 CE: HADRIAN RECONSTRUCTS

The Pantheon was rebuilt by Hadrian (in Rome).

This may have given birth to the legend reported in a *midrash* (*Bereshit Raba*, 44): In the days of Rabbi Joshua ben Hananiah, the emperor* had decided to rebuild the Temple, but that Samaritan opposition had aborted the plan. The Jews then assembled in the valley of Rimmon, angrily demanding to revolt. Rabbi Joshua ben Hananiah calmed their turbulence with a fable about a bird who with its long beak had removed a bone stuck in a lion's throat; like that bird, he said, the Jews should be satisfied with the fact that they had entered the lion's jaw and come away unharmed.

The lion (Rome) should not be expected to reward such a frail creature (the Jewish people). This legend vividly expresses the national and religious fermentation in Palestine, which persisted even after the destruction of the Temple and the wars waged against Trajan. (A *Histrorical Atlas of the Jewish People*)

130 CE: HADRIAN DROPS IN

Hadrian visits Judea; the Jews are forbidden to practice circumcision; the honeymoon between the emperor and the Jews is over.

131 CE: HADRIAN RE–NAMES

Emperor renames Jerusalem "Aelia Capitolina" and forbids the Jews to set foot there. When he departs the region in 131 CE, the Jews gear–up for revolt.

132 CE: *FULL–SCALE REVOLT*: BAR KOCHBA REVOLT (JEWISH–ROMAN WAR II)

a.k.a. Revolt III

* Hadrian

132 CE: FULL-SCALE REVOLT: BAR KOCHBA REVOLT (JEWISH-ROMAN WAR II)

The Jewish–Roman wars were a series of revolts by the Jews against the Roman Empire.

I. **First Jewish–Roman War** (66–73) —
    also called the First Jewish Revolt or the Great Jewish Revolt.

II. **Kitos War** (115–117) —
    sometimes called the Second Jewish–Roman War.

III. **Bar Kokhba revolt** (132–135) —
     also called the Third Jewish–Roman War.

IV. **War against Gallus** (351) —
    the Jewish revolt originating in Sepphoris.

V. **Revolt against Heraclius** (613) —
    the Jewish revolt originating in Tiberias.

The reverse of the coin displays a lulav (myrtle, palm branch, and willow tied in a bundle) and ethrog (citrus fruit), which are used in the celebration of the Jewish holiday Sukkot or Feast of Tabernacles. The inscription reads: "Year 2 of the freedom of Israel.

[Note: Many histories do not count the Kitos/ Mediterranean rebellions noted just above as Jewish–Roman War II, in which case the Bar Kochba Revolt is numbered by them as Jewish–Roman War II. Note that (tens of) thousands of Jews perished in the Kitos rebellions (115–117 CE) against Rome.]

The Jews rise up in revolt (132–135 CE) after the Romans build a temple to (the Roman god) Jupiter on the site of the Jewish Temple, and subsequent to Hadrian's abolishment of circumcision c. 130–131 CE.

While the Roman forces are originally forced out of Jerusalem by the forces of Bar Kochba, the Romans regroup. Detachments of Roman legions are brought from Egypt, Arabia, Syria, Asia Minor, and the Danubian countries. (Jewish–minted) coins bearing the inscription "Second Year of the Freedom of Israel" have been discovered in contemporary (20–21st Century) times.

c. 135 CE Roman armies under the command of Julius Severus retake Jerusalem and sack it.

According to Roman historian Cassius Dio, during the war 580,000 Jews are killed, 50 fortified Jewish towns destroyed, and 985 villages razed. On the other side of the ledger, an entire Roman Legion, the XXII Deiotariana apparently was destroyed by the Jewish rebels.

Bar Kochba's "last stand" was at Beitar, a fortified city 10 km southwest of Jerusalem.

Bar Kochba's prime backer, Rebbe Akiva, and the other leading rabbinics (to be known for posterity as the Ten Martyrs) are tortured and executed by the Romans...

135 CE: POST–REVOLT III

^
Hadrian's plenipotentiary

∨
Jerusalem Jewish group

Expulsion of the Jews (from Jerusalem) in the Reign of the Emperor Hadrian (135 CE): "How Heraclius turned the Jews out of Jerusalem."

– Facsimile of a Miniature in the "Histoire des Empereurs," Manuscript of the Fifteenth Century, in the Library of the Arsenal, Paris.

to be memorialized in Yom Kippur liturgy to this day—
"The Ten Martyrs" (*Aseret Harugei Malchut*).

135 CE: POST–REVOLT III

The crushing of the (Bar Kochba) revolt is followed by
a series of religious persecutions. Many Jews choose to
die for their faith. When Rabbi Hananiah ben Teradyon
is asked by a Roman judge why he studied the Torah in
defiance of the prohibition, his reply is: "I follow my God's
commandment." The Romans immediately condemn
him to be burned at the stake, his wife to be killed, and
his daughter to be taken to the prostitutes (Babylonian
Talmud, *Avoda Zara*, 17b). Hananiah was but one of
many martyrs. (A *Historical Atlas of the Jewish People*)

The Romans sustains severe battle casualties from the
forces of Bar Kochba. According to (Roman chronicler)
Dio Cassius, Hadrian's casualties are so severe, that when
he formally informs the Senate of his ultimate victory,
he omits the usual formal advisement to the Senate:
"I and my army are well." Bar Kochba had inflicted severe
punishment on the Roman Army.

135 CE: (REBBE) AKIVA

Executed by Rome (as noted above).

Tannaic sage, rabbi, martyr at the hands of Romans,
political/rabbinical backer of Jewish rebel Bar Kochba—
and his revolt—during the Jewish–Roman War III. Both
protagonists – Akiva and Bar Kochba – are tortured and/
or killed in Judea by forces of Roman Emperor Hadrian.

c. 150 CE: THE GOSPEL OF JUDAS

Surfaced in the 1970–1993 CE time frame; partially

135 CE: (REBBE) AKIVA

Rabbi Akiva, from the Mantua Haggadah (1568)

reconstructed by 2006; incendiary historical document; now *de facto* controlled by National Geographic Society; document turns Judas's alleged nefarious role on–its–head 2,000 years into the saga.

Somewhat in parallel to the Gospel of John, the Gospel of Judas has Jesus *de facto* choreographing his own crucifixion by Rome.

170 CE: IRENAEUS

(Saint) Irenaeus asserts/defends the concept that there are precisely four Canon Gospels.

Born in Asia Minor, now Turkey. (b. 120 CE; d. 202 CE)

Irenaeus was pivotal in codifying the four gospels noted above as being the exclusive Canon Gospels. This is more than a hundred years before the Constantine evolvement.

On another front, as relates to philosophy, there is the well–regarded "Irenaean theodicy" (philosophical response to Evil) very similar to the predecessor rabbinic *"nehama de–kissufa"* (*"un–earned bread"*) theodicy. See encyclopaedia entries for "Irenaean theodicy."

185 CE: "MISHNAH"

Completion of the "Mishnah"! (170–200 CE).

The embryonic discussions of the Mishnah started about 400 years earlier in Bavel (Babylon) and Jerusalem.

Exposition of the law by the scribes (*Soferim*)—particularly Hillel and Shamai (and their respective followings, noted above), and its elaboration by the Tannaim (high level

185 CE: "MISHNAH"

EXTRACT FROM *MISHNAH PEAH*

פאה א, משנה א; מסכת שבת קכז, א

אֵלּוּ דְבָרִים שֶׁאֵין לָהֶם שָׁעוּר: הַפֵּאָה, וְהַבְּכּוּרִים, וְהָרֵאָיוֹן,
וּגְמִילוּת חֲסָדִים, וְתַלְמוּד תּוֹרָה. אֵלּוּ דְבָרִים שֶׁאָדָם אוֹכֵל
פֵּרוֹתֵיהֶם בָּעוֹלָם הַזֶּה וְהַקֶּרֶן קַיֶּמֶת לוֹ לָעוֹלָם הַבָּא, וְאֵלּוּ
הֵן: כִּבּוּד אָב וָאֵם, וּגְמִילוּת חֲסָדִים, וְהַשְׁכָּמַת בֵּית הַמִּדְרָשׁ
שַׁחֲרִית וְעַרְבִית, וְהַכְנָסַת אוֹרְחִים, וּבִקּוּר חוֹלִים, וְהַכְנָסַת
כַּלָּה, וְהַלְוָיַת הַמֵּת, וְעִיּוּן תְּפִלָּה, וַהֲבָאַת שָׁלוֹם בֵּין אָדָם
לַחֲבֵרוֹ; וְתַלְמוּד תּוֹרָה כְּנֶגֶד כֻּלָּם.

Mishnah Peah 1:1; *Talmud Shabbath* 127a

These are the things for which no limit is prescribed: the
corner of the field, the first-fruits, the pilgrimage offerings, the
practice of kindness, and the study of the Torah. These are the
things the fruits of which a man enjoys in this world, while the
principal remains for him in the hereafter, namely: honoring
father and mother, practice of kindness, early attendance at the
schoolhouse morning and evening, hospitality to strangers, visiting
the sick, dowering the bride, attending the dead to the grave,
devotion in prayer, and making peace between fellow men; but
the study of the Torah excels them all.

Exhibit source: Philip Birnbaum, *Daily Prayer Book, Ha–Siddur Ha–Shalem*. New York: Hebrew
Publishing Company, © 1999, p. 15

sages) of the first and second centuries, particularly Akiva (noted above).

Final compilation was by Rabbi Yehudah Hanassi— Rabbi Judah, The Prince.

c. 195 CE: DE–LINKING EASTER FROM PASSOVER

The Christian controversy concerning the date for celebrating Easter (whether on the same day as the Jewish Passover or on a Sunday); St. Irenaeus mediates.

c. 200 CE: YEHUDA HA–NASSI: Focus

Rabbi Judah the Prince, born 135 CE, dies in 219 CE in Eretz Israel.

Rav Yehuda ha–Nassi is referred to as *"Rebbe"* and "Rabbeinu ha–Kodesh." He was the son of Rebbe Gamaliel II, and his life was intertwined, according to lore, with that of Roman ruler Marcus Aurelius.

202 CE: ROMAN EMPEROR SEVERUS

Severus forbids conversion to both Judaism and Christianity. He reigns 193-211 CE.

219 CE: THE ERA OF (RABBI) RAV

After a long period of study in Palestine, the Babylonian sage Rav returns to Babylon. In the tradition of the Babylonian sages, this date inaugurates a new era, the period of the Talmud: "When Rav came to Babylon, we became there like the Land of Israel" (Babylonian Talmud, Gittin, 1:1). According to them this date also

185 CE: "MISHNAH"

Mishnah Avot: Chapter 4

4:1

BEN ZOMA SAYS, 'WHO IS WISE?
HE WHO LEARNS FROM ALL MEN,
AS IT IS SAID: "FROM ALL MY
TEACHERS I GAINED WISDOM"
[PSALMS 119:99]. WHO IS MIGHTY?
HE WHO CONQUERS HIS EVIL IN-
CLINATION, AS IT IS SAID: "HE
WHO IS SLOW TO ANGER IS BETTER
THAN THE MIGHTY, AND HE WHO
CONTROLS HIS WILL IS BETTER
THAN THE ONE WHO CONQUERS A
CITY" [PROVERBS 16:32]. WHO IS
RICH? HE WHO REJOICES WITH HIS
PORTION, AS IT IS SAID: "WHEN
YOU ENJOY' THE WORK OF YOUR
HANDS, YOU WILL BE HAPPY AND IT WILL BE WELL WITH YOU"
[PSALMS 128:2]. "HAPPY" IN THIS WORLD, "AND IT WILL BE WELL
WITH YOU" IN THE WORLD TO COME. WHO IS WORTHY OF HONOR?
HE WHO HONORS HIS FELLOWMAN, AS IT IS SAID: "THOSE WHO
HONOR ME, I WILL HONOR, AND THOSE WHO DESPISE ME WILL BE
HELD IN CONTEMPT" [1 SAMUEL 2:30].

בֶּן זוֹמָא אוֹמֵר אֵיזֶהוּ חָכָם הַלּוֹמֵד
מִכָּל אָדָם שֶׁנֶּאֱמַר מִכָּל מְלַמְּדַי
הִשְׂכַּלְתִּי כִּי עֵדְוֹתֶיךָ שִׂיחָה לִי.
אֵיזֶהוּ גִבּוֹר הַכּוֹבֵשׁ אֶת יִצְרוֹ
שֶׁנֶּאֱמַר טוֹב אֶרֶךְ אַפַּיִם מִגִּבּוֹר
וּמוֹשֵׁל בְּרוּחוֹ מִלֹּכֵד עִיר. אֵיזֶהוּ
עָשִׁיר הַשָּׂמֵחַ בְּחֶלְקוֹ שֶׁנֶּאֱמַר יְגִיעַ
כַּפֶּיךָ כִּי תֹאכֵל אַשְׁרֶיךָ וְטוֹב לָךְ
אַשְׁרֶיךָ בָּעוֹלָם הַזֶּה וְטוֹב לָךְ
לָעוֹלָם הַבָּא. אֵיזֶהוּ מְכֻבָּד הַמְכַבֵּד
אֶת הַבְּרִיּוֹת שֶׁנֶּאֱמַר כִּי מְכַבְּדַי
אֲכַבֵּד וּבֹזַי יֵקָלּוּ:

Exhibit source: Rabbi Avrohom David, *The Wisdom of the Fathers.* New Jersey: Metsudah Publications, ©
1986, pp. 5 and 115

Mishnah Avot: Chapter 1

I:I

MOSES RECEIVED THE TORAH AT SINAI AND TRANSMITTED IT TO JOSHUA, AND JOSHUA TO THE ELDERS, AND THE ELDERS TO THE PROPHETS, AND THE PROPHETS HANDED IT DOWN TO THE MEMBERS OF THE GREAT ASSEMBLY. THEY [THE LATTER] STATED THREE PRINCIPLES: BE DELIBERATE IN JUDGMENT; EDUCATE MANY DISCIPLES; AND SET PROTECTIVE BOUNDS FOR THE TORAH.

מֹשֶׁה קִבֵּל תּוֹרָה מִסִּינַי וּמְסָרָהּ לִיהוֹשֻׁעַ וִיהוֹשֻׁעַ לִזְקֵנִים וּזְקֵנִים לִנְבִיאִים וּנְבִיאִים מְסָרוּהָ לְאַנְשֵׁי כְנֶסֶת הַגְּדוֹלָה. הֵם אָמְרוּ שְׁלֹשָׁה דְבָרִים הֱווּ מְתוּנִים בַּדִּין וְהַעֲמִידוּ תַלְמִידִים הַרְבֵּה וַעֲשׂוּ סְיָג לַתּוֹרָה:

Books of the Mishnah/Talmud

185 CE: "MISHNAH"

	Sedarim (Sections)	Theme	Tractates (Books)
1	ZERAIM (Seeds)	Agriculture	Berakoth (Benedictions) Peah (Gleanings) Demai (Produce not certainly tithed) Kilaim (Diverse Kinds) Shebiith (The Seventh Year) Terumoth (Heave-offerings) Maaseroth (Tithes) Maaser Sheni (Second Tithe) Challah (Dough-offering) Orlah (The Fruit of Young Trees) Bikkurim (First-fruits)
2	MOED (Set Feasts)	Calendar and Ritual	Shabbath (Sabbath) Erubin (The Fusion of Sabbath Limits) Pesachim (Feast of Passover) Shekalim (The Shekel Dues) Yoma (The Day of Atonement) Sukkah (Feast of Tabernacles) Yom Tov or Betzah (Festival-days) Rosh HaShanah (Feast of the New Year) Ta'anith (Days of Fasting) Megillah (The Scroll of Esther) Moed Katan (Mid-Festival Days) Chagigah (The Festal Offering)
3	NASHIM (Women)	Marriage	Yebamoth (Sisters-in-Law) Ketuboth (Marriage Deeds) Nedarim (Vows) Nazir (The Nazirite-vow) Sotah (The Suspected Adulteress) Gittin (Bills of Divorce) Kiddushin (Betrothals)
4	NEZIKIN (Damages)	Civil and Criminal Law	Bava Kamma (The First Gate) Bava Metzia (The Middle Gate) Bava Bathra (The Last Gate) Sanhedrin (The Sanhedrin) Makkoth (Stripes) Shebuoth (Oaths) Eduyoth (Testimonies) Abodah Zarah (Idolatry) Avoth (The Sayings of the Fathers) Horayoth (Instructions)
5	KODASHIM (Hallowed things)	Sacrifices and Offerings	Zebahim (Animal-offerings) Menachoth (Meal-Offerings) Chullin (Animals killed for food) Bekhoroth (Firstlings) Arakhin (Vows of Valuation) Temurah (The Substituted Offering) Kerithoth (Extirpation) Meilah (Sacrilege) Tamid (The Daily Whole-offering) Middoth (Measurements) Kinnim (The Bird-offerings)
6	TAHAROTH (Cleannesses)	Defilement	Kelim (Vessels) Oholoth (Tents) Nega'im (Leprosy-signs) Parah (The Red Heifer) Toharoth (Cleannesses) Mikvaoth (Immersion-pools) Niddah (The Menstruant) Makshirin (Predisposers) Zabim (They that suffer a flux) Tebul Yom (He that immersed himself that day) Yadaim (Hands) Uktzin (Stalks)

marks the creation of the two great Babylonian *yeshivot* – the Nehardea Academy (later transferred to Pumbedita) headed by Shmuel, and that of Sura, founded by Rav himself.

220 CE: THE AMORAIM PERIOD

Start of 280–year Amoraim Period (220–500 CE)

The *Amoraim*—the rabbis of the Talmud—redact the *Mishnah* (of the *Tannaim*) noted above. Their debates, discourses and discussions are eventually codified in the *Gemara*.

The Amoraim followed the Tannaim (10 CE–220 CE) both sequential–time–wise, and rabbinical "*standing–wise.*"

224 CE: PARTHIA FALLS

Fall of the Parthian kingdom and accession of the Sassanians who will rule over all of Persia. After a brief period of uncertainty, the Jews establish cordial relations with the new regime.

259 CE: NEHARDEA JEWISH ACADEMY DESTROYED

Destruction of Nehardea during a Palmyrene invasion. The academy is transferred to Pumbedita (Both locations are in Persia/Babylon).

c. 270 CE: MONASTICISM

(St.) Antony's retirement to the Egyptian desert marks the beginning of *monasticism*.

224 CE: PARTHIA FALLS

Marcus Aurelius receiving the homage of the Parthians

276 CE: MANI

The theologian Mani is crucified by the Sassanids in Mesopotamia for (platonically) preaching the incorporation of Judaism, Christianity and Zoroastrianism into one religion—to be known as "Manichaeism."

c. 300 CE: CONSTANTINE!

Emperor Constantine morphs into a "force multiplier" for Christianity, in general—but also for the Canon Gospels, in particular. And the Canon Gospels carried within their corpus their intense toxicity towards the array of Jewish icons laced through their pages.

(b. 272 CE; d. 337 CE).

300–900 CE: MAYAN CIVILIZATION APEX

Primarily Yucatan Peninsula, Mexico.

Important sites include Chichen Itza, Uzmal, Edzna and Cordoba.

Late 3rd century: ZOROASTRIAN IMPACT

The Babylonian Jewish community feels the oppression of the Zoroastrian church during its expansion.

303 CE: DIOCLETIAN DECREES

Persecution of Christianity under Roman Emperor Diocletian (reigns 284–305 CE).

c. 300 CE: CONSTANTINE!

Bust of the Emperor Constantine;
Palazzo dei Conservatori, Rome.

Constantine reversed the persecutions of his predecessor, Diocletion, and issued (with his co–sponsor Licinius) the Edict of Milan in 313 CE, which proclaimed religious toleration throughout the empire.

Born: Flavius Valerius Aurelius Constantinus

Commonly known in English as Constantine I and as Constantine the Great

Among Eastern Orthodox and Byzantine Catholics known as Saint Constantine

Destruction of Christian churches and texts. (See
Roman Rulers chart at 63 BCE in the book).

311 CE: EDICT OF TOLERATION

Issued in the last days of the rule of Emperor Galerius.
At that point there was a tetrarchy Galerius–Constantine–
Licinius. Roman luminary Maxentius, is, as well, a
party to the edict. The edict grants universal religious
toleration and restitution (306–313 CE). However,
Constantine will later backtrack (see 312 CE, just
below) on the universal aspect of the toleration.

[*As regards Galerius, the Edict of Toleration represented an
about–face in his posture towards Christianity.*]

312 CE: ROMAN EMPEROR CONSTANTINE *DE
FACTO* CONVERTS!

Constantine at least informally converts to Christianity.
He also folds paganism into a morphed Christianity. This
new pagan–infused Christianity speedily spreads across
the empire.

Meaning, therefore, that Rome converts to the religion
whose *de facto* progenitor it had originally condemned to
death and executed by crucifixion 300 years earlier.

Constantine I enacts restrictive legislation against the Jews

  – conversion of Jews to Christianity is banned
  – non–Christian congregations for religious purposes
    are curtailed

c. 300 CE: CONSTANTINE!
"CONSTANTINE'S DREAM"
PAINTER: PIERO DELLA FRANCESCA

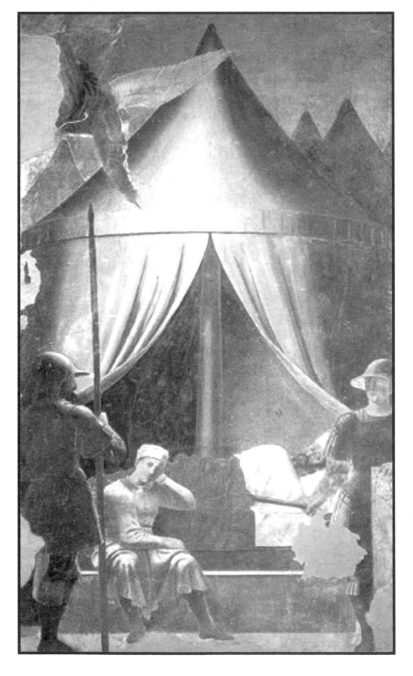

The morphing of the Roman Empire to Christendom, under the aegis of the Church Fathers, will radically negatively impact the Jews scattered throughout the Roman Empire—for centuries to come.

The Christians controlling the empire will promulgate an intensely negative portrayal of the Jews, and will promulgate the "Passion" (saga)—constructed selectively from most intense vignettes of the Canon Gospels—revolving around the last several days of Jesus.

As the Passion Saga is easily transmitted both to the small educated elite of Christendom—as well as to its millions of masses—a toxic view of the Jew is disseminated ongoing through Europe, for seventeen centuries through the Nazi era in mid–1900s.

This *demonization* of the Jews will set them up to be the *scapegoat of choice* for any demagogue making an appearance on the European stage for seventeen centuries. As the Jews declined to disappear as a distinct entity, they remained time and again, as a *prime–and–easily–identified* target.

313 CE: BYZANTINE RULE OF JERUSALEM COMMENCES

323–year Byzantine rule 313–636 CE, followed by 463–year Arab rule 636–1099 CE.

324 CE: CONSTANTINE'S EMPERORSHIP EXTENDS EASTWARD

Constantine's victory over Licinius gives him possession of the eastern provinces of the empire. For the first time Palestine comes under the rule of a Christian monarch.

Church "Ecumenical" Councils
325 CE – 787 CE

Several doctrinal disputes from the fourth century onwards led to the calling of Ecumenical councils.

There are seven councils authoritatively recognized as Ecumenical:*

1. The First Ecumenical Council was convoked by the Roman Emperor Constantine at Nicaea in 325 and presided over by the Patriarch Alexander of Alexandria, with over 300 bishops condemning the view of Arius that the Son [Jesus] is a created being inferior to the Father [God].

2. The Second Ecumenical Council was held at Constantinople in 381, presided over by the Patriarchs of Alexandria and Antioch, with 150 bishops defining the nature of the Holy Spirit [as equal to that of God] against those asserting His [his] inequality with the other persons of [parties to] the Trinity.

3. The Third Ecumenical Council is that of Ephesus in 431, presided over by the Patriarch of Alexandria, with 250 bishops, which affirmed that Mary is truly "Birthgiver" or "Mother" of God (*Theotokos*), contrary to the teachings of Nestorius.

4. The Fourth Ecumenical Council is that of Chalcedon in 451, Patriarch of Constantinople presiding, 500 bishops, affirmed that Jesus is truly God and truly man, without mixture of the two natures, contrary to Monophysite** teaching.

5. The Fifth Ecumenical Council is the second of Constantinople in 553, interpreting the decrees of Chalcedon and further explaining the relationship of the two natures of Jesus; it also condemned the teachings of Origen on the pre-existence of the soul, etc.

6. The Sixth Ecumenical Council is the third of Constantinople in 681; it declared that Jesus has two wills of his two natures, human and divine, contrary to the teachings of the Monophysites. **

7. The Seventh Ecumenical Council was called under the Empress Regent Irene of Athens in 787, known as the second of Nicaea. It supports the veneration of icons while forbidding their worship. It is often referred to as "The Triumph of Orthodoxy."

---

* http://www.goarch.org/ourfaith/ourfaith8071

** Monophysitism is the Christological [essentially, Christian theology] position that Jesus has only one nature, his humanity being absorbed by his Deity, as opposed to the Chalcedonian position which holds that Jesus maintains two natures, one divine and one human.

312 CE: ROMAN EMPEROR CONSTANTINE *DE FACTO* CONVERTS!

"THE BAPTISM OF CONSTANTINE"

PAINTER: RAPHAEL

Author's note: It is not at all clear that Constantine *formally* converted.

325 CE onwards: CONSTRUCTION OF CHURCHES IN PALESTINE

Construction of churches in Palestine: Constantine and his mother Helena order churches to be built in the most important Christian sites: Bethlehem, Jerusalem, Mount of Olives (inaugurated in 326), and Allon–Moreh near Hebron.

330 CE: CONSTANTINOPLE

Refounding of Constantinople on the site of an already existing city, Byzantium, settled in the early days of the Greek colonial expansion around 671–662 BCE. The new walled capital of the Roman Empire is built–up by Constantine I and named after him.

Constantinople is astride the Bosporus and the Marmara Sea. The western side of Constantinople (the walled part) on the Bosporus is Europe, and the eastern side, Asia. The city is astride the route from the Black Sea to the Mediterranean. The sequential sea route north to south is: Black Sea > Bosporus Strait > Sea of Marmara > Dardanelles Strait > Aegean Sea in the Mediterranean.

Constantinople was renamed "Istanbul" in 1930 by Ataturk.

335 CE: PALESTINE HAPPENINGS

Inauguration of the basilica of the Holy Sepulchre in Jerusalem on the site identified by Christian tradition as Jesus' burial place; the probable renewal of the interdict on Jews to reside in Jerusalem which has been in force since Hadrian's days; about the same time, an attempt was made by a converted Jew known as Joseph the Apostate to build

330 CE: CONSTANTINOPLE

Coin struck under Constantine I to commemorate the founding of
Constantinople

churches in the Galilee; his failure demonstrates that the Galilee is still a predominantly Jewish region where, unlike Judea and the center of Palestine, Christianity has not yet taken root. (*A Historical Atlas of the Jewish People*)

347 CE: JOHN CHRYSOSTOM

"The paramount tasks of the emerging Christianity were to overthrow the theological dominance of Judaism, to establish itself as a separate and self–sustaining religion, and to situate Christians as the new and authentic chosen people. The Christian Fathers believed that they were fighting a war with the Jews in which only the victor would reap the reward of eternal life; Judaism was a standing insult and threat to Christianity's image of itself. Jerome once wrote to Augustine that if converted Jews were allowed to practice even one fragment of their former religion, "they will not become Christians, but they will make us Jews... The ceremonies of the Jews are pernicious and deadly; and whoever observes them, whether Jew or Gentile, has fallen into the pit of the devil. For Christ is the end of the Torah..." John Chrysostom was blunt about it, "Don't you realize, if the Jewish rites are holy and venerable, our way of life must be false... The Jews... pay honor to the avenging demons, the foes of out life."

Through anti–Jewish theological myths and defamations, the Church Fathers pictured the Jews no longer as the chosen people, no longer heroes of holiness and moral living; they were instead the earthly representatives of the powers of evil."

—Robert Michael, *Holy Hatred*, *New York*: Palgrave Macmillan, p. 21

347 CE: JOHN CHRYSOSTOM

The Chrysostom Monastery in Moscow (1882).

John Chrysostom (c. 347–407 CE), Archbishop of Constantinople, was an important Early Church Father…. After his death (or, according to some sources, during his life) he was given the Greek surname *chrysostomos,* meaning "golden mouthed", rendered in English as Chrysostom.*[a][b]

The Orthodox and Eastern Catholic Churches honor him as a saint and count him among the Three Holy Hierarchs….

*a "St John Chrysostom" in the Catholic Encyclopedia,
   available online http://www.newadvent.org/cathen/08452b.htm; retrieved March 20, 2007.
*b Pope Vigilius, *Constitution of Pope Vigilius,* 553

It is not clear how a religion gets away with venerating with "sainthood" – over seventeen centuries ongoing – *demagogues* in clerical robes who promulgate hatred and demonization as core tenets.

Presumably, different morality rules apply to the Church.

351–352 CE: JEWISH REVOLT IV

a.k.a. War Against Gallus

A Jewish uprising in the Galilee under the command of a certain Patricius; provoked by local conflicts with the representatives of the Roman regime (of Emperor Constantius Gallus) rather than by a desire to overthrow the foreign yoke, the revolt broke out at Sepphoris and spread to other towns (Acre, Tiberias, Bet She'arim, and Lydda); it was crushed by an experienced commander Ursicinus, dispatched especially for this purpose. Ursinicus meets with Jewish sages, and he is mentioned, not unfavorably, in the Jerusalem Talmud. (*A Historical Atlas of the Jewish People*)

354 CE: (SAINT) AUGUSTINE

Augustine of Hippo. Pillar of Catholic Church. Frames the concept of "original sin."

Canonized by Christian popular acclaim. In the Greek Orthodox Church he is called the Blessed Augustine, or St. Augustine the Blessed.

358 CE: HILLEL II

Creates a mathematical calendar for calculating the lunar months.

351–352 CE: JEWISH REVOLT IV

Gallus coin

Hillel ha–Nassi, Hillel the Prince.
Nassi can be translated as President/Prince/Leader.
An amalgam of the three English terms probably best
communicates its intent.

Hillel II was preceded as *Nassi* by Judah II, and was
succeeded as *Nassi* by Gamliel V.

Hillel held the position of Head of the Sanhedrin
between 320–385 CE.

The Sanhedrin was the supreme rabbinical assembly,
which had different morphings and levels–of–authority
over the ages. When Judea/Israel was autonomous, the
Sanhedrin would tend to have (far greater) judicial and
political power. For instance, under Rome in 33 CE,
when Jesus was executed by Pontius Pilate, it had no
substantive judicial power whatsoever. Its *halachic* power
(power of adjudicating Jewish religious doctrine and
related) over the centuries depended on many factors,
including primarily its prestige at the moment.

In 33 CE Rome illegitimately appointed Caiaphas as the
High Priest. Next, instead of the Jews appointing the
top leader of the (already-neutered) Sandhedrin, Rome
then inserted the same Caiaphas into this top position.
And finally, the High Priest position was supposed to be
totally separate from the Sanhedrin in any event. Thus,
Caiaphas not only contaminated the Temple (and its
hierarchy), he contaminated any institution he touched.

361–363 CE: ROMAN EMPEROR JULIAN

–allows the Jews to return to Jerusalem (361–363 CE)

–and gives permission (not exercised by the Jews) to
rebuild the Temple.

358 CE: HILLEL II

The Jewish (lunar) Calendar has the following months/breakdown:

Hebrew	English	Number	Length	Gregorian Equivalent
נִיסָן	Nissan	1	30 days	March-April
אִיָּיר	Iyar	2	29 days	April-May
סִיוָן	Sivan	3	30 days	May-June
תַּמּוּז	Tammuz	4	29 days	June-July
אָב	Av	5	30 days	July-August
אֱלוּל	Elul	6	29 days	August-September
תִּשְׁרִי	Tishri	7	30 days	September-October
חֶשְׁוָן	Cheshvan	8	29 or 30 days	October-November
כִּסְלֵו	Kislev	9	30 or 29 days	November-December
טֵבֵת	Tevet	10	29 days	December-January
שְׁבָט	Shevat	11	30 days	January-February
אֲדָר	Adar I (leap years only)	12	30 days	February-March
אֲדָר ב	Adar (called Adar II in leap years)	12 (13 in leap years)	29 days	February-March

Emperor Julian the Apostate: In his enterprise of anti–
Christian restoration, the philosopher–emperor proposes
to make Jerusalem a Jewish city and to rebuild the Temple;
in a letter to the Jews he asks them to pray to their God
for his success in the war against the Persians, "So that
I should restore the holy city of Jerusalem with my own
money"; but Julian is killed during his Persian campaign
and the reconstruction of Jerusalem is brought to a
halt, probably also because of an earthquake which the
Christians see as a manifestation of God's wrath at the
apostate emperor.

375 CE: APOGEE OF RAV ASHI

Rav Ashi [b. 352; d. 427], head of the Sura Academy (till
424), is one of the principal redactors of the Babylonian
Talmud.

380 CE: OFFICIAL RELIGION OF THE ROMAN EMPIRE

Shortly before his "division of the Roman Empire,"
Emperor Theodosius codifies the legacy of Constantine,
and makes Christianity the official religion of the empire
February 27, 380 CE.

Rosemary Ruether describes the Christian Roman
Emperors as follows:

"In the laws of the Christian emperors enforcing a
status of reprobation on the Jewish community, one notes
a language of clerical vituperation. The synagogue is
referred to in one early law of the Theodosian Code by a
Latin slang word meaning "brothel," a word which never
before had been used for a place of religious worship in
Roman law.*A The Jews are referred to constantly in the

361 CE: ROMAN EMPEROR JULIAN

Julian the Apostate

laws as a group hated by God, to be regarded by Christian society as contemptible and even demonic. The laws bristle with negative and theologically loaded epithets. Judaism is called a *feralis secta* and a *Synagoga Satanae*. Their meetings are *sacrilegi coetus*.*[B] The very name of Jew is "foul and degrading." To marry a Jew is adultery and to be under their authority is "an insult to our faith." It becomes common to speak of Judaism in the language of pollution, contagion, and disease. The Third Novella, which promulgated the Theodosian Code, calls it a "desperate illness" that is beyond curing. Judaism is called "dangerous," "abominable," "evil teachings," "madness," while Jews themselves are described by such terms as "sly," "shameful," "foul," "insolent," "detestible," "blind," and "perverse."*[C] Jews are said to be the "enemies of the Heavenly Majesty and the Roman Laws," and to break the laws against judaizing is equivalent to a crime of *lèse majesté*. In short, the Christian emperors do not legislate as secular rulers…. Rather, the emperors speak here as exponents of the Christian theological view of the Jews, acting in their own right as priest–kings of the Christian theocratic empire."

---

*[A] *CTh*. 16, 8, 1 (13/8/339).
*[B] Seaver, *Persecution of the Jews*, p. 54
*[C] See the summary of Theodosian laws printed in Marcus, *Jew in the Medieval World*, pp. 4–6.

— Rosemary Ruether, *Faith and Fratricide*, Oregon: WS Publishers, © 1995, Chapter 3, pp. 194–195.

Rosemary Radford Ruether (b. 1936) is an American feminist scholar and theologian.

Rosemary Ruether

Faith and Fratricide

*The
Theological
Roots
of
Anti-Semitism*

Introduction by Gregory Baum

380 CE: THE EASTERN CHURCH FATHERS PILE–ON

Vitriolic slander and demonizations of the (minority) Jews ratchet–up significantly via Christian luminaries and would be luminaries, across the Roman Empire, as Christianity is now "official."

The book, *Holy Hatred*, p. 20, by Robert Michael, notes–

> "Christian writings were part of a theological war to the death, and beyond. Although several Church Fathers knew individual Jews, they portrayed Jews as satanic adversaries. They imagined that Jews insulted Christ and the Blessed Virgin each day in their synagogue prayers. For these crimes, Christian theologians argued, Jews must suffer continual punishment on earth and eternal damnation in the afterlife, unless they sought salvation through the one true faith, Christianity. They proclaimed that the Jews are, have always been, and will always be, paragons of evil.
>
> Christian theologians depicted the Jews as hateful to make Judaism repulsive to the Christian faithful or pagans. The stubborn persistence of Judaism and Jews constantly questioned Christian claims of earthly and spiritual triumph."

382 CE: VULGATE

–Latin translation of the Bible (directly from the Hebrew) commissioned by Pope Damasus I.

Completed early in the 400s largely due to the efforts of Church Father Jerome.

c. 380 CE: THE EASTERN CHURCH FATHERS PILE–ON

The intensity of anti–Jewish language in portions of the
Christian Scriptures and from almost every Christian
theologian from the Church Fathers forward—their writings
became almost as authoritative as Scripture—was both the
cause and the result of this concern for the potential loss of
Christian and pagan souls. In the writings and sermons of
these early Christian propagandists, no evil was too great
for the Jews not to revel in, no crime too appalling for the
Jews not to rejoice in. Hilary, bishop of Poitiers, wrote in the
fourth century, Judaism was "ever…mighty in wickedness:…
when it cursed Moses; when it hated God; when it vowed
its sons to demons; when it killed the prophets, and finally
when it betrayed to the Praetor and crucified our God
Himself and Lord… And so glorying through all its existence
in iniquity…"

source: Robert Michael, *Holy Hatred*, New York: Palgrave Macmillan, © 2006, p. 20.
"Tractatus in LI Psalmum," 6; J.–P. Migne, ed., *Patrologiae, Cursus Completus*, Series Latina
(Paris 1844–)
(unless otherwise indicated, translations were executed by the author).

The Vulgate became the official Bible (translation) of the Roman Catholic Church.

 c. 383 CE: (SAINT) JEROME LEAVES FOR PALESTINE

He leaves Rome for Palestine and begins translation of the Bible into Latin (the Vulgate). From 385 to 420 CE he lives in Bethlehem and takes an active part in religious controversies and in the development of monasticism in Palestine, mainly in the Judean desert.

c. 400 CE (Saint) Jerome (374–419 CE), Catholic Saint (the patron of Catholic theological learning) and Doctor of the Church, joins the newly emboldened Jew-baiters, demonizing via public diatribe:

"Judaic serpents of whom Judas was the model"

Jerome commissioned the "horned Moses" statue, as well (exhibit later).

387 CE: ADVERSUS JUDAEOS SERMONS

–by (SAINT) JOHN CHRYSOSTOM

"Against the Judaizers": Eight homilies by Chrysostom, The homilies are quite virulently anti–Semitic.

The Eastern Orthodox Church honors him as a saint and counts him among the Three Holy Hierarchs. The Roman Catholic Church regards him as a saint and as a "Doctor of the Church" (see exhibit for sample excerpts).

According to James Carroll in *Constantine's Sword*, p. 191:

"Chrysostom, (c. 349–407), the bishop of Antioch, still

c. 383 CE: (SAINT) JEROME LEAVES FOR PALESTINE
"ST. JEROME, CARDINAL"
PAINTER: EL GRECO

revered as the patron saint of preachers, was the master of the sermon genre known as *Adversus Judaeos*. Such words inevitably led to actions: assaults on synagogues, the exclusion of Jews from public office, expulsions."

After his death, the bishop of Antioch was named by the Church as Chrysostom, derived from the Greek, which means "golden–mouthed."

It should be clearly understood that (only) at this point in time, with the Jews, exiled, dispersed and disenfranchised, and symbolically, already "down on the mat," "down for the count," isolated in pockets across the Roman Empire, that the "Church Fathers" become most virulent. Only at the point that the Jews are totally defenseless.

It is (only) at this point that these "Church Fathers," emboldened by their own new–found protection within the totalitarian state alliance of the newly consolidated Church–State morphing of the Roman Empire, now ramp-up the vitriol.

It is at this point, that they now open wide the faucet and the engines full–throttle of unfiltered raw and virulent anti–Semitism. Meaning, the Early Church Fathers theologically embrace virulent race–baiting proportional to their power to *get away with it* risk–free.

*

Post–Holocaust, with outright anti–Semitism no longer "politically correct," a massive Church effort to *whitewash* the records of many of the Church Fathers is ongoing. Vituperative sermons of various Doctors of the Church seem to be magically disappearing from the online record....

SCULPTOR: MICHELANGELO

Jerome's statue MOSES
San Pietro in Vincoli, Rome

Translation Manipulation –
Jerome's statue MOSES

Commissioned by Pope Julius II in 1505, and sculpted in 1513–1515 CE for St. Peter's Basilica in Vatican City, the statue MOSES by Michelangelo presents a problem. The statue bizarrely portrays the Jewish icon Moses with two (animal) horns. The statue ended up in the tomb of Pope Julius II.

The *horns of Moses* are based on a (convenient) 'misinterpretation' of the bible (*Shemot* / Exodus 34:29) by (Saint) Jerome. Considering that retaining Michelangelo was not easy, presumably careful pre–thought was given by the statue's patron, Pope Julius II.

The biblical Hebrew phrase *koran* **orr** – applied by the Torah to the visage of Moses in one phrase of the Torah – means *rays of light.* Not *animal horns.* The *horned Moses* commissioned by Jerome, however, conveniently dovetails with the Church's multi–century demonization and dehumanization of Jewish icons via pseudo history.

The correct translation of **orr** can only mean *light,* not *animal horns.* There is no room for misunderstanding. Certainly (Saint) Jerome was, as well, familiar with the very first paragraph of the entire Torah (a.k.a the Old Testament) Bereshith / Genesis I, sentence 3 commences: "And God said : *yi–hi* **orr** – *Let there be Light.*" Not, *Let there be animal horns.* The same word **orr** is used four additional times before the iconic paragraph is complete. In each instance the meaning of **orr** is *light.* And only *light.*

The very, very saintly Jerome (c. 347–420 CE), is known as *the patron saint of translators* in the Roman Catholic Church. And, of course he ended up as a full–fledged *Doctor of the Church.* Both titles for Jerome now make perfect sense – if you are intent on demonizing the Jews.

***

Re–Engineering History

The more one researches the events relating to the crucifixion of Jesus, the more it becomes apparent that history was *re–engineered* by the early "Church Fathers."

Jesus was, of course, Jewish. And an integral member of the greater Orthodox Jewish/Pharisee community.

He was crucified by the Roman procurator (Pontius Pilate) on a Roman Cross – as a potential threat to Rome.

Rome held 99 percent of the *power–cards* in Judea at that time.

35 years later, the Jews rebelled against Rome. The Christians did not.

The early Christians had an interest in distancing Rome from its crucifixion of the Christian icon Jesus, and of somehow off–loading blame for the Roman crucifixion onto the Jews. This would serve multiple political and recruiting purposes.

By a sort of historical *sleight of hand*, and a concerted and focused Church effort, the early Christian Fathers 'tag' the Jews for the Roman crucifixion, even though the Jew Jesus was, of course, crucified by Rome (the new political target of Christianity).

Inasmuch as post–Constantine, in the 300s CE, for several centuries at a minimum, the Church thoroughly controlled the media organs of the Roman Empire unfettered, the Church was in a position to aggressively re–spin and re–write history. And scapegoat the geographically isolated, vastly outnumbered, and politically powerless Jews.

* * *

388 CE: (SAINT) AMBROSE

Bishop of Milan, defends synagogue burning.

392 CE: THEODOSIUS I

Division of the Roman Empire by Theodosius I...

Theodosius, Emperor of Rome, bequeaths –

- the eastern half of the Roman Empire to his son, Arcadius, with its capital in Constantinople, and

- the western half of the empire to his son Honorius, with its capital in Milan, and later Ravenna.

393 CE: THE ANCIENT OLYMPIC GAMES SUPPRESSED

Roman Emperor Theodosius I ends the Olympic Games, as part of his campaign to impose Christianity as the state religion. The Olympics were viewed by the Church as neo–pagan.

The consensus is that the quadrennial Olympics had commenced c. 786 BCE in Olympia, Greece, and apparently lasted in this phase for almost 1200 years. Olympia, Greece was not a classic town or city, but rather a religious sanctuary site dedicated to the Greek gods, Zeus in particular.

The normative guideline over the 1200 year tenure of the games was that only free men who spoke Greek were allowed to compete. All competitors were male. Competition was generally nude subsequent to c. 720 BCE.

Branded

Branding the Jewish leadership – or any leadership – as being a major accessory to the killing of the progenitor of another Religion, is not a light matter. Politically convenient or not, the libel is as serious and as incendiary a charge as can be leveled.

Pontious Pilate, Roman Procurator of Judea, had sole judiciary power in Judea. His word was law. Pilate ordered the crucifixion Jesus – on a Roman cross. Roman centurions nailed in the nails. But the Christian populace across the Roman Empire and Greater Europe, will be sold the canard that the Jews of Roman–occupied Judea were somehow responsible.

Blame the Jews. Plausible or not, disproportionate or not, corroborated or not, sequentially possible or not, the alleged (and fabricated) Sanhedrin Trial libel (and the consequent charge of *deicide* – against the Jews as a whole), combined with the parallel full–spectrum *demonization* of the Jews, will lead to the multi–century suffering and deaths of millions of Jews as a consequence.

The Church hierarchy will play with this theme for centuries.

With twenty centuries of cynical manipulation involved, one can only stand amazed.....

***

Respectfully, the Church has still not to this day (March 2010) *'come clean'* on this sordid matter.

[Another view on the endpoint of the Ancient Olympics is that an earthquake – either in 393 CE or in the sixth century – destroyed Olympia and effectively terminated the Ancient Olympics.]

399 CE: ROMAN INJUNCTION v. APOSTOLI

April 11: A Roman law (under Theodosius) prohibiting sending emissaries (*apostoli*) to collect donations on behalf of the *nassi*: [the (Jewish) Sanhedrin President back in Judea] "That the Jews should know that we have delivered them from this iniquitous tribute" (C. Th.XV, 8, 14).

End of 4ᵗʰ century: TOSEFTA CLOSED

The final editing of the *Tosefta* (compilation commenced c. 200 CE by Rabbis Chiya and Oshaiah) probably in Palestine. This is a collection of commentaries containing material excluded from the Mishnah, mostly unedited "raw material".

400 CE: "EXCALIBUR"

Legendary sword—of legendary King Arthur (Celtic) in legendary Camelot—in Fifth–Sixth century CE

400 CE: SACKING OF ROME BY ALARIC, KING OF THE VISIGOTHS

Some historians mark the beginning of the Middle Ages, a.k.a. The Dark Ages, with this 400 CE point. Others demarcate the commencement of the Middle Ages with the deposing of Romulus Augustus as Emperor of Rome (76 years later) in 476 CE, which marked the end of the Western Roman Empire, the "fall of Ancient Rome."

400 CE: EXCALIBUR
ILLUSTRATOR: AUBREY BEARDSLEY

Sir Bedivere cast the sword Excalibur into the water.

---

* CYRIL OF ALEXANDRIA

400 CE: Cyril of Alexandria

➢ Pope of Alexandria 412-444 CE

➢ Church Father

➢ Doctor of the Church

➢ February 9 is his official "Feast Tridentine Day" on Roman-Catholic (Tridentine) Calendar

412 CE: CYRIL OF ALEXANDRIA*

"To provide the Church with a clear identity for itself, Christian theologians transvaluated Judaism. The Church Fathers turned Jewish values and practices on their heads by misrepresenting them as their opposites. Cyril of Alexandria wrote, "Note that the shadow of the law is reversed and the ancient things of the law are made ineffective."

"Christian theologians attacked the essential values and practices of Jewishness—the Jews Covenant with the One God, their Chosenness, circumcision, ethical laws, God–wrestling, Messiah, dietary obligations, Sabbath, holy days, patriarchs, and Holy Scriptures. The Church Fathers did this by reinterpreting, modifying, and adapting them to fit the requirements of the Christian self–image and theology. In effect, the Latin and Greek Fathers said to the Jews, "We'll take your God, your Scriptures, your Messiah, and some of your Law; as for you, you are disinherited, cast into a limbo.""

—Robert Michael, *Holy Hatred. New York:* Palgrave Macmillan, p. 21.

415 CE: ALEXANDRIA FESTERS

Temporary expulsion of Jews from Alexandria by Patriarch Cyril.

415 CE: HYPATIA MURDERED

March: Roman–ruled Egypt: Scientist "Hypatia of Alexandria" murdered by Coptic Christian mob, possibly Nitrian monks, affiliated with (St.) Cyril of Alexandria

400 CE: SACKING OF ROME BY THE VISIGOTHS

Ages of Man (400 CE - 2000 CE)

THE CRUCIFIXION

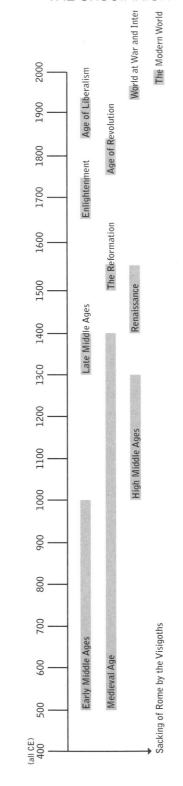

(all CE)

400 · 500 · 600 · 700 · 800 · 900 · 1000 · 1100 · 1200 · 1300 · 1400 · 1500 · 1600 · 1700 · 1800 · 1900 · 2000

Sacking of Rome by the Visigoths

Early Middle Ages

Medieval Age

High Middle Ages

Late Middle Ages

Renaissance

The Reformation

Enlightenment

Age of Revolution

Age of Liberalism

World at War and Inter

The Modern World

(a.k.a. "The Pope of Alexandria, a.k.a. "The Pillar of Faith").

Hypatia was considered the first notable woman in mathematics. A world–class polymath, she also taught and wrote on philosophy and astronomy.

Socrates of Scholasticus describes her in his *Ecclesiastical History*.

"There was a woman at Alexandria named Hypatia, daughter of the philosopher Theon, who made such attainments in literature and science, as to far surpass all the philosophers of her own time. Having succeeded to the school of Plato and Plotinus, she explained the principles of philosophy to her auditors, many of whom came from a distance to receive her instructions. On account of the self–possession and ease of manner, which she had acquired in consequence of the cultivation of her mind, she not infrequently appeared in public in presence of the magistrates. Neither did she feel abashed in going to an assembly of men. For all men on account of her extraordinary dignity and virtue admired her, the more."

Born around 360 CE into an academic family, she leaves a corpus of commentaries as well as her own academic works of note, including "The Astronomical Canon." Events surrounding her murder have achieved notoriety, and have apparently been a focus of historians for centuries
(see exhibit "The murder of Hypatia": 3 chronicles).

c. 425 CE: ROMAN INJUNCTION v. NASSI

Roman abolition of the Office of the Patriarch (*nassi*)

415 CE: HYPATIA MURDERED
THE MURDER of HYPATIA: 3 CHRONICLES

Socrates Scholasticus (5th–century)	John of Nikiû (7th–century)	Edward Gibbon (18th–century)
Yet even she fell a victim to the political jealousy which at that time prevailed. For as she had frequent interviews with Orestes, it was calumniously reported among the Christian populace, that it was she who prevented Orestes from being reconciled to the bishop. Some of them therefore, hurried away by a fierce and bigoted zeal, whose ringleader was a reader named Peter, waylaid her returning home, and dragging her from her carriage, they took her to the church called Caesareum, where they completely stripped her, and then murdered her by scraping her skin off with tiles and bits of shell. After tearing her body in pieces, they took her mangled limbs to a place called Cinaron, and there burnt them.	And in those days there appeared in Alexandria a female philosopher, a pagan named Hypatia, and she was devoted at all times to magic, astrolabes and instruments of music, and she beguiled many people through Satanic wiles...A multitude of believers in God arose under the guidance of Peter the magistrate... and they proceeded to seek for the pagan woman who had beguiled the people of the city and the prefect through her enchantments. And when they learnt the place where she was, they proceeded to her and found her...they dragged her along till they brought her to the great church, named Caesarion. Now this was in the days of the fast. And they tore off her clothing and dragged her...through the streets of the city till she died. And they carried her to a place named Cinaron, and they burned her body with fire.	A rumor was spread among the Christians, that the daughter of Theon was the only obstacle to the reconciliation of the prefect and the archbishop; and that obstacle was speedily removed. On a fatal day, in the holy season of Lent, Hypatia was torn from her chariot, stripped naked, dragged to the church, and inhumanly butchered by the hands of Peter the Reader and a troop of savage and merciless fanatics: her flesh was scraped from her bones with sharp oyster–shells and her quivering limbs were delivered to the flames.

in Palestine, and suppression of formal scholarly/rabbinic ordination.

c. 425 CE: JERUSALEM TALMUD CLOSED

The "closing" of the Jerusalem Talmud (in Tiberias), primarily as a consequence of the suppression of the Patriarchate (425 CE) just–noted above, by Theodossius II.

[The text of *Talmud Yerushalmi* is mostly a discussion of the orders (sections) of *zer'im*, *mo'ed*, *nashim*, and *nezikin* of the Mishnah.]

c. 425 CE: MIDRASH BERESHITH RABBAH

Composition of the Midrash *Genesis Rabbah* which interprets verses from Genesis in aggadic style.

434 CE: ATTILA THE HUN

–leads the Hunnic Empire:

Attila lived 406–453 CE, and was also known as Attila the Hun or the Scourge of God. Attila led the Huns from 434 until his death 19 years later. He was leader of the Hunnic Empire, which stretched from Germany to the Baltic Sea. During his rule, he was one of the most feared of the Western and Eastern Roman Empires' enemies, but he never actually attacked either Rome or Constantinople. His propaganda was that the Sword of Attila had come to his hand by miraculous means.

In much of Western Europe, he is remembered as the epitome of cruelty and rapacity. In contrast, some Northern European histories and Chronicles lionize him

434 CE: ATTILA THE HUN

Roman Empire Segment
413 CE – 476 CE
highlighting Attila the Hun

	413–26	Saint Augustine writes *The City of God*.
	420s	Emperor Aetius begins a policy of hiring one mercenary barbarian band to attack other barbarian bands—Roman army now ineffective.
	425	Scattered raids by Angles, Saxons, and Jutes on Britain. Valentinian III declared "Roman Emperor" in the West—though much of the old Empire is in ruins—with communication breaking down and widespread depopulation.
	429	Vandals cross the Straights of Gibraltar and conquer Roman holdings in North Africa. Vandal kingdom forms in northern Africa. It lasts until 535. The Arian heresy dominates this region.
	432	Saint Patrick begins mission to Ireland.
> > >	434	Attila rules the Huns. He dies in 453.
	439	Vandal forces under King Gaiseric capture Roman Carthage.
	440	Pope Leo the Great elected Pope. He serves until 461.
	449	Traditional date the Angles, Saxons, and Jutes invade the part of Britain that will become England, introducing Old English as a language to the Celtic–speaking island. The Jutes under Hengest and Horsa conquer Kent (south-eastern section of modern England).
	450	Folklore attributes Saint Patrick with the invention of whiskey—though Romans probably brewed "aqua vitae" as early as 50 BCE. Establishment of the seven liberal arts as regular course of study in medieval colleges. Probably no connection to earlier events this year.
> > >	451	Attila the Hun invades Gaul. Franks, Romans, and Alemanni repulse him at the battle of Châlons.
> > >	452	Attila the Hun invades northern Italy
> > >	453	Death of Atilla the Hun.
	455	Gaiseric and the Vandals sack Rome. Death of Emperor Valentinian.
	465	The so–called "White Huns" dominate northern India.
	471	Theodoric the Great, King of the Ostrogoths. He rules until 526.
	475	Romulus Augustus declared Roman Emperor. He will be the last one.
	476	Rome falls in its final death spasms under Romulus Augustulus. Odovacar the Goth and his forces depose Romulus Augustus. Traditional end of the Western Roman Empire, though the Eastern half continues and grows into the Byzantine Empire.

as a great and noble king. He plays a major role in three Norse sagas.

435–438 CE: ROMAN INJUNCTION v. SYNAGOGUES

The Theodosian Code prohibits, among other things, the construction of new synagogues.

442 CE: JEWISH QUARTER IN CONSTANTINOPLE

Jews concentrate in the copper–workers' quarter of Constantinople, situated near the church of Hagia Sophia.

c. 450 CE: LEVITICUS RABBAH

Composition of *Leviticus Rabbah* in the Galilee – a homiletic *Midrash* devoted mainly to the themes of reward and punishment, God's love for the poor, and the praise of peace.

455 CE: ROME IS SACKED

–by Geiseric, King of the Vandals

c. 475 CE: MORE MIDRASH

Composition of *Midrash Pesikta derav Kahana* in the Galilee – homilies for all the festivals, taken from various books of the Pentateuch or Prophets.

476 CE: FALL OF THE ROMAN EMPIRE

The year generally accepted as the end of the (western) Roman Empire, although it actually fell after multiple attacks over several decades.

455 CE: ROME IS SACKED

Geiseric sacking Rome
[Note the (Jewish) Menorah in background]

476 CE: THE DARK AGES a.k.a. THE EARLY MIDDLE AGES COMMENCES

–demarcated (somewhat arbitrary) ending: 1000 CE

485 CE: ALARIC II

Beginning of the reign (485–515 CE) of Visigoth King Alaric II who reigned, as well, over Spain and Portugal.

See our created–link www.IberianVisigoth.com for – **Persecution of the Jews Under Visigoth Rule of the Iberian Peninsula 400s CE – 711 CE.**

499 CE: ARYABHATA, 23, FINISHES WRITING *ARYABHATIYA*

–probably in central or southern India

Aryabhata (476 CE–550 CE) is the first in the line of great mathematician–astronomers from the classical age of Indian mathematics and astronomy. Aryabhata is the father of the Hindu–Arabic (decimal) number system, which has, of course, become universal today.

His most famous work, aside from the Aryabhatiya just–noted, is the *Arya–Siddhanta.*

500 CE: RAVINA DIES

Death of Ravina, head of the Sura Academy, considered to be the last of the *Amoraim* (the Babylonian sages of that generation).

510 CE: (SAINT) RUSPE AND "ETERNAL FIRE" FOR THE JEWS

(Saint) Fulgentius of Ruspe (c. 467–533 CE), Bishop of

499 CE: ARYABHATA, 23, FINISHES WRITING HIS *ARYABHATIYA*

Statue of Aryabhata on the grounds of Inter–University Center for Astronomy and Astrophysics (IUCAA), Pune, India.

Ruspe, North Africa, (later canonized as a Catholic saint) in his "Writings":

"Hold most firmly and no doubt that not all the pagans, but also all the Jews, heretics and schismatics, who depart from the present life outside the Catholic Church, are about to go into eternal fire prepared for the devil and his angels."

527 CE: JUSTINIAN

Justinian from the Eastern Roman Empire attempts to wrest control of major portions of the western empire, including the reconquest of Rome.

Justinian commissions a uniform rewriting of Roman law, 529 CE, supervised by Tribonian 529–534 CE – and to be known through the ages as "the Justinian Code" *Corpus Juris Civilis* (Body of Civil Law).

The title *Corpus Juris Civilis* sounds magisterial, but unfortunately it incorporates, as well, severe restrictions and discriminations against the Jews ("*Servitus Judaeorum*"). Thus, about two hundred years after the Roman Empire began morphing to Christianity, anti–Judaism now gets enshrined into Roman law itself.

These now–codified [Church-inspired] Roman Empire discriminations, ["they (the Jews) shall enjoy no honors"] would severely impact Jews throughout Europe for many hundreds of years. Among other abominations, using Hebrew at all was forbidden and reciting the core–prayer the *Shema* ("Hear O, Israel, the Lord is our god, the Lord is One…") was totally banned in particular. Among its more Machiavellian features: A Jew who converted to Christianity was entitled to inherit his or her father's estate, to the exclusion of the still–Jewish siblings.

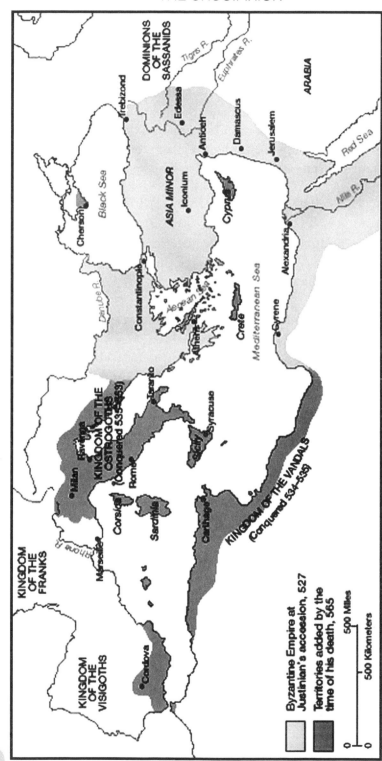

527 CE: JUSTINIAN

KINGDOM OF THE FRANKS

KINGDOM OF THE VISIGOTHS

Córdova

Marseille

Milan

Ravenna

KINGDOM OF THE OSTROGOTHS
(Conquered 535-553)

Rome

Corsica

Sardinia

Taranto

Syracuse

Sicily

Carthage

KINGDOM OF THE VANDALS
(Conquered 534-535)

Rhône R.

Danube R.

Black Sea

Chersan

Constantinople

Aegean Sea

Athens

Crete

Mediterranean Sea

ASIA MINOR

Iconium

Trebizond

Edessa

Antioch

Damascus

Jerusalem

Cyprus

Cyrene

Alexandria

DOMINIONS OF THE SASSANIDS

Tigris R.

Euphrates R.

ARABIA

Red Sea

Nile R.

Byzantine Empire at Justinian's accession, 527

Territories added by the time of his death, 565

500 Miles

500 Kilometers

The Byzantine Empire under Justinian. Justinian's re-conquests of North Africa, Italy, and the coast of Spain severely strained the empire's resources.

540 CE: JUSTINIAN'S PLAGUE

The Bubonic Plague rampages throughout Justinian's empire and surrounding Europe. In many areas 50 percent of the population dies (estimates range up to 100 million dead). Jews were often blamed and harassed or killed as a consequence. This was a dire saga in Jewish history.

Justinian suppresses all non–Christians, including the Jews. The Jews of Borium (in Italy), who had politically challenged his military policies, are forcibly converted.

540 CE: GREGORY THE GREAT BORN

Papacy of (Saint) Gregory the Great (c. 540 CE – 604 CE).

Pope St. Gregory I...better known historically as Gregory the Great, was pope from September 590 until his death.

He is also known as Gregory the Dialogist in Eastern Orthodoxy because of his Dialogues. He was the first of the popes to come from a monastic background. Gregory is a Doctor of the Church and one of the six Latin Fathers. He is considered a saint in the Roman Catholic Church and in the Eastern Orthodox Church.

Gregory is the patron saint of musicians, singers, students, and teachers.

*

[This is the same Gregory who codified the pejorative version of Mary Magdalene (i.e. the vilification that Mary Magdalene was a prostitute).

540 CE: GREGORY THE GREAT BORN
PAINTER: FRANCISCO DE ZURBARÁN

Jewish traditions, in the very rare cases where they encounter the issue, do not "buy–into" the pejorative version of the Magdalene saga. If anything, they are intrigued by the female disciple Mary Magdalene.

As noted above, Gregory's actions mystify. He comes perilously close to undermining Christendom itself with his undermining of pivotal Mary Magdalene, the asserted "sole witness" (of the "resurrection" of Jesus).]

Rosemary Ruether writes:

> "Gregory the Great, reigning as Roman pontiff at the end of the sixth century, represents a perfect model of the anti–Judaic theory, as this had been embodied in Christian Roman law and carried on by the Church through Roman law. In contrast to the view of medieval Christians and even medieval popes, Gregory the Great is often cited as a "friend" of the Jews, but this is a misunderstanding of the context in which he himself worked. It is true that Gregory opposed forced baptism and synagogue burning, but he did so as an executor of Roman law which protected Jewish religious institutions and forbade violence.*" (Ruether, *Faith and Fratricide*, p. 199).

---

* Solomon Katz, "Pope Gregory The Great and the Jews," JQR

The pontificate of Gregory the Great (590-604 CE):

–who adopts a "moderate" policy towards the Jews. He condemns forced conversions, but approved of conversions attached by material inducements; he first formulates the principle which was reiterated from the twelfth century onwards in all papal bulls 'benign' to the Jews that "and one should not accord the Jews in their synagogues any

550-700 CE: TALMUD BAVLI FINAL-EDIT

PRINCIPLES OF TALMUDIC EXEGESIS OF THE TORAH

TALMUDIC EXPOSITION OF THE SCRIPTURES

Sifra, Introduction

Rabbi Ishmael says: The Torah is interpreted by means of thirteen rules:

1. Inference is drawn from a minor premise to a major one, or from a major premise to a minor one.

2. From the similarity of words or phrases occurring in two passages it is inferred that what is expressed in the one applies also to the other.

3. A general principle, as contained in one or two biblical laws, is applicable to all related laws.

4. When a generalization is followed by a specification, only what is specified applies.

5. When a specification is followed by a generalization, all that is implied in the generalization applies.

6. If a generalization is followed by a specification and this in turn by a generalization, one must be guided by what the specification implies.

7. When, however, for the sake of clearness, a generalization necessarily requires a specification, or when a specification requires a generalization, rules 4 and 5 do not apply.

8. Whatever is first implied in a generalization and afterwards specified to teach us something new, is expressly stated not only for its own sake, but to teach something additional concerning all the instances implied in the generalization.

9. Whatever is first implied in a general law and afterwards specified to add another provision similar to the general law, is specified in order to alleviate, and not to increase, the severity of that particular provision.

10. Whatever is first implied in a general law and afterwards specified to add another provision which is not similar to the general law, is specified in order to alleviate in some respects, and in others to increase the severity of that particular provision.

11. Whatever is first implied in a general law and is afterwards specified to determine a new matter, the terms of the general law can no longer apply to it, unless Scripture expressly declares that they do apply.

12. A dubious word or passage is explained from its context or from a subsequent expression.

13. Similarly, if two biblical passages contradict each other, they can be harmonized only by a third passage.

ספרא, פתחה

רַבִּי יִשְׁמָעֵאל אוֹמֵר: בְּשָׁלֹשׁ עֶשְׂרֵה מִדּוֹת הַתּוֹרָה נִדְרָשֶׁת:

א) מִקַּל וָחֹמֶר;

ב) וּמִגְּזֵרָה שָׁוָה;

ג) מִבִּנְיַן אָב מִכָּתוּב אֶחָד, וּמִבִּנְיַן אָב מִשְּׁנֵי כְתוּבִים;

ד) מִכְּלָל וּפְרָט;

ה) וּמִפְּרָט וּכְלָל;

ו) כְּלָל וּפְרָט וּכְלָל אִי אַתָּה דָן אֶלָּא כְּעֵין הַפְּרָט;

ז) מִכְּלָל שֶׁהוּא צָרִיךְ לִפְרָט, וּמִפְּרָט שֶׁהוּא צָרִיךְ לִכְלָל;

ח) כָּל דָּבָר שֶׁהָיָה בִּכְלָל וְיָצָא מִן הַכְּלָל לְלַמֵּד, לֹא לְלַמֵּד עַל עַצְמוֹ יָצָא, אֶלָּא לְלַמֵּד עַל הַכְּלָל כֻּלּוֹ יָצָא;

ט) כָּל דָּבָר שֶׁהָיָה בִּכְלָל וְיָצָא לִטְעוֹן טֹעַן אַחֵר שֶׁהוּא כְעִנְיָנוֹ, יָצָא לְהָקֵל וְלֹא לְהַחֲמִיר;

י) כָּל דָּבָר שֶׁהָיָה בִּכְלָל וְיָצָא לִטְעוֹן טֹעַן אַחֵר שֶׁלֹּא כְעִנְיָנוֹ, יָצָא לְהָקֵל וּלְהַחֲמִיר;

יא) כָּל דָּבָר שֶׁהָיָה בִּכְלָל וְיָצָא לִדּוֹן בַּדָּבָר הֶחָדָשׁ, אִי אַתָּה יָכוֹל לְהַחֲזִירוֹ לִכְלָלוֹ עַד שֶׁיַּחֲזִירֶנּוּ הַכָּתוּב לִכְלָלוֹ בְּפֵרוּשׁ;

יב) דָּבָר הַלָּמֵד מֵעִנְיָנוֹ, וְדָבָר הַלָּמֵד מִסּוֹפוֹ;

יג) וְכֵן שְׁנֵי כְתוּבִים הַמַּכְחִישִׁים זֶה אֶת זֶה, עַד שֶׁיָּבוֹא הַכָּתוּב הַשְּׁלִישִׁי וְיַכְרִיעַ בֵּינֵיהֶם.

*more precisely – from Baraita Sifri

source: Philip Birnbaum, *Daily Prayer Book, ha-Siddur ha-Shalem*. New York: Hebrew Publishing Company, © 1996, pp. 45-49.

liberty beyond what is fixed by law, thus they should not suffer, within what they were accorded, any infringement of their rights."

 550 CE: TALMUD BAVLI FINAL–EDIT

–and reaches its present form by 700 CE

Babylonian Talmud reaches its present form.

Rabbinics Ravina and Rav Ashi play key roles in its final organization. As noted, the Talmud is a record of rabbinic discussions and debates pertaining to Jewish law, ethics, customs and history. The Talmud has two major components: the Mishnah, which is the first written compendium of Judaism's Oral Law; and the (much more extensive) Gemara, a discussion of the Mishnah and related Tannaic writings that often ventures onto other subjects and expounds broadly on the Tanach (*Torah–Neveim–Ketuvim* i.e. the entire Jewish canon).

The Gemara, in turn, is the basis for all codes of rabbinic law and is much–quoted in other rabbinic literature. The whole Talmud is traditionally also referred to as the *shas* (a Hebrew quasi–abbreviation of, the "six orders" of the Mishnah). Talmud Bavli is the same as Talmud Babli which, as noted above, is the Babylonian Talmud. The Talmud – as it reached its core form in 700 CE – represented an approximately 1000–year effort.

As redaction and commentary have been added–on subsequently, as of the year 2,000 the Talmud and ongoing commentary represent a 2300–year continuous endeavor.

The focused two millennia endeavor has not been

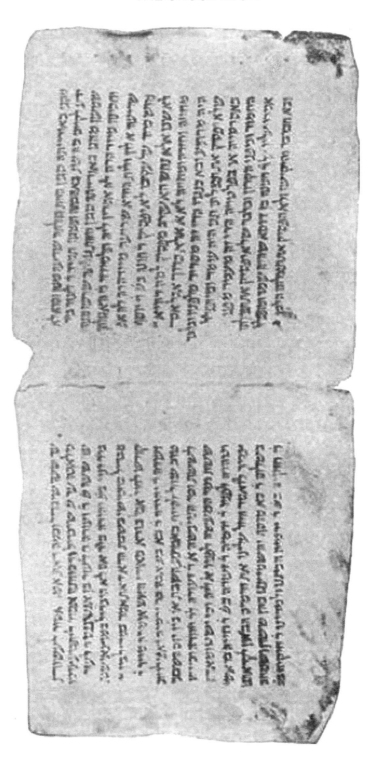

550-700 CE: TALMUD BAVLI FINAL-EDIT

A page of a medieval Jerusalem Talmud manuscript, from the Cairo Genizah.

unhinged by pogrom, plague, persecution, exile or communal displacement.

*

Daf Yomi is a daily regimen undertaken to study the entire 5,422–page Talmud Bavli, one *daf* (one sheet, i.e. two actual pages) per day. On that daily basis, it can be completed in seven years and five months.

The pages are complex and long.

140,000+ people worldwide (as of 2008) participate in a synchronized endeavor of daily study of the same exact Talmud page worldwide. The next official culmination of the (7–year and 5–month) study cycle is scheduled on August 2, 2012. Note that the cycle–commencement and structure were conceived and set by the organizers of the current (international) program, and not in antiquity.

550 CE: SAVORAIM

–the Jewish sages of Persia (550–700 CE).

–who fine–tuned the Talmud Bavli (the Babylonian Talmud).

550 CE: *JEWISH* REVOLTS IN JUDEA

Under Byzantine rule (550 CE – 700 CE):
    –two Jewish revolts
    –three Samaritan revolts

570 CE: MOHAMMED

Islam founded.

570 CE: MOHAMMED
"PROPHET MUHAMMAD AT THE KA'BA"
ILLUSTRATOR: NAKKAŞ OSMAN

The historic "Hegira" of Mohammed from Mecca to Medina. Mohammed, prophet of Islam, one of the most influential religious and political/military leaders of all time.

The rise of Islam in the Arabian Peninsula, constrains the growth of competing movements, particularly Christianity.

589 CE: GEONIM

Beginning of the period of the *Geonim*, heads of the academies in Babylon.

600 CE: THE KHAZARS

Establish a Jewish kingdom in the seventh century.

The Khazars, a semi–nomadic Turkic people from Central Asia founded an independent Khaganate in the Northern Caucasus along the Caspian Sea (southeastern part of Europe) where over time Judaism became the state religion. At their height they and their tributaries controlled most of what is today Southern Russia, western Kazakhstan, eastern Ukraine, Azerbaijan, large portions of the Caucasus (including Dagestan, Georgia) and the Crimea.

610 CE: THE EASTERN ROMAN EMPIRE EASES

–into the rule of the Greeks

–and morphs into the (Middle Age) Byzantine Empire a.k.a. Romania or Basileia Romaion.

The Byzantines continue to call themselves Romans, however. This Byzantine–Greek–Roman Empire falls, in

Comparison of Sunni and Shia Islam

	Sunnah	**Shia (or Shi'ah)**
adherents called	Sunnis	Shiites, Shi'i
meaning of name	"well–trodden path" or "tradition"	"party" or "partisans" of Ali
current adherents	940 million	120 million
percentage of total Muslims	90 percent	10 percent
primary locations	most Muslim countries	Iran, Iraq, Yemen
subsects	none, but four major schools of Muslim law are recognized	Ithna 'Ashariyah (Twelvers; the largest), Isma'iliyah and Zaydiyah
origins	c. 632 CE; theology developed especially in 10th cent.	c. 632–650 CE; killing of Ali's son Husayn in 680 CE is major event
did Muhammad designate a successor?	no	yes
true successor of the Prophet	Abu Bakr, father of the Prophet's favoured wife, 'A'ishah (elected by people of Medina)	'Ali ibn Abi Talib, husband of the Prophet's daughter Fatimah (designated by the Prophet)

cont'd

Comparison of Sunni and Shia Islam   [continued]

	Sunnah	Shia (or Shi'ah)
qualifications for ruler of Islam	tribe of the Prophet (Quraysh); later, any qualified ruler	family of the Prophet
current leaders	imams	mujtahids
identity of imams	human leaders	infallible manifestations of God and perfect interpreters of the Qur'an
Al Mahdi	will come in the future	was already on earth, is currently the "hidden imam" who works through mujta-hids to intepret Qur'an; and will return at the end of time
religious authority other than the Qu'ran	ijma' (consensus) of the Muslim community	infallible imams
concealing faith for self– protection (taqiya)	affirmed under certain circumstances	emphasized
temporary marriage (mut'ah)	practiced in the Prophet's time, but now rejected	still practiced
holy cities	Mecca, Medina	Mecca, Medina, Najaf, Karbala
major holidays	Eid al–Adha, Eid al–Fitr	Eid al–Adha, Eid al–Fitr, Ashura

Timeline of Mohammed in Medina

Important dates and locations
in the life of Mohammed in Medina

c. 618 CE	Medinan Civil War
622	Emigrates to Medina (Hijra)
622	Ascension to heaven
624	Battle of Badr: Muslims defeat Meccans
624	Expulsion of Banu Qaynuqa
625	Battle of Uhud: Meccans defeat Muslims
625	Expulsion of Banu Nadir
627	Battle of the Trench
627	Demise of Banu Qurayza
628	Treaty of Hudaybiyyah
c. 628	Gains access to Mecca shrine Kaaba

cont'd

Timeline of Mohammed in Medina

Important dates and locations
in the life of Mohammed in Medina
[continued]

628 CE	Conquest of the Khaybar oasis
629	First hajj pilgrimage
629	Attack on Byzantine Empire fails: Battle of Mu'tah
630	Bloodless conquest of Mecca
c. 630	attle of Hunayn
c. 630	Siege of Ta'if
c. 631	Rules most of the Arabian peninsula
c. 632	Attacks the Ghassanids: Tabuk
632	Farewell hajj pilgrimage
632	Death (June 8): Medina

600 CE: THE KHAZARS

Scale: 1:20,700,000

300 Miles

300 Kilometers

850 c.e.

BULGARS

Bulghar
Samar

KHWARIZM

GHUZZ

Caspian Sea

R. Ural

R.

KHAZARIA

Saksin
Volga
Don-Volga Portage
Atil

Samandar

Balanjar

Tbilisi

Sarkel

R. Don

R. Don

R. Don

R.

Tmutorakan

Kerch

CRIMEA

Sherson

Trebizond

Black Sea

Kiev

R. Dnieper

Constantinople

Sougdea

BYZANTINE

turn, to the Ottoman Turks in 1453 CE, approximately 850 years later.

Consequently, start to finish, if one counts from the beginning of the Roman Republic in 510 BCE (centered in Rome) to the very end (in 1453 CE) of the morphed eastern "Roman Empire" – the Byzantine–Greek–Roman Empire (centered in Constantinople), we are talking about a "run" of well over 2,000 years.

At its territorial peak, under Trajan in 116 CE, (43 years after Masada) Rome controlled c. 2,300,000 square miles of land surface. As a frame–of–reference, modern–day Italy is 116,000 square miles.

 610–625 CE: JEWISH REVOLT V

Revolt against Byzantine Emperor Heraclius (reign 610– 641 CE). The Jewish revolt originated in Tiberius (Judea).

The Jewish revolt came to the aid of the Persian Sassanid invaders of the Byzantine Empire, Judea in particular. Jerusalem fell to the combined Persian– Jewish forces after a 20–day siege. The Persians gave the Jews authority to control the city, and they effectively controlled it for five years. However, at that point, Jerusalem swung back into Christian control c. 626 CE. Betrayals and massacres ensued, resulting in a huge Jewish exodus to Egypt.

632 CE: FORCED CONVERSIONS

Forced conversions of Byzantine Jews ordered by Emperor Heraclius after the Jews of Judea had allied with the Persian invaders, particularly in Jerusalem c. 614 CE.

610–625 CE: JEWISH REVOLT V
"THE EMPEROR HERACLIUS CARRIES THE CROSS TO JERUSALEM"
PAINTER: MICHELE DI MATTEO LAMBERTINI

634–642 CE: ISLAMIC EXPANSION

Palestine, Syria and Egypt—where the majority of Jews live—come under Arab domination.

636 CE: ARAB RULE OVER JUDEA COMMENCES

463 year Arab rule: 636–1099 CE.

661–680 CE: MU'AWIYA

The Caliph Mu'awiya, the first Umayyad caliph, transforms the Arab world into a secular state in which religion takes second place. For the first time leadership is in the hands of a person who was not one of the Prophet's associates. Mu'awiya settles Jews, whom he considers to be faithful allies of the Arabs, in Tripoli and Syria; a period of prosperity for the Jews and Christians in Palestine under a regime which is very tolerant.

691 CE: DOME OF THE ROCK

Completed (by Caliph Abd al–Malik ibn Marwan), Old City, Jerusalem… will emerge as the third holiest site in Islam…

–atop the ruins of the Jewish Holy Temple (the very holiest site in Judaism).

End of 6th century: UPHEAVAL IN TURKEY

Expulsion of Jews from Antioch (Turkey): anti–Jewish riots in Syria and Anatolia; (Turkey) the center authorities of the empire are too weak to protect the Jews nor can they force them to adopt Christianity.

Caliphates

Muhammad (623-632)
Abu Bakr (632-634) father-in-law (Arabic, khalifah, [successor]), khalifat Rasul Allah, [successor to the Messenger of God]), 1st Caliph
Umar I (634-644) amir-al-mum-inin (Arabic, [commander of the believers], 2nd Caliph
Uthman ibn Affan (644-656) Muhammad's son-in-law, 3rd Caliph
Ali Ben Abu Talib (656-661) a cousin and son-in-law of Muhammad, 4th Caliph

(Shi'ites, Shi'a)	
Ali Ben Abu Talib (656-661) (1st Imam) **al-Hasan** (661-669) (2nd Imam) **al-Husayn** (669-680) (3rd Imam) **Ali Zayn al-'Abidin** (680-713) (4th Imam) **Muhammad al-Baqir** (713-733) (5th Imam) **Ja'far al-Sadiq** (733-765) (or Jafar ibn Muhammad) (6th Imam)	
Ismailis, Isma'iliyyah (Sevener Shi'ites) **Ismail** (died before, 760,) (7th imam, last for Ismailis) or **Muhammad,** his son (either is considered to still be alive, hiding)	**Twelver Shi'ites, Imamiyyah** (Ithna Ashariyya) **Musa al-Kazim** (765-799) (7th imam) **'Ali al-Rida** (799-818) (8th Imam) **Muhammad al-Jawad** (818-835) (9th Imam) **'ali al-Hadi** (835-868) (10th Imam) **al-Hasan al-'Askari** (868-874) (11th Imam) had student **Ibn Nusayr** (d.868), began Nusayris, Nusayriyyah **Muhammad al-Mahdi** (12th Imam, last) (considered to still be alive, hiding)
(Fatimids) (through Ismail) **Ubayd Allah al-Mahdi** (909-) **al-Qa'im** **al-Mansur** -972) **Moizz** (972-) **Al-Hakim** (3rd Fatimid Caliph) **Abu 'Ali al-Mansur al-Hakim** (985-1021) (6th Fatimid Caliph) **al-Mustansir** (-1094) **al-Mustali** (1094-) began Musta'liyyah he killed brother, **Nizar**, began Nizariyyah, Nizaris, Khojas (-1171) (overthrown by Saladin 1171) (but endures as the Druzes)	**(Buwayhids)** (945-) Adid (-1171) (conquered by Saladin 1171)
	Ayyubids Saladin (1171-1193) al-Adil (1193-1218) al-Kamil (1218-1238) (-1249) (conquered by Mamelukes 1249)
	(Babis) (1830-) Ali Muhammad Shirazi (-1850), started Babism Mirza Husayn Ali Nuri (c.1863), started Ba'hai

cont'd

Caliphates
[continued]

Allah and four noble caliphs

(Kharijites, Kharijiyyah)

(c. 650 - c.720) Often called the Puritans of Islam, as they demanded purity of conscience as well as body. They tended to brand everyone who did not agree with them as unbelievers. A sub-sect, the Azraqites, believed in such rigid following of the Koran as to massacre large groups of Muslims who had allegedly committed grave sins. Interestingly, Kharijites were very tolerant of non-Muslims.

(Sunni, Sunnites)

Umayyad Caliphs (661-750)

Muawiyah I ibn Abu Sufyan (661-680)
related to Uthman

Yazid I ibn Muawiyah (680-683)
Muawiya II ibn Yazid (683-684)
Marwan I (684-685)
Abd al-Malik ibn Marwan (685-705)
al-Walid I ibn Abd al-Malik (705-715)
Suleiman ibn Abd al-Malik (715-717)

Umar ibn Abd al-Aziz (717-720)
Yazid II ibn Abd al-Malik (720-724)
Hisham ibn Abd al-Malik (724-743)
al-Walid II ibn Abd al-Malik (743-744)
Yazid III ibn Abd al-Malik (744)
Ibrahim ibn Abd al-Malik (744)
Marwan II (744-750)
(end of Umayyad)
(conquered by Abbasids 750)

Umayyad Caliphs of Cordoba
(Spanish Umayyads) (929-1031)

Abd-ar-rahman I, escaped to Spain, 756-788

Abd-ar-rahman III, as caliph, 929-961
Al-Hakam II, 961-976
Hisham II, 976-1008
civil war (1008-1028)

Mohammed II, 1008-1009
Suleiman, 1009-1010
Hisham II, restored, 1010-1012
Suleiman, restored, 1012-1017
Abd-ar-rahman IV, 1021-1022
Abd-ar-rahman V, 1022-1023
Muhammad III, 1023-1024
Hisham III, 1027-1031

Abbasid Caliphs of Baghdad (750-1258)
descendants of Prophet's uncle Abbas Sunnites

Abu'l Abbas Al-Saffah 750-754
Al-Mansur 754-775
Al-Mahdi 775-785
Al-Hadi 785-786
Harun al-Rashid 786-809
Al-Amin 809-813
Al-Ma'mun 813-833
Al-Mu'tasim 833-842
Al-Wathiq 842-847
Al-Mutawakkil 847-861
Al-Muntasir 861-862
Al-Musta'in 862-866
Al-Mu'tazz 866-869
Al-Muhtadi 869-870
Al-Mu'tamid 870-892
Al-Mu'tadid 892-902
Al-Muktafi 902-908
??? (908, one day)
Al-Muqtadir 908-932
Al-Qahir 932-934
Al-Radi 934-940
Al-Muttaql 940-944
Al-Mustakfi 944-946
(by about 950, very little power)

Al-Muti 946-974
Al-Ta'i 974-991
Al-Qadir 991-1031
Al-Qa'im 1031-1075
Al-Muqtadi 1075-1094
Al-Mustazhir 1094-1118
Al-Mustarshid 1118-1135
Al-Rashid 1135-1136
Al-Muqtafi 1136-1160
Al-Mustanjid 1160-1170
Al-Mustadi 1170-1180
An-Nasir 1180-1225
Az-Zahir 1225-1226
Al-Mustansir 1226-1242
Al-Musta'sim 1242-1258
(conquered by Mongols in 1258)

Mamelukes

(first Dynasty, Bahri) (1250-1382)
(second Dynasty, Burji) (1382-1517)
[two Caliphs, but just symbolic]
(defeated by Selim, 1517)

691 CE: DOME OF THE ROCK

Dome of the Rock built by Ummayyad caliph
(right on top of the ruins of the Jewish Temple).

700 CE: GUNPOWDER

The Chinese invent gunpowder by combining saltpeter, sulphur and carbon.

It is initially used primarily for fireworks.

711 CE: WESTWARD MUSLIM CONQUEST / IBERIA

–beginning of the 7–year Muslim conquest of the Iberian Peninsula

711 CE: GOLDEN AGE OF JEWS OF SPAIN COMMENCES

711 CE is the earliest "start date" used by historians for the "Golden Age of the Jews of Spain." Others place the "start date" at 912 CE (the rule of Abd–ar–Rahman III).

Depending on the historian, this ("Golden Age") period ends either in 1031 CE (when the Caliphate of Cordoba ended)
or
1066 CE (the year of the Grenada massacre)
or
1099 CE (when the Almoravides invade)
or the
mid–1100s CE (when the Almohades invade)

So, at a minimum, 100 years;
at a maximum, almost 450 years.

Now, there is much disagreement as to just how "golden" this "Golden Age" was.

700 CE: GUNPOWDER

五重裹衣以麻縛定更別鎔松脂傳之以砲放復有

清油桐油濃油同煎成膏入前藥末旋和勻以砲放復有

研乾漆搗為末竹茹即微炒碎末黃蠟松脂

右以晉州硫黃窩黃焰硝同搗羅硫黃定粉黃丹同

桐油半兩 松脂十四兩 濃油一分

竹茹一兩 黃丹一兩 黃蠟半兩 清油一分

麻茹一兩 乾漆一兩 硫黃一兩 定粉一兩

晉州硫黃十四兩 窩黃七兩 焰硝二斤半

火藥法

右題砲預備用以蓋覆及防火箭

鍬三具 鍤一領 鍬三具 火索一十條

卻筒四箇 土布袋一十五條 界搭索一十條

水濺二箇 拒馬二 麻搭四具 小水桶二隻

鐵鈎十八箇 大末樞二箇 界扎索一十條

散子末二百五十條 救火大桶二

搭頭挂一十八條 皮廉八片 皮索一十條

The earliest known written description of the formula for gunpowder, from the Chinese Wujing Zongyao military manuscript, during the Song Dynasty.

Was it
objectively "golden"?
or
just **relatively** golden – as compared to Christian Europe?

Probably, the latter.

But, "relatively golden" may have been a quantum–leap significantly better "neighborhood" for a Jew to live in – and bring up his family. That would be my estimation. Furthermore, one needs to assume that the level of "golden–ness" oscillated over the span.

However, one should not underestimate the political capital expended by sundry Muslim rulers extending various levels of protection, tolerance, respect and harmony to the Jews.

Of course, historically there have been extraordinary cultural and economic—and often scientific and political—benefits to shielding "those Jews." But the Muslim rulers as a general rule clearly acted responsibly and often quite nobly.

Life for a Jew in contiguous Christian Europe spanning the widest demarcation of this period was more often than not a hellish existence. The breadth and depth of Christian toxicity towards the Jews is numbing.

*

Maimonides, oft–cited as the exemplar of a Jew in this (Spanish) Golden Age, was only born in 1135 CE, so his own zenith does not truly catch even the fourth and last possible historical cut–off date (mid–1100s CE) noted

711 CE: BEGINNING OF THE 7–YEAR MUSLIM CONQUEST OF THE IBERIAN PENINSULA

Image of a cantor reading the Passover story in Al Andalus, from the 14th century Haggadah of Barcelona.

above for the era. We include him in Golden Age of Jewish Philosophy (1200s–1400s), but not in the Golden Age of the Jews of Spain. See 1200 CE below.

732 CE: BATTLE OF TOURS

Poitiers, France: Frankish warlord Charles Martel ("the Hammer") turns back the Muslims under the command of Abdul Rahman Al Ghafiqi.

Note: The appellation "the Hammer" echoes (Jewish liberator) Judas Maccabeus, Judah the Hammer, 900 years prior.

c. 750 CE: GAONIM PERIOD

The earliest Talmud commentaries (750–1000 CE).

The associated yeshivas of *Sura and Pumbeditha* (both in modern–day Iraq) achieve *Diaspora*–wide prominence in this period. (*Diaspora* meaning "exile," referring to the Jews spread around the globe, post Babylonian–exile c. 586 BCE, and Roman–exile c. 70 CE)

Rav Amram Gaon of *Sura* compiles his *Siddur* (prayer book) in 846 CE; Rav Saadia Gaon, his own in 940 CE.

760 CE: THE KARAITES

The Karaites reject the Oral Law, and split off from now mainstream Rabbinic Judaism.

Major Karaite personages include Anan ben David, Benjamin of Nahawandi (830 CE), Daniel al–Kumsi (900 CE).

732 CE: BATTLE OF TOURS
PAINTER: CHARLES DE STEUBEN

A triumphant Charles Martel (mounted) facing Abdul Rahman Al Ghafiqi (right) at the Battle of Tours.

After mainstream Rabbinic Saadia Gaon of Egypt (noted above) ascends to the head of Sura Academy in Babylonia in 928 CE, and writes his masterwork "Beliefs and Opinions" (*Emunoth ve–Deoth*), which traces and elucidates the philosophical basis for Rabbinic Judaism, Karaism fades from the stage.

793 CE: LINDISFARNE

Vikings (from Scandinavia) raid the British island monastery of Lindisfarne.

This marks the start of the Viking Age, particularly in the British Isles.

The Vikings also conquer and settle parts of France. Several generations later, in 1066 CE, the Norman (France–based) descendants of these Vikings, now speaking French and identifying themselves as French, effect the watershed Norman Conquest (of England) and become the ruling aristocracy of England. Thus the Vikings project across Europe and down through world history, albeit in morphed form.*

800 CE: CHARLEMAGNE

The son of King Pepin the Short and grandson of Charles Martel is crowned Imperator Augustus (Holy Roman Emperor) by Pope Leo on Christmas Day. He reigns 46 years. Lore has it that he had 5 wives, 20 children and 5 mistresses.

Sometimes referred to as the Father of Europe, Charlemagne conquers Italy and is regarded by many as the founding father of both France and Germany.

---

*including their potential "discovery" of America

793 CE: LINDISFARNE

VIKINGS
793 – 1066 A.D.

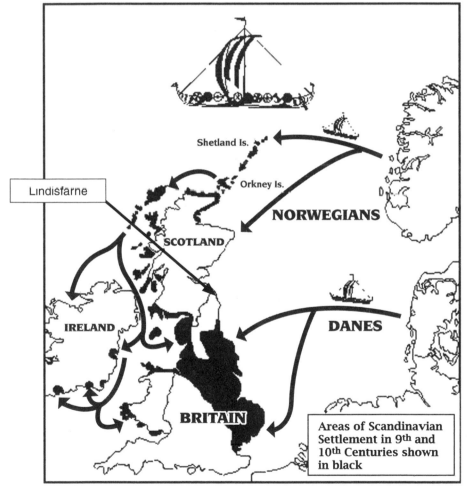

Lindisfarne

Shetland Is.

Orkney Is.

NORWEGIANS

SCOTLAND

DANES

IRELAND

BRITAIN

Areas of Scandinavian
Settlement in 9th and
10th Centuries shown
in black

Charlemagne Christianizes Europe, including the Saxons, at the point of the sword.

Charlemagne maintains a protective posture and very close ties with the Pope. Each will re–enforce the other.

His rule is associated with the Carolingian Renaissance, a revival of the arts and education in the West.

806 CE: CHARLEMAGNE DIVIDES HIS KINGDOM AMONG HIS THREE SONS

873 *or* 874 CE: PERSECUTION UNDER BASIL I

Persecution of the Jews and forced baptisms by order of Byzantine Emperor Basil I (reign 867 – 886 CE). Basil I founds the Byzantine "Macedonian Dynasty."

c. 928 CE: SAADIA GAON

Heads the legendary Sura Academy in Babylonia. Authors many important Jewish works, primarily in Arabic. [Noted in the 760 CE section on the Karaites above]

As of 2006 the oldest complete manuscript of the Haggadah is in a prayer book compiled by Saadia Gaon. [We alluded to his siddur in the 750 CE section on the Gaonim above.]

c. 930 CE: THE "ALEPPO CODEX"

The Aleppo (Syria) Codex is a manuscript set of the *Tanach*. It was at one time the oldest complete manuscript of the *Tanach**; however approximately one–

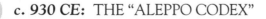

*excluding the Dead Sea Scrolls

THE CRUCIFIXION

806 CE: CHARLEMAGNE DIVIDES HIS KINGDOM

France (800 CE - 2000 CE)

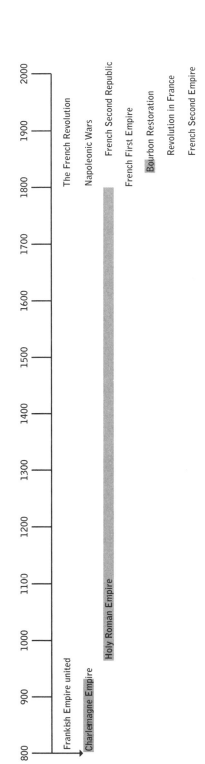

third of it, including nearly all of the Torah, has been missing since 1947.

It is considered by many to be the most authoritative document in the *masorah* ("the Jewish transmission"), the tradition by which the Hebrew Scriptures, law and tradition have been preserved and passed–on from generation to generation.

After its creation in the tenth century, the codex was given to the Jewish community of Jerusalem during the mid–eleventh century. However, it was among the works held ransom by the Crusaders during the First Crusade.

After being rescued by the elders of Ashkelon (Judea), it was transported to Egypt along with Jewish refugees. It later resurfaced in the Rabbanite synagogue in Cairo, where it was referenced by Maimonides; Maimonides' descendants brought it to Aleppo, Syria, at the end of the fourteenth century.

The Codex remained in Syria for five hundred years, until Muslim anti–Jewish riots desecrated the synagogue where it resided. The Codex disappeared, and re–emerged in 1958, when it was smuggled into Israel by Syrian Jew Murad Faham, and presented to the president of the state, Itzhak Ben–Zvi.

On arrival, it was found that parts of the codex had been lost. The Aleppo Codex was entrusted to the Ben–Zvi Institute and the Hebrew University in Jerusalem. As noted, the beginning (nearly all of the Torah) and end of the manuscript are missing, as well as are some pages in between.

c. 930 CE: THE "ALEPPO CODEX"

"The Aleppo Codex is a medieval manuscript of the Hebrew Bible (*Tanach*), associated with Rabbi Aaron Ben Asher. The Masoretic scholars wrote it in the early 10th century, probably in Tiberias, Israel. It is in book form and contains the vowel points and grammar points (nikkudot) that specify the pronunciation of the ancient Hebrew letters to preserve the chanting tradition. It is perhaps the most historically important Hebrew manuscript in existence."   – Wikipedia

932– c. 944 CE: LECAPENUS

Persecutions by Emperor Romanus I Lecapenus (reign 920–944 CE). Jewish community leaders are executed and Hebrew manuscripts are burned.

1000 CE: "DARK AGES" ENDPOINT

–End of the so–called Dark Ages 476–1000 CE)

An approximate mid–point of the Middle Ages (476 CE* – 1492 CE***)

*   Fall of the Roman Empire
*** Columbus discovers the New World

Not particularly dark intellectually, as far as sophisticated Jewish philosophical output was concerned. In the midst of abject poverty, persecutions, pogroms, blood libels, Black Deaths, and expulsions, the Jews are writing—for their contemporaries—and for posterity.

Somehow, many of these texts have been protected to this day. Interestingly, the themes and writings are overwhelmingly quite sophisticated and nuanced, picking up where Aristotle left off. Seamlessly.

Nahmanides, Abba Mari ben Moses, Simon ben Zemah Duran, Joseph Albo, Isaac Arama, and Joseph Jaabez intellectually arm–wrestle with Maimonides on a range of metaphysical issues. They generally come down on the side of a much smaller "core" of so–called "principles of faith."

1000 CE: "DARK AGES" ENDPOINT
"THE EXPULSION OF THE JEWS"
PAINTER: EMILIO SALA

Isaac Abravanel response to the Edict of Expulsion of the Jews from Spain in front of Ferdinand and Isabella.

Ferdinand   Isabella

Isaac Abravanel

Maimonides had articulated 13 core principles of (Jewish) faith.

1) To know the existence of the Creator
2) The unity of God
3) The denial of physicality in connection with God
4) God's Antiquity
5) The "worthiness" of God
6) Prophecy
7) The prophetic aspect of Moses
8) The divinity of the Torah
9) The completeness of the Torah
10) Divine omniscience
11) Reward & Punishment
12) The era of the Messiah
13) Resurrection of the Dead

However, just three core beliefs manifest with this above–noted group of philosophers (Nahmanides *et al.*)

1) Belief in God
2) Belief in Revelation
    (that God revealed himself at Sinai)
3) Belief in Providence (God's protection)

Hasdai Crescas, David ben Samuel Estella, David ben Yom Tov ibn Bilia, Jedaidah Penini, and Isaac Abravanel, among other notables then join the particular intellectual fray with full–scale expositions.

 c. 1000 CE: RABBEINU GERSHOM

a.k.a. Rabbeinu Gershom Me'Or Hagolah ("our teacher Gershom the Light of the Exile").

c. 1000 CE: RABBEINU GERSHOM

Synagogue in Mainz, Germany

His unilateral edicts are pretty unique in Jewish tradition, but by the force of his stature, his will has prevailed over the centuries.

Takkanot of Rabbeinu Gershom [The Legal Adjustments (into Orthodox Jewish Law) of Gershom ben Judah]:

1) A prohibition on polygamy
2) A prohibition on summarily divorcing a woman against her will [but Divorce *per se*, after discussion and/or mediation remains thoroughly permissible, as prior]
3) A prohibition on reading the private mail (emails would be included – *wink*) of others

His bans are considered binding on (Ashkenazic, in particular) Jewry to this day.

1008 CE: THE "LENINGRAD CODEX"

The Leningrad Codex (or Codex Leningradensis) is perhaps the oldest *complete* manuscript of the complete *Tanach*.

The Aleppo Codex (c. 930 CE), was the first notable such manuscript and is several decades older, but as noted, key parts of it have been missing since 1947, making the Leningrad Codex the oldest complete codex that has survived intact to this day. Essentially all of Jewry has integrated them both over the last millennia.

In modern times, the Leningrad Codex is most important as the Hebrew text reproduced in Biblia Hebraica (1937) and Biblia Hebraica Stuttgartensia (1977).

1008 CE: THE "LENINGRAD CODEX"

Leningrad Codex (cover page E, folio 474a)

The city of St. Petersburg was founded in 1703 by Tsar Peter I of Russia. It was called Petrograd 1914–1924, and Leningrad 1924–1991.

The Leningrad Codex, in extraordinarily pristine condition after a millennium, also provides an example of medieval Jewish art. Sixteen of the pages contain decorative geometric patterns that illuminate passages from the text. The Signature Page shows a star with the names of the scribes on the edges and a blessing written in the middle (see exhibit).

The order of the books in the Leningrad Codex follows the Tiberian textual tradition, which also matches the later tradition of Sephardic biblical manuscripts. This order for the books differs markedly from that of most printed the *Tanach* for the books of Ketuvim.

The Leningrad Codex (a manuscript as opposed to a scroll) is so named because it has been housed at the Russian National Library in Saint Petersburg since 1863. After the Russian Revolution scholars renamed it the "Leningrad Codex."

[Author's note: July 7, 2009, when I was in Leningrad, I went to the museum at 11 A.M. on a Tuesday morning (meaning, well after opening time on a regular non–Holiday weekday) and tried to view the codex. I was stopped cold. First I was told that I needed a letter from a university; then I "discussed the situation"; then I was told I might be able to pay for a special guided tour; then the Front Desk was unable to make any contact whatsoever with the department in the same main building which I was in, which oversees the codex—or its "private tours," in any event. Everyone, including the Front Desk Manager and the apparently important Security Desk Manager—all "shrugged their shoulders." The Leningrad Codex may just as well have been on the moon. It was inaccessible.]

1023 CE: PAPER MONEY

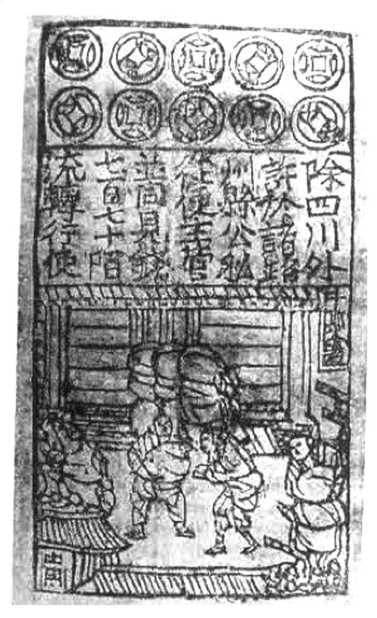

Early paper money

1023 CE: PAPER MONEY

–printed in China.

1040 CE: RASHI

Over his 65–year lifespan, Rashi writes legendary and
enduring Aramaic commentary
- on the Torah (Jewish Bible/Five Books of Moses)
- on most of Neveim (Prophets)
- on Ketuvim (Biblical Writings),
- as well as on most of the oft–studied tractates of the
  Talmud.

A giant in Judaism.

1041 CE: MOVABLE TYPE (CLAY)

The Chinese invent the printing press.

1045 CE: ALFASI

Rabbi Isaac ben Jacob Alfasi (a.k.a. Isaac Hakohen Alfasi)
moves to Fes, Morocco from an outlying region.

His works include *The Rif* and *Sefer ha–Halachot (Book of
Jewish Laws)*.

Alfasi was the teacher of Rav Yehuda Halevi, who in turn
was the author of *The Kuzari*.

1048 CE: OMAR KHAYYAM

Distinguished poet and mathematician, born in Persia
(modern day Iran).

 **1040 CE: RASHI**

An interior view of *RASHI Synagogue;*
Worms, Germany

He authors the legendary poetic work *The Rubaiyat of Omar Khayyam*, among others.

1054 CE: "THE GREAT SCHISM"

The major blocks of the Eastern Orthodox Church split–off from Roman Catholic hegemony.

Their center of gravity will be Constantinople. In 2008 there are now about 250 million constituents affiliated with a total of 14–15 separate autocephalous hierarchical churches, which recognize each other as "canonical" Orthodox Christian churches.

1066 CE: HASTINGS

Battle of Hastings: Norman conquest of England.

William the Conqueror (Norman) defeats King Harold II (Saxon).

The actual battle and breakthrough were less majestic than one would surmise, but, in any event, Harold was killed, and William will set the course for Britain's destiny.

Thus, in 1066 the Normans launch their assault (700 ships, 20,000 men) on England—from the beaches of French Normandy.

In 1944, eight hundred and seventy–eight years later, the historic invasion "Overlord" is launched in the opposite direction: the Allies (including the British) launch their assault (5,000 ships; 175,000 invasion troops) onto (the Third Reich via) the beaches of French Normandy—from England.

1066 CE: BATTLE OF HASTINGS

THE CRUCIFIXION

British Isles (4000 BCE - 2000 CE)

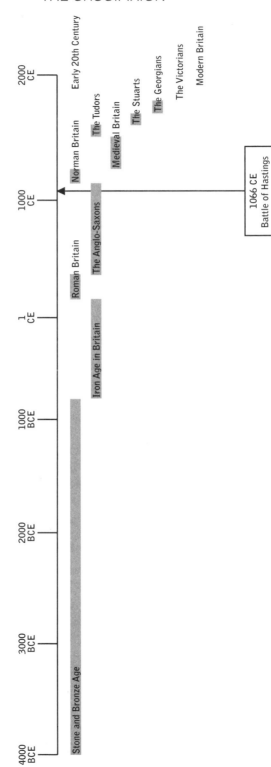

Stone and Bronze Age

Iron Age in Britain

Roman Britain

The Anglo-Saxons

Norman Britain

The Tudors

Medieval Britain

The Stuarts

The Georgians

The Victorians

Modern Britain

Early 20th Century

4000 BCE
3000 BCE
2000 BCE
1000 BCE
1 CE
1000 CE
2000 CE

1066 CE
Battle of Hastings

1066 CE: GRENADA MASSACRE

Muslim Berber mob storms the royal palace in Grenada (now in Spain), crucify the Jewish vizier (of the Berber king Badis) Joseph ibn Naghrela and massacres 4,000 Jews, most of the Jewish population of the city.

The massacre is not unique in the history of the Jews in the Muslim world, but horrendous as they were, these deadly events were more of an acute and isolated aberration than the rule, over the several thousand–year span.

In the Grenada bloodbath itself, it is not clear what percentage of the fury was politically–driven to eliminate the (Jewish) political allies of (Jewish) ibn Naghrela, rumored in Berber circles, from whence the uprising came, to be controlling the Berber king and rumored to be intending him quite serious harm.

1068 CE: OXFORD

Oxford College is built in 1068, though it is not formally founded until 1282, in England.

Perhaps they were day–dreaming of the future Harry Potter in the 214 year interlude between *building* and *founding*.

1070 CE: ibn GABIROL'S (c. 1050 CE) METAPHYSICS

–published in Arabic

–plus once in Latin (1070 CE)—*Fons Vitae*—with no attribution to ibn Gabirol;

–plus once in Hebrew (c. 1250–1275 CE) with no attribution to ibn Gabirol.

1066 CE: BATTLE OF HASTINGS
PAINTER: FRANCOIS HIPPOLYTE DEBON

The last stand of King Harold

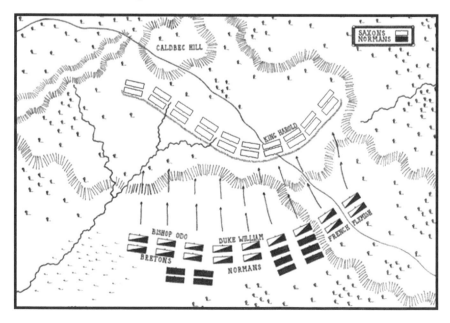

Fons Vitae (1070 CE), a Latin neo–Platonic metaphysical work which portrays creation as a cosmic struggle between form and matter.

"…was widely circulated among Catholic scholars who did not know the true religious or actual identity of its author"

–James Carroll, *Constantine's Sword*, p. 302.

The Latin work *Fons Vitae* (thought for centuries to be the work of a Christian cleric) Avicebron, was discovered in 1846 CE (776 years after its original publication) to be a translation from an earlier Arabic text.

The original Arabic work, in turn, was written by the Jewish philosopher Solomon ibn Gabirol.

There was a Hebrew version of Fons Vitae, as well, translated from the original Arabic into Hebrew by Shem–Tov Palquera (Falaquera) (c.1225–1290 CE). A Spanish Jewish philosopher and poet, well–versed in Greek and Arabic, whose (1225 CE) birth post–dated the 1070 CE posthumous publication of the Latin *Fons Vitae* version. (It is not clear whether the Palquera Hebrew version unearthed was fully intact, and whether it included the introductory pages, and whether they showed any attribution to ibn Gabirol or any disclaimer of original authorship by Palquera.)

Solomon ibn Gabirol was a poet and philosopher and ethicist, who wrote his metaphysics in Arabic and his poetry in Hebrew. He was born in Malaga, Spain around 1021 CE, and died in Valencia, Spain around 1058 (in his late 30s). His time, place and body–of–works would place him in the *Andalucian* school of Jewish personages. Ibn Gabirol's philosophical works are neo–Platonic, and he is considered

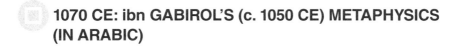 1070 CE: ibn GABIROL'S (c. 1050 CE) METAPHYSICS (IN ARABIC)

ibn Gabirol's metaphysics
Arabic text
(no title)
by
Solomon ibn Gabirol
(1021–1058 CE)

↓

ibn Gabirol's metaphysics
Latin Text
Fons Vitae*
1070 CE
[authorship signed
"Avicebron"]**
[actually written
by Solomon ibn Gabirol]

↓

ibn Gabirol's metaphysics
Hebrew Text
(no title)
Shem–Tov Palquera***
(1225–1290 CE)
receives the credit for
700+ years
[actually written
by Solomon ibn Gabirol]

* distributed with no attribution to ibn Gabirol authorship

** Many encyclopedia entries consider ibn Gabirol and Avicebron to be one–and–the–same

*** Palquera was a quite–distinguished author in his own right (see Palquera exhibit 2 pages hence).

as having been a "bridge" between Hellenic philosophy and the Eastern world.

Solomon ibn Gabirol has been enshrined hitherto in the Jewish pantheon primarily for his Hebrew poetry. His best known poem is *Keter Malchut* – Royal Crown (see exhibits for 1070 CE).

1095 CE: CRUSADES COMMENCE

–with widespread killings of Jews as a backdrop.

*

Nine Crusades would be launched (between 1095–1272 CE) into the Middle East, with Jerusalem, and Christian control thereof, as the penultimate target.

*

The Ninth Crusade, the last major medieval Crusade, ended with the fall to the (Arab) Mamluks of Tripoli [now Libra] (1289) and Acre [Holy Land] (1291). Those Christians unable to leave the cities were massacred and the last traces of local Christian rule in the Levant disappeared.

1095–6 CE: FIRST CRUSADE "DETOUR"

The First Crusade sets out to "liberate" Jerusalem. But a 10,000–man German Crusader army, instead of heading southeast towards Jerusalem, marches first north into the Rhine Valley, into well–known Jewish communities such as Cologne. The Jews were to be held individually culpable for the Crucifixion of Jesus by Rome 1062 years earlier.

1070 CE: ibn GABIROL'S (c. 1050 CE) METAPHYSICS (IN ARABIC)

Palquera's works include:

- *Iggeret Hanhagat ha–Guf we ha–Nefesh*, a treatise in verse on the control of the body and the soul.
- *Eri ha–Yagon*, on resignation and fortitude under misfortune. Cremona, 1550.
- *Iggeret ha–Wikkua*, a dialogue between an orthodox Jew and a philosopher on the harmony of philosophy and religion, being an attempt to prove that not only the Bible, but even the Talmud, is in perfect accord with philosophy. Prague, 1810.
- *Reshit okmah*, treating of moral duties (and giving the so–called "ethical epistles" of Aristotle), of the sciences, and of the necessity of studying philosophy. In this Shem–⬛ob treats of the philosophy of Aristotle and Plato. This and the preceding work have been translated into Latin (Bibliothèque Nationale, Paris, MS. Latin, No. 6691A).
- *Sefer ha–Ma'alot*, on the different degrees of human perfection; ed. I. Venetianer, 1891.
- *Ha–Mebaesh*, a survey of human knowledge in the form of a dialogue in rimed prose interspersed with verse. This work is a remodeling of the Reshit okmah. Amsterdam, 1779.
- *Sefer ha–Nefesh*, a psychological treatise according to the Arabian Peripatetics, especially Avicenna. Brody, 1835.
- *Moreh ha–Moreh*, commentary on the philosophical part of the Moreh Nebukim (Guide to the Perplexed) of Maimonides, with an appendix containing corrections of the Hebrew translation of Samuel ibn Tibbon. Presburg, 1837.
- *Letter in defense of the Moreh Nebukim*, which had been attacked by several French rabbis; published in the Minat ena'ot. Presburg, 1838.
- Extracts from Ibn Gabirol's *Meor ayyim*, published by Solomon Munk in his Mélanges de Philosophie Juive et Arabe. Paris, 1859.
- *De'ot ha–Filusufim*, containing Aristotle's Physics and Metaphysics according to Ibn Roshd's interpretations (Steinschneider, Cat. Hebr. MSS. Leyden, No. 20).
- *Iggeret ha–Musar*, a compilation of ethical sentences (comp. Orient, Lit. 1879, p. 79).
- *Megillat ha–Zikkaron*, a historical work, no longer in existence, quoted in the Mebaesh.
- *Iggeret ha–alom*, a treatise on dreams, mentioned in *Moreh ha–Moreh*, iii, ch. 19, p. 131.

With the Crusaders often giving the Jewish communities a choice between conversion and death, according to the historical record many Jewish communities committed mass–suicide in horrific scenes.

***

Today, many contemporary Christian books and many online encyclopedias relating events of the Middle Ages, often have a small segment included relating/asserting how the local bishop attempted to protect the Jews from the *low–level* Christian mobs or from the fancy Christian mob—the Crusaders.

In all these segments, the bishop is inevitably overcome by the mob or yields to the mob or is outflanked by the mob. The Catholic bishop, however, does not seem to ever actually "stand–down" the Catholic mob. Correct me if I'm wrong.

Be that as it may, where was all this hatred sown initially? It was sown in Church-related and texts—in the very cathedral of this very same bishop—whether or not during his precise tenure.

***

Having provided the "kindling wood, the gasoline and the matches" for a *bonfire mob scene* of hatred, the Church is then postured in contemporary Catholic texts as having shown up at the conflagration in the person of the bishop, to nobly protest. In addition, many of these vignettes seem to have made an appearance in Catholic texts *after* the Holocaust, after which, damning the Jews and other assorted genocidal tendencies, all tended to no

1070 CE: ibn GABIROL'S (c. 1050 CE) METAPHYSICS (IN ARABIC)

Keter Malchut – Royal Crown
by Solomon Ibn Gabriol

My God, I know that those who plead
To thee for grace and mercy need
All their good works should go before,
And wait for them at heaven's high door.
But no good deeds have I to bring,
No righteousness for offering,
No service for my Lord and King.

Yet hide not thou thy face from me,
Nor cast me out afar from thee;
But when thou bidd'st my life to cease,
O may'st thou lead me forth in peace
Unto the world to come, to dwell
Among thy pious ones, who tell
Thy glories inexhaustible.

There let my portion be with those
Who in eternal life arose;
There to purify my heart aright,
In thy light to behold the light.
Raise me from deepest depths to share
Heaven's endless joys of praise and prayer,
That I may evermore declare:

Though thou wast angered, Lord, I will give thanks to thee,
For past is now thy wrath, and thou dost comfort me.

source: Wikipedia (Shem–Tov ibn Falaquera)

longer play–well in "polite society" of the West. So, best, apparently, to tamper with the texts.

The Vatican may be a little slow in contemporary times when it comes to updating various Catholic texts to *neuter* hatred towards the Jews as per the humanistic thrust of *Nostre Aetate*, but its numeraries seem to have alacrity at "*updating*" its texts and online references post–Holocaust, to "distance" the Vatican from the inevitable "*mob*," whether Crusader Christian or Nazi.

Both the bishops and the cathedrals, in parallel to the Church itself, will have two "faces," two diametrically different agendas and projections.

The bishops will be postured as devoted servants of Jesus, advancing humanism. But the bishops are simultaneously also the subtle "enablers" of hatred—towards the Jewish nation, the fount of Jesus, as well as towards other "politically incorrect" groups.

1096–1099 CE: FIRST CRUSADE

Launched by Pope Urban II in 1095 and encompassing greater Christian Europe, to retake 'Christian lands,' including ultimately Jerusalem, from the Muslim conquest.

Severe massacres of (civilian) Jews during the First Crusade.

Rosemary Ruether writes:

> "The pogroms of the Crusades were met with stoic heroism by the Jewish communities of the Rhineland. Refusing the baptism offered at sword's point by the Crusaders, they regularly submitted to death or

1095–6 CE: FIRST CRUSADE "DETOUR"

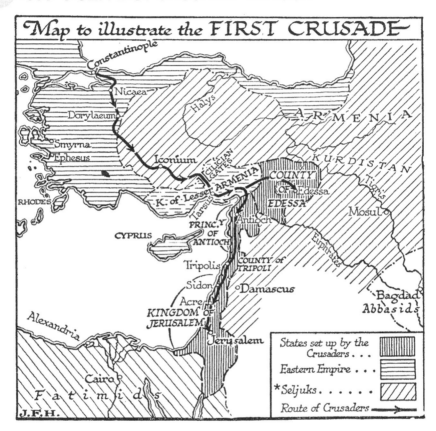

* Seljuks refers to Muslim Empire

committed mass suicide rather than be baptized. A martyr ethic was forged in European Jewry. The Christian doctrine of the Trinity was regarded as polytheism and its view of Jesus' divinity as idolatry. To resist baptism was comparable to the witness of the ancient martyrs of Israel, who resisted to the death the assaults of paganism at the time of the Maccabees. Jews died uttering the *Shema'* as witnesses to the unity of God's Holy Name.*A This resistance of the Jews to baptism was inexplicable to Christians." (Ruether, *Faith and Fratricide*, p. 207).

---

*A For medieval Jewish martyr theology, see especially Jacob Katz, *Exclusiveness and Tolerance* (New York: Schocken, 1969; reprint), pp. 82–92.

1096 CE: JEWISH MARTYRDOM AT MAINZ (GERMANY) CATHEDRAL

From *Constantine's Sword* –

"The crusaders were unleashed, storming through the city, looking for "the circumcised." Jews who had eluded crusaders, or bribed them during the early phase of the Rhineland incursion, had been succeeded, especially in Speyer and Worms, by Jews who were murdered in cold blood. By the time of Mainz, crusader ferocity was at its peak, fueled by a cross–inspired righteousness, for, as the [medieval] chronicler recounts it, they declared of their Jewish prey, 'You are the children of those who killed our object of veneration, hanging him [Jesus] on a tree [Cross]; and he [Jesus] himself had said: There will yet come a day when my children will come and avenge my blood. We [the Crusaders] are his children and it is… therefore obligatory for us to avenge him since you [the Jews] are the ones who rebel and disbelieve him.'"

1095–6 CE: FIRST CRUSADE

Crusades (Christian Warfare with Islam in Palestine)
(1095 CE – 1258 CE)

1096	Participants in the First Crusade massacre Jews in several Central European cities, beginning centuries of pogroms linked to the Crusades.
1096	More than 5,000 Jews were murdered in Germany in several different attacks.
May 3, 1096	Count Emico of Leiningen, on his way to join a Crusade, attacked the synagogue at Speyers and killed all the defenders.
May 27, 1096	1,200 Jews commit suicide in Mayence to escape Count Emico, who tried to forcibly convert them.
1085–1140	Judah Halevi (Jewish author).
1099	Crusaders (European Christians) capture Jerusalem and massacre tens of thousands of the city's Jews.
1100	Germans, including German Jews, migrate to Poland. It is seen as "the land of opportunity."
1107	Moroccan Almoravid ruler Yoseph Ibn Tashfin orders all Moroccan Jews to convert or leave.
1109	Tiberias falls to the Crusaders.
1115	After reconquering Toledo, Spain from the Muslims, Alphonso I invited all Jews to return.
1120	Jews from Muslim countries begin to settle in Byzantium.
1124	Records of a Jewish gate in Kiev attest to the presence of a Jewish community there.
1135–1204	Maimonides (Rabbi Moses ben Maimon; Jewish scholar).
1139	Judah Halevi completes his influential philosophy of Judaism known as *The Kuzari*. He is a friend of commentator Abraham Ibn Ezra, who also left Spain for the life of a wandering Jewish scholar.
1143	150 Jews killed in Ham, France.
1144	Jews in Norwich, England, are accused of murdering a Christian child in what is believed to be the first ritual murder charge. The blood libel, as well as others in England that follow in the 12th century, incites anti–Jewish violence.
1160–1173	Benjamin of Toledo, *The Itinerary of Benjamin of Toledo*.
1163	Benjamin of Toledo writes of 40,000 Jews living in Baghdad, complete with 28 synagogues and 10 Torah academies.
1171	Saladin (1138–1193) overthrows Fatimid dynasty in Egypt.
1187	Saladin recaptures Jerusalem from Crusaders grants Jews permission to re–enter.
March 16, 1190	Jews attacked, over 150 die after a six day standoff in York, England.

"The theology of anti–Jewish hatred could not be more clearly stated. Its meaning could not have been more firmly grasped than it was then by the Jews of Mainz. More than one thousand men, women, and children huddled in the courtyard of the archbishop's palace. They knew very well what had happened elsewhere in the preceding weeks, how bribes and flight had failed, finally, to protect even children. In Mainz, Jews had time to reflect on what was coming, and they knew that the only possible escape was through apostasy. Some few took that way out, but to most conversion to Christianity was more unthinkable than ever."

"There is an ancient arcaded courtyard beside the cathedral that dates to within a century of 1096, and it is certainly at or near the place where the Jews awaited the crusader. Not long ago, on balmy summer morning, I sat on a stone bench in that courtyard, with the Gothic arches of the church on one side, the pointed leaded windows of the present chapter house on another. The ornate chapter house formerly served as the archbishop's palace, on or near the site of Ruthard's. A large granite crucifix dominated yet another side of the yard. A stone fountain, a vestige of a well, stood in the center of a grassy rectangle, altogether the size, say, of a basketball court. A pair of relatively young trees cast a filigree of shadows towards the fountain. The trees reminded me that everything I was looking at had been reconstructed from the rubble of World War II. A scattering of rose bushes was in bloom that morning, and the red shimmered against the gray stone, a contrast that emphasized the dark weight of a multilayered past."

1095–6 CE: FIRST CRUSADE *[continued]*

Crusades (Christian Warfare with Islam in Palestine)
(1095 CE – 1258 CE)

1190	Approximately 2,500 Jews live in England, enjoing more rights than Jews on the continent.
1191	French King Phillip starts the Third Crusade, cancels debts to Jews, drives many Jews out of France, confiscates their property.
1194–1270	Scholar and Jewish leader Moses Ben Nachman (Nachmanides).
1195	Moses Maimonides completes *The Guide to the Perplexed*, considered the most important work of medieval Jewish thought.
1211	A group of 300 rabbis from France and England settle in Palestine (Eretz Yisrael), beginning what might be interpreted as Zionist *aliyah*.
1198–1216	Pope Innocent III (Christian).
1204	First synagogue built in Vienna, a city where Jews enjoyed more freedom than in other areas of Austria.
1215	Fourth Lateran Council expands anti–Jewish decrees in Europe, forces Jews to wear the Yellow Patch, the "Badge of Shame."
1222	Doacon Robert of Reading, England, was burned for converting to Judaism, setting a precedent for the burning of "heretics".
1222	Stephen Langton, Archbishop of Canterbury and a prime mover of the Lateran Council, forbids Jews from building new synagogues, owning slaves or mixing with Christians.
ca. 13th cen.	*The Zohar* (a Jewish kabbalistic book): .
1227	Death of Genghis Khan (roving Mongol conqueror).
ca. 1230	Inquisition by Christians in Spain.
1232	The Jewish community of Marrakech, Morocco, is reestablished, leading to massacres of Jews caused by Islamic political revolt and grassroots hatred.
1239	Pope Gregory IX orders the kings of France, England, Spain and Portugal to confiscate Hebrew books, Following this edict, the Talmud is condemned and burned in France and Rome.
1225–1274	Thomas Aquinas (Christian scholar).
1240–1292	Spanish Kabbalist Abraham Abulafia.
1243	First accusation of desecration of the Host (the wafers used is Christian Mass) – the blood libel – in Berlitz, Germany.
1244–1517	Rule by Tartars, Mongols, Ayybids, and Mamelukes.
1247	Pope Innocent IV issued a Bull refuting blood libels and sent it throughout Germany and France.
1254–1517	Mamluk Islamic rule (new dynasty) in Egypt.
1258	Fall of Islamic Abbasid dynasty to Hulagu (Mongol).

"Solomon bar Simson wrote [in 1096 CE]:

The hand of the Lord rested heavily on His people,
and all the Gentiles assembled against the Jews in the
courtyard to exterminate them…When the people of
the Sacred Covenant saw that the Heavenly decree had
been issued and that the enemy had defeated them and
were entering the courtyard, they all cried out together
– old and young, maidens and children, menservants
and maids – to their Father in Heaven…"There is no
questioning the ways of the Holy One, blessed be He and
blessed be His Name, Who has given us His Torah and
has commanded us to allow ourselves to be killed and
slain in witness to the Oneness of His Holy Name…"

"Then in a great voice they all cried out as one: "We
need tarry no longer, for the enemy is already upon us.
Let us hasten and offer ourselves a s sacrifice before
God. Anyone possessing a knife should examine it to
see that it is not defective, and let him then proceed to
slaughter us in sanctification of the Unique and Eternal
One, then slaying himself – either cutting his throat or
thrusting the knife into his stomach."

"In April 1942, Nazis swarmed into the Warsaw
Ghetto, hauling Jews to Umschlag Platz, where the
boxcars waited. The yellow building behind the high
fence at 60 Sienna Street was a children's hospital.
One of its doctors was Adina Blandy Szwajger. She
survived to tell what happened as the Germans began
"taking the sick from the wards to the cattle trucks…I
took morphine upstairs…and just as, during those two
years of real work in the hospital, I had bent down
over the little beds, so now I poured this last medicine

Yizkor

Memorial Service   הזכרת נשמות

In memory of Jewish martyrs:

יִזְכּוֹר אֱלֹקִים נִשְׁמוֹת הַקְּדוֹשִׁים וְהַטְּהוֹרִים שֶׁנֶּהֶרְגוּ,
שֶׁנִּשְׁחֲטוּ וְשֶׁנִּשְׂרְפוּ, וְשֶׁנִּטְבְּעוּ וְשֶׁנֶּחְנְקוּ עַל קִדּוּשׁ הַשֵּׁם. בַּעֲבוּר
שֶׁנּוֹדְרִים צְדָקָה בְּעַד הַזְכָּרַת נִשְׁמוֹתֵיהֶם, בִּשְׂכַר זֶה, תִּהְיֶינָה
נַפְשׁוֹתֵיהֶם צְרוּרוֹת בִּצְרוֹר הַחַיִּים עִם נִשְׁמוֹת אַבְרָהָם יִצְחָק
וְיַעֲקֹב, שָׂרָה רִבְקָה רָחֵל וְלֵאָה, וְעִם שְׁאָר צַדִּיקִים,
וְצִדְקָנִיּוֹת שֶׁבְּגַן עֵדֶן, וְנֹאמַר אָמֵן.

May God remember the souls of the saintly martyrs who have
been slaughtered, burned, drowned or strangled for their loyalty
to God. We pledge charity in their memory and pray that their
souls be kept among the immortal souls of Abraham, Isaac, Jacob,
Sarah, Rebekah, Rachel, Leah, and all the righteous men and
women in paradise; and let us say, Amen.

source: *Daily Prayer Book, ha-Siddur ha-Shalem,* pp. 669 and 670.

down those tiny mouths…and downstairs there was screaming."

"Or, as Solomon bar Simson wrote of those in the archbishop's courtyard (in 1096 CE):

The women girded their loins with strength and slew their own sons and daughters, and then themselves. Many men also mustered their strength and slaughtered their wives and children and infants. The most gentle and tender of women slaughtered the child of her delight. They all arose, man and woman alike, and slew one another…Let the ears hearing this and its like be seared, for who has heard or seen the likes of it? In quire and seek: was there ever such a mass sacrificial offering since the time of Adam? Did it ever occur that there were one thousand and one hundred offerings on one single day – all of them comparable to the sacrifice of Isaac, the son of Abraham?…For since the day on which the Second Temple was destroyed, their like had not arisen, nor shall there be their like again… Happy are they and happy is their lot, for all of them are destined for eternal life in the World–to–Come – and may my place be amongst them!"

—James Carroll, *Constantine's Sword*, New York: Houghton Mifflin © 2001, pp. 261–263

1096 CE: 300 JEWS OF TRIER COMMIT MASS–SUICIDE

Surrounded by a Crusader–inspired mob demanding, under pain of death, that they convert to Christianity, one group of 300 Jews of Trier, Germany, in an echo of Masada, elect

1099 CE: FIRST CRUSADE CAPTURES JERUSALEM

The capture of Jerusalem marked the First Crusade's success

five of their number to slay all the rest, rather than convert or be slain by the hounding mob. "Jewish mass suicide reenters history" –James Carroll, *Constantine's Sword*, p. 251.

1097 CE: HENRY IV

Note that there were several European rulers named Henry IV, including kings of France and England, as well.

We are focusing here on Henry IV (1050–1106 CE), King of Germany (from 1056 CE) and Holy Roman Emperor (from 1084 CE).

Henry IV allows Jews who were forcibly converted in the previous year to return to their (Jewish) faith.

1099 CE: FIRST CRUSADE CAPTURES JERUSALEM

According to Christian accounts, all of Jerusalem's Muslims and Jews are slaughtered. The "Latin Kingdom of Jerusalem" begins.

Godfrey of Bouillon emerges as the ultimate authority in Jerusalem (*Advocatus Sancti Sepulchri*, or "Protector of the Holy Sepulchre"). When Godfrey dies in 1100 CE, he is succeeded by his brother, Baldwin (of Edessa), who takes the title King of Jerusalem.

1100s CE: TOSEFOT, FRANCE

–Authoritative commentary on the Babylonian Talmud by a school of French rabbis.

Late 1100s CE: ROBIN HOOD SAGA UNFOLDS

illustration
Robin Hood (Robin of Sherwood)

This commentary is generally presented in all gemaras (Talmud editions).

They are linked on several levels to the works of the commentator Rashi, which also appear in all complete Talmuds.

Late 1100s CE: ROBIN HOOD SAGA UNFOLDS

In popular culture, (perhaps mythical, perhaps based on fact) Robin Hood is driven to outlawry during the misrule of King John of England, the "bad guy" brother of Richard the Lion–Hearted (who was *"out of town"* leading the Third Crusade).

Robin Hood and his Merry Men hung out in Sherwood Forest. They often tangle with the Sheriff of Nottingham when Robin Hood is not busy giving away his "winnings" to the poor, or flirting with Maid Marian.

And just where is Friar Tuck when you need him?

1110 CE: ibn DAUD

Abraham ibn Daud, Spanish–Jewish astronomer, historian, and philosopher (1110–1180 CE).

His works include the philosophical work "Emunah Ramah" (*The Sublime Faith*), a religious tradition chronicle "Sefer ha–Kabbalah" (*Book of Tradition*), plus others.

Ibn Daud deals extensively with the theological theme of *hashgacha pratit* (divine intercession in daily life).

1120 CE: *SICUT JUDAEIS* ISSUED BY POPE CALIXTUS II

Extracts from the oldest existing version of the bull,
from Pope Alexander III

"[The Jews] ought to suffer no prejudice. We, out of the meekness of Christian piety, and in keeping in the footprints or Our predecessors of happy memory, the Roman Pontiffs Calixtus, Eugene, Alexander, Clement, admit their petition, and We grant them the buckler of Our protection.

For We make the law that no Christian compel them, unwilling or refusing, by violence to come to baptism. But, if any one of them should spontaneously, and for the sake of the faith, fly to the Christians, once his choice has become evident, let him be made a Christian without any calumny. Indeed, he is not considered to possess the true faith of Christianity who is not recognized to have come to Christian baptism, not spontaneously, but unwillingly.

Too, no Christian ought to presume...to injure their persons, or with violence to take their property, or to change the good customs which they have had until now in whatever region they inhabit.

Besides, in the celebration of their own festivities, no one ought disturb them in any way, with clubs or stones, nor ought any one try to require from them or to extort from them services they do not owe, except for those they have been accustomed from times past to perform.

...We decree... that no one ought to dare mutilate or diminish a Jewish cemetery, nor, in order to get money, to exhume bodies once they have been buried.

If anyone, however, shall attempt, the tenor of this degree once known, to go against it...let him be punished by the vengeance of excommunication, unless he correct his presumption by making equivalent satisfaction."

1120 CE: *SICUT JUDAEIS* ISSUED BY POPE CALIXTUS II

An expansive papal bull delineating protections and rights of the Jews.

Sicut Judaeis literally means *"and thus to the Jews,"* but it is generally referred to as *"the Constitution of the Jews."*

Reactive to the persecutions, houndings and slaughters of the First Crusade, Pope Calixtus II moves forcefully. His papal bull forbids Christians, among other things, from coercing Jews to convert, to harm them, to take their property, to interfere with their cemeteries – **on pain of excommunication** (this last point regarding excommunication being key).

This papal bull was reaffirmed intermittently by assorted popes in the period 1191 CE to 1447 CE.

There is a "catch" here, however; many times, if not always, preambles or post–texts to the papal bulls existed, which alerted Christian followers, nevertheless, to "deficiencies" of the Jews, whether as pertaining to their Christian–alleged role in the crucifixion of Jesus, their Christian–alleged "assigned role" by God to suffer, or whatever. Thus, on the one hand, the Jews are formally "protected," but on the other hand, the lower clergy and masses are fed toxic *fuel for the fire*.

This pattern, of leaving the "top of the pyramid" (the popes and cardinals *et al.*) with "clean hands," while the lower clergy and masses are given ample toxic fuel, is a pattern repeated ongoing to this very day even in much–celebrated *Nostre Aetate* in the late twentieth century.

1120 CE: *SICUT JUDAEIS* ISSUED BY POPE CALIXTUS II

Burdinus* (right), was a challenge to Calixtus II (not shown).
(b. 1118; d. 1121)

* a.k.a. Gregory VIII, a.k.a. Maurice Burdanus, a.k.a. Papa Gregorius octavus

It is not the refined and erudite Vatican functionaries who are rampaging with battle axes against unarmed Jewish housewives and Jewish school children; rather, it is the very basest component of the Catholic masses that are preying on the weak and the isolated and unarmed. This base–component layer receives all the "green light" it needs from the "mixed message." Basically, no light at all. Rather, *business as usual.*

Basically, everyone "hears" what he or she wants to hear. The Jews "hear" protection, of sorts. The basest component of the Christian masses, on the other side, hears a rationale to persecute the Jews. Many Catholic apologists centuries later post–Holocaust "scrub" history, and discern only the pristine segment.

By the time of Calixtus II, however, the degradation of the Jews fomented by the Church Fathers in the 100 CE – 500 CE period, had been coursing through Europe for over 600 years. In the case of the "good popes," as in the case of many exceptional individual Catholics over the centuries to come, the diabolical institutional posture of the Church Founders of the 100–500 CE period, previously spread through the far reaches of Christendom, would most often overwhelm individual good will, papal or otherwise. A spreading cancer of hatred and denigration against the Jews had been embedded in the *corpus* of Europe by the Church Fathers. Once implanted, intermittent benign cosmetic surgery or minor surgery or "mixed message" surgery would prove ineffective at stopping the cancer's virulent spread.

The worst was yet to come for the Jews of Europe.

And beyond Europe, the prognosis was bad, as well.

WHITE vs. BLACK

The amalgam of the inter–related – and almost unrelenting – defamations and diabolical imagery will achieve critical destructive mass. And will feed upon itself. The writers of the gospels will stitch–onto their writings various grotesque caricatures of sundry Jewish icons and figurative representatives, and then later proclaim this trashing as 'Holy Writ.' Passion–sagas will take these themes further.

Aside from the direct defamation of the Jews, these defamations will drive a moral wedge between Jesus and the Jews, his root–nation. While Jesus is portrayed as of Immaculate Conception and *all purity and saintly* attributes and basically representing the "Forces of Light", the Jews are painted, icon after icon, as diabolical and sinister, and basically as representing, the "Forces of Darkness."

Light vs. Darkness
Good vs. Evil
Saint vs. Sinner
Virgin purity v. Diabolical corruptness
Redemption vs. Damnation
Angelic vs. Demonic
Godly vs. Satanic
Selfless vs. Greedy
Pure vs. Impure
Martyr vs. Betrayer

No stone – or theme – or defamation – is left unturned. The facts are not allowed to interfere with the *demonizations.*

* * *

Ultimately, this "cancer," originally implanted across
the Roman Empire, would spread far beyond its original
boundaries, following in lockstep with global Catholic
missionary activity.

In turn, post–1948, the Arab and Muslim masses across the
Middle East and parts of Asia, would feed–off this poison,
in turn spread by their own politico–religious leaders and
demagogues. "Hate sells." Virulent hatred sells even better.

***

In the case of the extraordinary and valiant Calixtus II
however, the papal bull was enormously effective. The
blood orgies against the Jews of the First Crusade, were
quite radically blunted, albeit far from eliminated in the
Second Crusade.

The Calixtus bull warned of *excommunication* as
a consequence for transgressors of the papal bull's
prohibitions. This is language understood even by "the
masses." This is language "with teeth." It is meaningful—
and to a great extent, it worked.

Is the current pope listening?

The Jews at that East Side Manhattan synagogue visited by
the pope in 2008 do not need papal protection. The Jews
of Latin America and rural Russia surrounded, 40–50 years
after *Nostre Aetate*, by still–virulent anti–Semitism, might
not mind some proactive papal action – Unambiguous –
and "with teeth."

1135 CE: MAIMONIDES

Moses Maimonides

1123 CE: POPE CALIXTUS II: FIRST LATERAN COUNCIL / CELIBACY DECREE

–decrees that clerical marriages are invalid. And forbids clergy to have concubines.

Many believe that the Vatican policy of clerical celibacy has contributed to ongoing Catholic clerical sexual abuses over the centuries subsequent. The Vatican challenges this argument.

It should be noted that sexually abused young Catholic males [and the count over the millennia is not small], often filled with amorphous rage looking for a target, and simultaneously indoctrinated with focused hatred by the same Church, are not necessarily without consequence to society – and to isolated Jews in particular.....over the centuries subsequent to Calixtus.

c. 1135 CE: MAIMONIDES

Birth of Moses Maimonides, a.k.a. "Maimuni"; a.k.a. The "Rambam" (acronym for "Rabbi Moshe ben Maimon").

A towering figure in Judaism.

Authors: The Commentary on the Mishnah (Perush HaMishnayot); The Book of Commandments (Sefer Hamitzvot); Code of Jewish Law (Mishne Torah a.k.a. Sefer Yad HaChazakah); The Guide to the Perplexed (Moreh Nevuchim); Letter to Yemen (Iggeret Teiman).

Maimonides (and Aristotle) are later rigorously critiqued in classic Or HaShem by Hasdai Crescas of Barcelona in

First Crusade
"Massacre of the *Judenhut*"

French Christian bible illustration of 1250 CE depicts Jews (identifiable by the *Judenhut,* the "Jew hat" men were forced to wear) being massacred by Crusaders during the First Crusade, 1096 CE.

There are three Jewish men on the right depicted as being massacred. Two pray upwards to God; one looks to the left.

On the left, angels and/or Jesus are depicted as sanctifying the murders.

Second Crusade
"Murder/Drowning of the Daughter of Isaac"

A tombstone of a young Jewish woman, the 'Daughter of Isaac,'
one of the early victims of the Second Crusade.

The fragmented inscription reads:
"...Daughter of Isaac, [who was murdered] and drowned
in Sanctification of the Oneness of God, in the year 906 [1146 CE]
on the Friday, the fifth of Iyar [19 April].
May she rest in Eden, the Garden."

See *Jahrbuch der Vereinigung "Freunde der Universitat Mainz"*
8(1959): 71–72. (Courtesy of Professor Eugen Ludwig Rapp, Mainz.)

source: Shlomo Eidelberg, *The Jews and the Crusaders.* New Jersey: KTAV Publishing
House, © 1996, p. 126.

1135 CE: MAIMONIDES

Maimonides' 13 Principles of Faith

1. I believe with perfect faith that the Creator, Blessed be His Name, is the Creator and Guide of everything that has been created; He alone has made, does make, and will make all things.

2. I believe with perfect faith that the Creator, Blessed be His Name, is One, and that there is no unity in any manner like His, and that He alone is our God, who was, and is, and will be.

3. I believe with perfect faith that the Creator, Blessed be His Name, has no body, and that He is free from all the properties of matter, and that there can be no (physical) comparison to Him whatsoever.

4. I believe with perfect faith that the Creator, Blessed be His Name, is the first and the last.

5. I believe with perfect faith that to the Creator, Blessed be His Name, and to Him alone, it is right to pray, and that it is not right to pray to any being besides Him.

6. I believe with perfect faith that all the words of the prophets are true.

7. I believe with perfect faith that the prophecy of Moses our teacher, peace be upon him, was true, and that he was the chief of the prophets, both those who preceded him and those who followed him.

8. I believe with perfect faith that the entire Torah that is now in our possession is the same that was given to Moses our teacher, peace be upon him.

9. I believe with perfect faith that this Torah will not be exchanged, and that there will never be any other Torah from the Creator, Blessed be His Name.

10. I believe with perfect faith that the Creator, Blessed be His Name, knows all the deeds of human beings and all their thoughts, as it is written, "Who fashioned the hearts of them all, who comprehends all their actions" (Psalms 33:15).

11. I believe with perfect faith that the Creator, Blessed be His Name, rewards those who keep His commandments and punishes those that transgress them.

12. I believe with perfect faith in the coming of the Messiah; and even though he may tarry, nonetheless, I wait every day for his coming.

13. I believe with perfect faith that there will be a revival of the dead at the time when it shall please the Creator, Blessed be His name, and His mention shall be exalted forever and ever.

— Maimonides

the late 1300s, who in turn directly influences Spinoza in the 1600s.

Miamonides dies at age sixty–nine in 1204 CE

[I, among others, respectfully believe that the works of Maimonides are an unattributed key source of Aquinas's renowned *Summa Theologica* (written 1265-1274 CE). See entry later – Aquinas].

1146 CE: MURDER VICTIM: "DAUGHTER OF ISAAC"

–Second Crusade

Caption on Mainz, Germany tombstone, Old Jewish Cemetery, *Alt Israelitische Friedhof*, extant today, on hillside overlooking the Rhine River, as visited and viewed by chronicler James Carroll:

"Daughter of Isaac drowned and murdered. Martyred in sanctification of the oneness of God in the year 906 (1146 CE) on the Friday, the fifth of Iyar (19 April). May she rest in Eden, the Garden."

***

"That the daughter of Isaac was murdered in (April) 1146 CE indicates that she was a martyred victim of the Second Crusade, which was launched by a call of Pope Eugene III in March (the month prior) of that year. That the young woman died in April, within the month, suggests with what efficiency crusader terror returned to Mainz (after the First Crusade)."

–Shlomo Eidelberg, *The Jews and the Crusaders*, New Jersey: KTAV Publishing House © 1996, p. 126.

1135 CE: MAIMONIDES

Maimonides' Division of the Mitzvot

The *taryag* mitzvot: he divides the 613 commandments
into 14 books, with 83 sections

Book	Title	Number of Commandments	Contents
1	**The Book of Knowledge**	75	The laws concerning religious belief, character, Torah study, idolatry, and repentance.
2	**The Book of Adoration**	11	Recital of the Shma Yisrael, prayer, tefillin, mezuza, Torah scroll, tzitzit, blessings, and circumcision.
3	**The Book of Seasons**	35	The Shabbat, Yom Kippur, holidays, New Moon, and fast days.
4	**The Book of Women**	17	Marriage, divorce, seduction, and infidelity.
5	**The Book of Holiness**	70	Illicit sexual relations, forbidden foods, and ritual slaughter.
6	**The Book of Specific Utterances**	25	Oaths, vows, Nazirite restrictions, and devotion of property to the Sanctuary.
7	**The Book of Seeds**	67	The crossing of seeds, cattle and materials, laws of charity and tithing, and laws regarding the sabbatical and jubilee years.
8	**The Book of Divine Service**	103	The Sanctuary, how it is to be built, who serves in it and the nature of the service.
9	**The Book of Sacrifices**	39	The sacrifices brought on holidays and as atonement for sins.
10	**The Book of Purity**	20	All the causes of defilement and the requirements for purification.
11	**The Book of Injuries**	36	The laws of compensation for damages and theft, returning lost property, murder, and the preservation of life.
12	**The Book of Acquisition**	18	Commercial transactions, neighbors, and bondage.
13	**The Book of Judgments**	23	Labor relations, renting and borrowing, and inheritance.
14	**The Book of Judges**	74	The judicial system, rabbinic and parental authority, mourning, kings, and wars.

source: http://ohr.edu

Note the nuance of the subtly defiant inscription in full public view:

"In sanctification of the oneness of God"—as opposed to the trinity of her killers.

***

To the Jews, the Crusader cross was a symbol of evil and death. Church theology juxtaposed Catholicism against their metaphysical anti–Christ. To the Jews, as murderous Christian activity accelerated against them in the Middle Ages, the Church had *itself* morphed into the metaphysical anti–Christ, disguised and dressed in holy vestments, an occupation entity holding fancy cathedrals in its evil grasp.

From the Jewish perspective, a diabolical Church preached peace and love to the world, but simultaneously fostered and incited hatred and murder to its core constituents. Ongoing for centuries.

To the terrorized and brutalized Jews of the Middle Ages, the amorphous legacy of a loving Rabbi Jesus, whoever Jesus might actually have been, had clearly been hijacked by the manipulative Church. In turn, this increasingly empowered Church had morphed as increasingly murderous and merciless against the isolated and unarmed Jews. Notwithstanding the fact that Jesus had himself preached within Judaism or perhaps, because of that. For whatever combination of tactical, psychological, political or theological–justification motives, the Church had set out to undermine and brutalize the already–scattered and isolated Jews.

Christianity would "package" the New Testament as part of a 2–part set with the Jewish Bible, adding *gravitas*

1135 CE: MAIMONIDES

14 precepts relating to
Love and Brotherhood

Precept		
1	Not to put any Jew to shame	(Lev. 19:17)
2	To love all human beings who are of the covenant	(Lev. 19:18)
3	Not to stand by idly when a human life is in danger	(Lev. 19:16)
4	Not to wrong anyone in speech	(Lev. 25:17)
5	Not to carry tales	(Lev. 19:16)
6	Not to cherish hatred in one's heart	(Lev. 19:17)
7	Not to take revenge	(Lev. 19:18)
8	Not to bear a grudge	(Lev. 19:18)
9	Not to curse any other	(Lev. 19:14) (by implication: if you may not curse those who cannot hear, you certainly may not curse those who can)
10	Not to give occasion to the simple–minded to stumble on the road	(Lev. 19:14) (this includes doing anything that will cause another to sin)
11	To rebuke the sinner	(Lev. 19:17)
12	To relieve a neighbor of his burden and help to unload his beast	(Ex. 23:5)
13	To assist in replacing the load upon a neighbor's beast	(Deut. 22:4)
14	Not to leave a beast, that has fallen down beneath its burden, unaided	(Deut. 22:4)

and credibility to the New Testament. But would then simultaneously severely undermine the Jews as a whole in the very same New Testament.

Christianity via its iconic centerpiece Jesus, would co-opt "love thy neighbor" from the Hillel School of the Pharisees (normative Judaism).
While the mother of Jesus was positioned as the Virgin Mary, the balance of world Jewry, stretching forth many dozens of generations, outside his devotees, is assiduously demonized and dehumanized – as in–league with the Devil – by the Christian "Doctors of the Church," front and center.

The murder–drowning victim "the daughter of Isaac" was far from alone. The Rhine River alone would run red with Jewish blood intermittently over the centuries to come.

The Crusaders were a *very brave lot* – especially when it came to murdering defenseless Jewish children – and their parents...

1146–1147 CE: SECOND CRUSADE ABBOT SAGAS

Abbot Peter of Cluny ("Peter the Venerable", a.k.a. Peter of Montboissier), abott of the Benedictine abbey of Cluny, France, advises Louis VII to confiscate Jewish property to help finance the Crusade.

[Fast–Forward: At his weekly general audience in Saint Peter's Square on October 14, 2009, Pope Benedict XVI used Peter as an 'example of compassion and understanding,' citing Peter's "diplomacy and governance."]

*

1146–1147 CE: SECOND CRUSADE ABBOT SAGAS

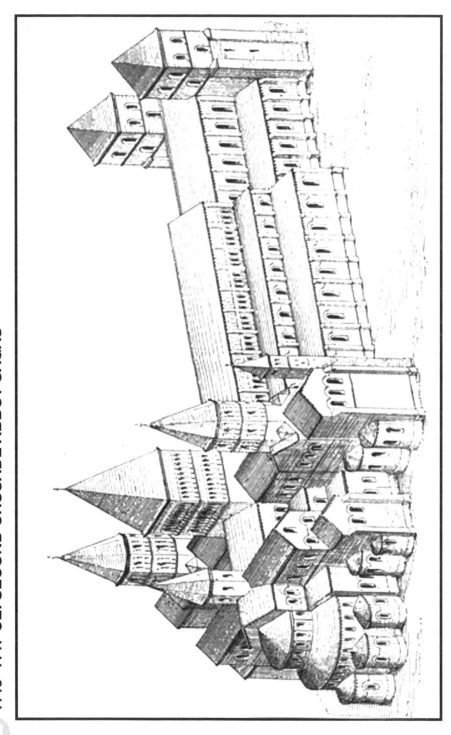

The abbey of Cluny as it would have looked in Bernard's time.

Abbot (and later saint) Bernard of Clairvaux (1090–1153 CE)
[French] apparently goes to the Rhine Valley [Germany]
to call for a stop to anti–Jewish massacres inspired and/or
conducted by the German monk Rudolphe a.k.a. Raoul in
Cologne, Mainz, Worms and Speyer.

Bernard of Clairvaux was a primary builder of the reforming
Cistercian monastic order.

It is not clear why murderous German Crusaders would
listen to a gentle French abott. It is also not clear why the
formidable Christian Archbishops of Cologne and Mainz
seem to be thoroughly impotent, had they wished to expend
political capital, to confront a cowardly murderous rabble
within the Christian religious enterprise. Presumably the
bloody corpses of the murdered Jewish men, women and
children were long swept down the Rhine by the time gentle
and decent Abott Bernard of Clairvaux made his trek from
France to Germany.

1147 CE: THE ALMOHADS

Conquest of Spain by the Almohads, a North–African
Berber dynasty, who force both Jews and Christians, to adopt
Islam at least outwardly.

1152 CE: ELEANOR OF AQUITAINE DIVORCES

–KING LOUIS VII OF FRANCE

–and takes back her lands, which now represented a good
portion of greater France, back with her to England.

On her return to England, a few weeks later she proposes

1152 CE: ELEANOR OF AQUITAINE DIVORCES

(left) the wedding of Louis VII and Eleanor; (right) troops of Louis leaving on Crusade headed by Louis.

to—and subsequently marries—the eleven years younger Henry, Duke of Normandy, who becomes King of England (King Henry II) two years later in 1154

In due course, two of their sons, King Richard the Lionheart and King John, also become kings of England, respectively.

There is more to the story of course:

Mid–way through King Henry II's reign, Eleanor had plotted with her son "Henry the Young King" (no need to digress further into this) to overthrow Henry II. The plot was foiled and Eleanor was imprisoned in 1173. Upon Henry's death, in 1189, the new king, her son Richard, freed his mom.

1170 CE: THOMAS BECKET

Archbishop of Canterbury, assassinated in Canterbury Cathedral, England, by knights allied with King Henry II.

Formerly a very close political ally of Henry II, Becket, upon becoming Archbishop in 1162 CE, asserts his independence and rectitude, shifts gears, and moves to dramatically advance Church rights and independence.

Canonized by Pope Alexander in 1173, four years after his assassination.

One year later, at the "guidance" of the pope, Henry II effects his famous "barefoot in the snow" penance at Becket's tomb in Canterbury. Shakespeare will later deal with this Canterbury.

1171 CE: BURNINGS–AT–STAKE

A medieval woodcut depicting Jewish communities burnt–at–the–stake as a direct result of blood libel accussations.

Projected by: Daniel S. Cutler

1171 CE: BURNINGS–AT–STAKE

May 26: First blood–libel case in France: Thirty–two Jews are burnt at the stake in Blois after the disappearance of a Christian child.

Rabbenu Tam (c. 1100 – 1171 CE), apparently in possibly the final year of his life, institutes a fast on the date of that event. He apparently also coordinated attempts by the Jewish communities in Paris and in Champagne to convince King Louis VII and the Duke of Champagne to halt the spread of anti–Jewish allegations.

1182 CE: BARBAROSA

Frederick I Barbarossa (b. 1122; d.1190 CE) stresses the duty of the emperor, prescribed by justice and reason, to defend the rights of his subjects, including non–Christians.

Barbarosa was elected King of Germany 1152 CE. He was crowned Holy Roman Emperor 1155 CE by Pope Adrian IV. Barbarosa was further crowned King of Burgundy in 1178 CE.

1185 CE: GENGHIS KHAN, 20, ASSUMES THE MONGOL THRONE

(See 1227 CE entry)

1187 CE: SALADIN!

–conquers Jerusalem from the Crusaders; allows Jewish settlement.

1190 CE: ENGLAND: MARTYRDOM AT YORK CASTLE

On the night of Friday 16 March 1190 some
150 Jews and Jewesses of York having sought
protection in the Royal Castle on this site
from a mob incited by Richard Malebisse
and others chose to die at each other's
hands rather than renounce their faith.

יָשִׂימוּ לַיָ כָּבוֹד וּתְהִלָּתוֹ בָּאִיִּים

ISAIAH XLII 12

source: Dobson, R.B. *Clifford's Tower and the Jews of Medieval York.* (London: English Heritage, 1995)

1190 CE: ENGLAND: MARTYRDOM AT YORK CASTLE (THIRD CRUSADE)

Mar 16: Alarmed by Crusader massacres of local Jews in surrounding towns, the Jews of York gain entry to Clifford Tower.

The tower is subsequently besieged by Crusaders demanding that the Jews convert to Christianity or die. The spiritual leader of the Jews, Rav Yom Tov of Joigny, directed his flock to kill themselves rather than convert. The political leader of the Jews, Josce, thereupon stepped forth and slew his wife and his two children. Then by pre-agreement Yom Tov slew Josce, and on it went until all but a few lay dead or dying.

The handful who did not commit suicide surrendered to the Crusaders at daybreak under promise, apparently, that enough blood had been spilled. Whereupon they were massacred. And the wooden Clifford Tower burnt down.

Then the Crusaders marched on towards Jerusalem.

1192 CE: SAMURAI

The Samurai warriors emerge as the ruling class in Japan.

This is the beginning of the Shogunate. There were ultimately (Bakufu) in Japan:

> Kamakura 1192–1333 CE
> Muromachi 1336–1573 CE
> Tokugawa (Edo) 1603–1868 CE

The Shogunate, (in parallel to the reigns of the Roman

1200 CE: MARCO POLO

ПУТЕШЕСТВИЯ МАРКО ПОЛО
1271–1295 гг.

Map of the journey

Empire) although romanticized, was a feudal military dictatorship.

1198–1231 CE: DELINEATING 'JEWISH RIGHTS'

Eighteen conventions between the respective kings of France (Augustus, Louis XVIII, Louis IX) and his barons define and clarify their respective 'rights' over "their Jews."

1200 CE: GOLDEN AGE OF JEWISH PHILOSOPHY

+/– 300 years (so, 900–1492 CE)
Zenith of Sephardic Jewry in Spain and surrounding countries. Abarvanel, Maimonides [Rambam], Nachmanides [Ramban], Gersonides [RaLbaG], Abraham Ibn Ezra, Ibn Daud Rabad I (a.k.a. Ravad I), Ibn Gabirol, Karo *et al*.

1200s CE: MARCO POLO

Travels to Emperor Kublai Khan's Chinese Court; signs–up for Chinese government service; returns home and produces "Travels of Marco Polo"; visits Jerusalem in 1275 CE.

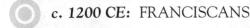

c. 1200 CE: FRANCISCANS

Franciscan Catholic Order of Friars is founded in Italy (by Saint Francis of Assisi).

Ordo Fratrum Minorum in Latin.

1204 CE: END OF THE FOURTH CRUSADE

–led by Western knights and by Venice.

c. 1200 CE: FRANCISCANS
"SAINT FRANCIS IN PRAYER"
PAINTER: EL GRECO

The Jewish quarter in Constantinople is burned down by the Crusaders.

1209–1211 CE: 300 (TOSAFISTS) RABBIS SETTLE IN PALESTINE

"The *aliyah* of the three hundred rabbis" – the name given in Jewish historiography to the migration to Palestine by many tosafists.

Tosafot rabbinics ultimately spanned Europe, but the cradle of the tosafot rabbinics was France, then Germany–Spain–Italy.

1215 CE: MAGNA CARTA SIGNED

King John of England muscled by barons. Some power shifts from the king to the nobles.

The Magna Carta required King John of England to proclaim certain rights (pertaining to freemen), respect certain legal procedures, and accept that his will could be bound by the law.

Most Western history books treat the Magna Carta as an epochal document.

It is far from clear that in the short run (before the English Civil War of 1641–1651), the rights of anyone except those of the nobles increased.

a.k.a. *Magna Carta Libertatum* (the Great Charter of Freedom).

It was amended several times, and it is the 1297 CE version which remains on the statute books of England and Wales.

1215 CE: MAGNA CARTA SIGNED
"JOHN OF ENGLAND SIGNS MAGNA CARTA"
ILLUSTRATION FROM CASSELL'S HISTORY OF ENGLAND (1902)

1215 CE: FOURTH LATERAN (CATHOLIC) COUNCIL

(Convoked by Pope Innocent III with a papal bull April 19, 1213 CE)

November 1215: Rome:

Present: 71 patriarchs and metropolitan bishops
          412 bishops
          900 abbots and priors

The council approved the decrees submitted to it by Pope Innocent III.

Included in the seventy–one decrees were commands that all Jews
  –wear distinguishing labels on their garments.
  –be confined to ghettos.

The politically dominant Vatican was in position to enforce its decrees.

Prior council: Third Council of the Lateran
Next council: First Council of Lyon

Rosemary Ruether writes:

> "The final expression of the Church's effort to segregate the Jew from any social contact with Christian society was the ghetto and the wearing of Jewish dress, conical hat, and "Jew badge" (usually a yellow circle, symbolic of the Jew as betrayer of Christ for "gold," an image which fused religious with economic anti–Semitism). These regulations were passed at the Fourth Lateran Council (1215), although the Church

1227 CE: GENGHIS KHAN DIES

Genghis Khan

source: *Dschingis Khan und seine Erben* (exhibition catalogue p. 304), München 2005.

only succeeded in enforcing them universally after the Council of Basel (1434).*A These marks had the effect of making Jewish ignominy visible and singling the Jew out for physical attack as never before, destroying further the ability of the Jew to travel the open roads as a merchant. Other canonical rules, such as those that insisted that the synagogue must be a low and miserable building, that Jews must not enter churches or come into the streets on holy days, especially during Passiontide, or work on Sunday, were intended to enforce the visible superiority of Christianity.*B But it also reinforced the popular idea that Jews secretly desired to mock and profane Christian symbols, even though the popes officially tended to discount the myths of ritual murder and host profanation. Finally, the Talmud itself was declared illegal. Successive inquisitions condemned it, despite the defense put up against Christian accusations by Talmudic scholars.*C The Talmud and Jewish works were burned publicly in France in the mid–thirteenth century, bringing to an end an important center of Talmudic scholarship. Like Justinian, the Church seems to have believed that without the rabbinic exegesis, the Jews would quickly come to acknowledge that the Christological exegesis of the Church was the correct one." (Ruether, Faith and Fratricide, pp. 209–210).

---

*A Poliakov, *History of Anti–Semitism*, p. 65. Also Grayzel, Church and the Jews, pp. 59–71.
*B Poliakov, *History of Anti–Semitism*, pp. 33–36.
*C Ibid., pp. 29–34.

1227 CE: GENGHIS KHAN DIES

CHINA: born *Temüjin* (1162 CE), the empire he carved–out is at its maximum at his death (1227 CE).

1230 CE: (SAINT) LOUIS
"TRIUMPH OF CHRISTIANITY OVER JUDAISM"

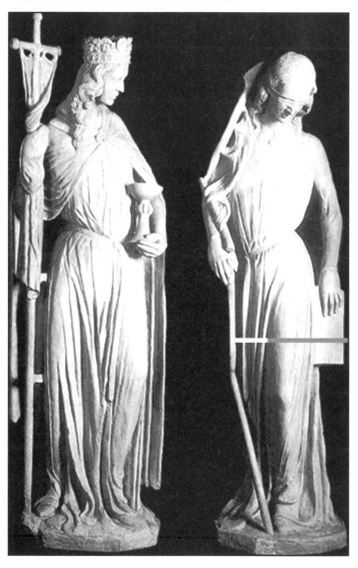

Degradation of the Jews is explained in theological terms of the wall of Strasbourg Cathedral. Depicted is the crowned Church while Synagogue, "blindfolded" to the truth of the Gospels, continues to lean on "the broken staff" of the "Old Testament."

Church Triumphant over Synagogue – relief of Strasbourgh Cathedral c. 1230

But his son …gedei Khan (the "Great Khan") stretches it still further (southward and westward)—and by 1279 CE the Mongols would control all China. The Mongol Empire is at this point physically the largest contiguous empire the world has ever known—stretching well into Europe, Russia, the Middle East and the Near East, as well.

1230 CE: (SAINT) LOUIS

Decree of Louis IX (reigns 1227–1270 CE) defining the subordination of the Jews to the king and to their lords "as if they were their serfs."

1230–1233 CE: MAIMONIDES PUBLISHES

The controversy over Maimonides' works rocks the Spanish and French communities; the rabbis of southern France pronounce an excommunication on anyone who reads the Guide of the Perplexed or seeks after "Greek wisdom": a counter–excommunication is proclaimed by the Maimonidean camps of "Provence" (southern France).
(A Historical Atlas of the Jewish People)

[Maimonides' Guide for the Perplexed is currently considered possibly the preeminent "establishment Jewish philosophical work."]

1231 CE: EXCOMMUNICAMUS

–issued by Pope Gregory IX.
Excommunicamus empowers Dominican and Franciscan religious–purity courts. The nefarious Holy Inquisition Courts have their genesis.

1242 CE: PARIS TALMUD BURNING

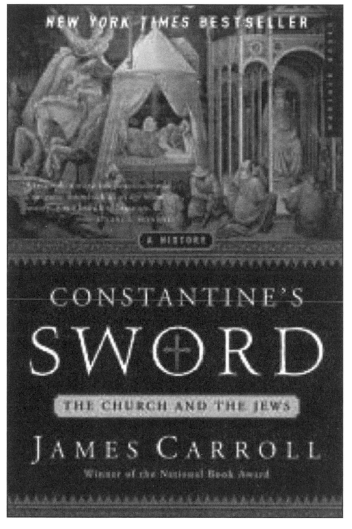

I am certain that the first time I would have heard the word "Jew" was from the pulpit of St. Mary's Church in Alexandria, Virginia, where I lived as a child. My father was an Air Force general working at the Pentagon, but we made our family life in the Old South river port down the Potomac, where the Catholic parish was the oldest in Virginia. It would have surely been one Holy Week when I was six or seven that I heard the mythic words proclaimed: "The Jews cried out with one voice, 'Crucify him!'"

source: book cover

Rosemary Ruether writes:

"The canonical legislation of the Church in
the thirteenth century effected a systematic social
degradation of the Jew. The Church struggled to
reimpose all the old canonical and imperial anti–Judaic
legislation back to Constantine. But it went beyond this
in forbidding even Christian servants or nurses to the
Jews under pain of excommunication.*A The Church's
basic position was that the Jew should occupy no place
of eminence or power in Christian society which would
ever put him in a position of authority over a Christian,
however modest. The basic principle for this, as we have
indicated, was that of the *Servitus Judaeorum*, as the
reprobate status of the Jew in history." (Ruether, *Faith
and Fratricide*, p. 209).

---

*A Grayzel, *The Church and the Jews*, p. 25, and documents 14, 15, 29,
69, and 104; also conciliar decrees: documents 3, 16, 25, and 33.

1242 CE: PARIS TALMUD BURNING

James Carroll writes the following in his book *Constantine's
Sword*, pp. 308–310:

"Only two blocks from Notre–Dame, on the right bank
of the Seine, there stands a lovely plaza, spread like an
apron before the dignified, mansard–roofed Hôtel de
Ville. Not long ago, I spent a quiet afternoon sitting at
a small table in one of the sidewalk cafés that line one
edge of the square. Visible to my right were the soaring
towers of the cathedral, their gargoyles alert. Just beyond
was the needle spire of the exquisite Sainte–Chapelle,
built as a reliquary for the crown of thorns, which made
me think of the Seamless Robe – Helena's legacy was a

1242 CE: PARIS TALMUD BURNING

The first page of the Babylonian Talmud

alive in Paris as in Trier. Anchoring the distance, across the square, was the congested bazaar of the weekend market. Despite this lively scene, my concentration was taken over by the layered history of the place. Near here was the mustering point for the Jews of Paris rounded up on July 16, 1942. Thirteen thousand were taken away that day, four thousand of them children. There was no protest. More than half of the eighty–five thousand Jews deported from France to Nazi extermination camps came from Paris – the streets around me. Their confiscated artworks, bank accounts, and apartments are still being adjudicated.

What is the line between that day and the day in 1242 when up to twenty–four cartloads of books, something like twelve thousand volumes, were dumped onto the pavement of this same plaza? Those books were all the known copies of the Talmud to be found in Paris and its environs, brought here by the soldiers of King Lous IX, also known as Saint Louis. His men had invaded and ransacked Jewish homes and synagogue to get at the books.

"The faculty of the University of Paris, heirs of Peter Abelard and teachers of Thomas Aquinas, had held its trial in the form of a debate, with conscripted Jewish sages speaking for the Talmud and Dominicans speaking against. The faculty rendered its verdict: The Talmud was a work of heresy. The Talmud was the reason Jews were refusing to convert. Destroy the Talmud, and the truth of "fulfillment" arguments from the Old Testament, rationally offered, would be clear to them at last. The king's men took their stations around the mountain of books, to keep back the Jews as the torchbearer approached. The two–sword theory of Saint Bernard was here given its first mature expression, as the kind carried

1242 CE: PARIS TALMUD BURNING
PAINTER: PEDRO BERRUGUETE

The Talmud is ordered (by Pope Gregory IX) confiscated and
burned (1239–1242).

out the physical sanction decreed by the spiritual court. The bonfire was lit. The Talmud burned. It would take one and a half days to consume all volumes..."

"Here is an indictment of the Talmud solemnly given by Gregory's successor, Innocent IV (1243–1254):

> Ungrateful to the Lord Jesus Christ, who, His forbearance overflowing patiently awaits their conversion, they manifest no shame for their guilt, nor do they reverence the dignity of the Christian faith. Omitting or condemning the Mosaic Law and the Prophets, they follow certain tradition of their elders. In Hebrew they call them "Thalamuth," and an immense book it is, exceeding the text of the Bible in size, and in it are blasphemies against God and His Christ, and against the blessed Virgin, fables that are manifestly beyond all explanation, erroneous abuses, and unheard–of stupidities – yet this is what they teach and feed their children, and render them totally alien to the Law and the Prophets, bearing patent testimony to the only–begotten Son of God, who was to come in flesh, they be converted to the faith, and return humbly to their Redeemer."

"The public burning in the great square of Paris was a first indication that a living, growing Judaism would not be allowed to survive in a Europe ever more under the sway of the sword–perverted cross. And what was written on those destroyed pages? Here are lines "picked from the Talmud at random," as distinguished rabbi Emil Bernhard Cohn put it, '...to lift a corner of the veil':

> Love of humanity is more than charity. The value of charity lies only in love, which lives in it. Love surpasses

LOVE, TRUTH & LAW

A sub–motif of the gospels is that 'LAW' (of Moses) is inherently trumped by 'LOVE.' The Jews, however, believe that the two (LAW – and LOVE) live side–by–side, with both imperatives – Law – and Love/Sensitivity – finding an entente.

Judaism does believe that *LOVE* carries with it, *responsibility*. Judaism would plead guilty to that charge.

Respectfully, it is only if one distorts Jewish Law, that can one trumpet 'insensitivity.'

> "This Pauline view fatally distorts Judaism's understanding of the Way of Torah. Judaism is not letter without spirit, but a way of life which knows the unresolved tension of letter and spirit."*

Unfortunately, Judaism is painted and caricatured icon–by–icon in far worse imagery than in the Gospel "*Synagogue–healing mini–saga*." Judaism and sundry Jewish icons are painted in the brushstrokes of 'the hellish and hell'.

"For the law was given by Moses, but grace and truth came by Jesus Christ." (John 1:17)

So, Moses, according to (Saint) John, alas, was not quite 'truth'. Only 'law'.

Read John 1:17 – and weep.

A simple – but lethal – stratagem: BLACKEN–the–Jews from every conceivable angle. And UNDERMINE everything about them. From days past – to the 'end of days.'

---

* Rosemary Reuther, Faith and Fratricide, Oregon: WS Publishers, © 1995, Chapter 1, p. 241.

charity in three respects: Charity touches only a man's money; love touches the man himself. Charity is only for the poor; love is for both poor and rich. Charity is only for the living; love is for both living and dead. Love without reproof of errors is no love. He who judges his neighbor leniently will himself be judged leniently by God. Let man always be intelligent and affable in his God–fearing. Let him answer softly, curb his wrath and let him live in peach with his brethren and his kin and with every man, yes, even with the pagan on the street, in order that he be beloved in heaven and on earth, and be acceptable to all men. The kindly man is the truly God–fearing man."

1247 CE: RETURN OF TALMUDS

August: Pope Innocent IV orders confiscated Talmud copies to be returned to the Jews.

1250 CE: KOREAN PRINTING PRESS

Korean Choe Yun–ui invents an iron movable type printing press; Gutenberg does the same 200 years later in Germany. Gutenberg commences printing the Bible and achieves immortality (in the West that is). Iron movable type defines the revolution.

1250 CE: MOSES DE LEÓN

–a.k.a, Moshe ben Shem Tov, born in León, Spain

Rav Moshe De León penned – or redacted – the extant version of the legendary Zohar, the preeminent iconic work of Kabbalah. De León ascribes the themes of his 1700 page opus to traditions from the spiritual giant

1250 CE: MOSES DE LEON

Statue of Moshe ben Shem-Tov a.k.a. Moses de León
Guadalajara, Spain

Rav Shimon bar Yochai of the second century (thereby anchoring the work in highly formidable spiritual legitimacy).

Scholem, the twentieth century kabbalistic historian, believes the work is more de León, and less bar Yochai, meaning, less grounded in quintessential historical legitimacy. Like many kabbalistic works, the reality may very well lie somewhere in–the–middle: part original, part lore.

Note that kabbalistic writings, like much of Jewish philosophy, are more often than not a creative continuum of thought/spirituality and creative hypothesis. Drawing from the past and from the going–wisdom to–date, but with the contemporary author's neo–kabbalistic signature on it. Any philosophical or kabbalistic work not tethered to the past, simply *does not fly* in Jewish tradition. The issue is balance; walking a fine line. Too much anchoring and the new work lacks dynamism; too little tethering, and the work is not taken seriously. De León might have wished to emphasize the tethering if he were afraid of attack from the "right wing" of Judaism.

By contemporary times, however, de León himself, in–any–event, has achieved quite formidable parallel iconic standing.

Note that while the Zohar is penned in Aramaic, de León's other known work, Sefer ha–Rimon (The Book of the Lemon) is penned in Hebrew. Meaning, if the Zohar is much more de León than bar Yochai, he (de León) certainly went to very formidable lengths to conceal the fact. Meaning, by writing it in his second or third or fourth language, not in his primary milieu, Hebrew, to incorporate

1263 CE: 1263 CE: "THE DISPUTATION OF BARCELONA" / RAMBAN

Rav Shimon bar Yaochai, De León who was an author in his own right, is investing quite heavily to anchor his works.

In his lifetime De León lived in the Spanish cities of Guadalajara, Valladolid, Avila and Arevalo, among others.

1263 CE: "THE DISPUTATION OF BARCELONA" / RAMBAN

Spain: In front of King James I of Aragon

–between the monk Pablo Christiani (a convert from Judaism), and Rabbi Nachmanides (the Ramban).

At the end of the disputation, the king awarded Nachmanides a monetary prize and declared, according to lore, that never before had he heard "an unjust cause so nobly defended."

Nevertheless, the Dominicans claimed victory and Nachmanides was exiled and his report of the proceedings was condemned and burned.

Other historic disputations (*disputationes*) include:

1240 CE: Disputation of Paris
(during the reign of Louis IX of France (St. Louis)

1375 CE: Disputation of 1375 in Burgos and Avila
(both in Spain)

1413 CE: Disputation of Tortosa, Spain
staged by the Avignon Pope Benedict XIII

1267 CE: THE RAMBAN REESTABLISHES *JEWISH COMMUNAL LIFE* IN JERUSALEM

רבינו משה בן נחמן זל רמבן
נולד תתקנד נפטר הכט לבע

R. MOSES NACHMANIDES

Rabbi Moshe Ben Nachman (Nachmanides)

These disputations—under the aegis of powerful Christian personages—tend not to have "happy endings" for Jewish interests.

It is a "lose–lose" proposition for the Jews. If the Jewish advocate prevails in the debate, there are persecutions; if the Jewish advocate does not prevail in the debate, there are persecutions.

Now, back to Nachmanides…

Nachmanides (1194 CE – c.1270 CE), "The Ramban" moves to Jerusalem, where he founds the now–historic Ramban Synagogue. His most famous work is *Commentary on the Torah*.

1267 CE: THE RAMBAN REESTABLISHES *JEWISH COMMUNAL LIFE* IN JERUSALEM

Jerusalem: Nahmanides, exiled from Aragon, Spain, for criticizing Christianity.

He makes *aliyah* to the land of Israel, where he establishes a synagogue, extant to this day, in the Old City, known, of course, as the Ramban Synagogue.

The Ramban's tenure in Jerusalem reestablishes rich cultural Jewish communal life in the Old City, which had been interrupted by the Crusades. The establishment of the Ramban Synagogue thus marks the beginning of almost 700 years of uninterrupted Jewish communal settlement in the Old City of Jerusalem, up until its temporary seizure by Jordan in the 1948 war.

1271 CE: AQUINAS

Thomas Aquinas

1270 CE: THE TUR

–a.k.a. Arb'ah Turim

–by Rav Jacob ben Asher (1270–1343 CE) a.k.a. *Baal ha–Turim*.

Halakhic code, rabbinic classic *Arba'ah Turim* (The Four Rows).

The 4–part structure and its division into chapters (*simanim*) was later adopted in the *Shulchan Aruch* (the enduring Code of Jewish Law).

The four Turim (rows) are as follows:

Orach Chayim –	laws of prayer and synagogue, Sabbath and Holidays
Yoreh De'ah –	*Schechita* (ritual slaughtering) and inter–related *kashrut*
Even Ha'ezer –	laws of marriage, divorce
Choshen Mishpat –	laws of finance, financial legal responsibility, damages, and legal procedure

c. 1271 CE: AQUINAS

Thomas Aquinas completes *Summa Theologica*.

Aquinas, born in 1225 CE in Naples, Italy, dies in 1274 CE at age 49 of illness while en route to the Second Council of Lyons. He is canonized 1323 CE. Writing metaphysics and philosophy in the Aristotelian tradition within a Christian framework, along with some anti–Jewish sub–themes, he is a towering figure in Church philosophical–religious tradition.

1285 CE: ABULAFIA PUBLISHES *LIGHT OF THE INTELLECT*

Abraham Abulafia's *Light of the Intellect* 1285,
Vat. ebr. 597 leaf 113 recto

Maimonides' works are most definitely disseminated through Europe preceding Aquinas by 70 years.

The striking parallels between the two corpuses are of significance.

"Aquinas would imitate Maimonides' methods and retrace his lines of inquiry [without any attribution to Maimonides], knowing full well he was a Jew." (i.e. without attribution to Maimonides)

—James Carroll in *Constantine's Sword*

1281 CE: ROYAL CASTILIAN EXTORTIONIST

January: Alfonso X of Castile, a region of Spain (reign 1252–1284 CE) orders the wholesale arrest of Jews and demands an enormous ransom for their release.

1285 CE: ABULAFIA PUBLISHES *LIGHT OF THE INTELLECT*

Jewish philosopher Abraham ibn Abulafia was born in Zaragoza, Spain, in 1240 CE and is considered the founder of the school of "Prophetic Kabbalah."

His works include:

- *Sefer ha–Ge'ulah* (1273), a commentary on *The Guide for the Perplexed*
- *Sefer ayyei ha–Nefesh*, a commentary on *The Guide for the Perplexed*
- *Sefer ha–Yashar* ("Book of the Upright/Righteous") (1279)
- *Sefer Sitrei Torah* (1280), a commentary on *The Guide for the Perplexed*

1288 CE: RALBAG

Rav Levi ben Gershon

- *Ayyei ha–Olam ha–Ba* ("Life of the World to Come") (1280)
- *Or ha–Sekhel* ("Light of the Intellect")
- *Get ha–Shemot*
- *Mafte'a ha–Re`ayon*
- *Gan Na'ul*, a commentary on *Sefer Yetzirah*
- *Otzar Eden Ganuz*, another commentary on *Sefer Yetzirah*
- *Sefer ha–eshek*
- *Sefer ha–Ot* ("Book of the Sign") (1285 x 1288)
- *Imrei Shefer* ("Words of Beauty") (1291)

1288 CE: RALBAG

Rav Levi ben Gershon (1288 CE – 1344 CE), better known as Gersonides

–rabbi, philosopher, mathematician, astronomer/astrologer, and Talmudist.

Born at Bagnols in Languedoc, France. His philosophical classic is "Sefer Milhamot Ha–Shem" (The Wars of the Lord).

In the twentieth century, the astronomical community names a crater on the moon after him – "the Levi Crater."

1290 CE: JEWS EXPELLED FROM ENGLAND

…by Edward I

The "legal" vehicle was the "Statute of Jewry."

1291 CE: SACREANS (MUSLIMS) CAPTURE ACCRE

–last Christian stronghold in Palestine; **end of Crusades after 200 years.**

1291 CE: SACREANS (MUSLIMS) CAPTURE ACCRE

The Siege of Accre

1294 CE: KUBLAI KHAN DIES

–after 35–year reign establishing Ming dynasty.

1295 CE: ENGLAND'S MODEL PARLIAMENT—
EDWARD I

...summons bishops, knights, and burgesses from all
parishes for first representative parliament.

1296 CE: A GENOESE PRISONER

Marco Polo, writes about his travels to the Orient.

1300 CE: START: JEWISH PERSECUTION AND
MASSACRES: SPAIN

Span of this round of Spanish persecutions:
1300–1391 CE

Massacres: 1366 and 1391 CE
Forced conversions: 1391 > 1492 CE
(see 1492 CE *Jews, Church & Civilization* Volume III)

1302 CE: FINAL END OF THE CRUSADES

The iconic (Christian Crusaders) Knights Templar retreated
to a small island (Ruad) off the coast of Syria for several
years. However, they were ultimately routed by the (Muslim) Mamluks in a preemptive Mamluk attack September
26, 1302 CE.

* end *

*

end of Book 1

An Integrated
Jewish/Christian/Universal
focused timeline

*

The Crucifixion is
continued in Book 2

*

www.Harvard1000.com

(master site)

---

www.Philosophy1000.com

www.History1000.com

www.Spinoffs1000.com

www.YouTubeX1000.com

www.AmazonX1000.com

www.eReader1000.com

Is The U.S.
Mideast Policy
Fumbling?
Page 4

Reports Of
Cons. Judaism's
Demise Premature
Page 6

JEWISH TRIBUNE

Vol. 69 #12 April 1-7, 2011 • 26 Adar II-3 Nisan 5771   *One Dollar*

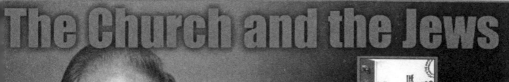

The Church and the Jews

Birnbaum fences with the Church

- and Pope Benedict

Reviews and articles, pages 8-12

David Birnbaum's *The Crucifixion* (of the Jews)

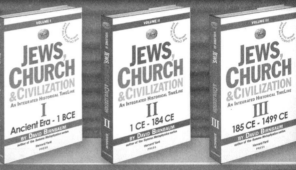

works by **David Birnbaum** Mar.1.2012

DBprivate@aol.com

$40.00 for two-book set

The Crucifixion
Book 1

ISBN: 978-0-9843619-0-8